Fluent English

ACKNOWLEDGMENTS

Thanks to the Living Language staff: Tom Russell, Christopher Warnasch, Zviezdana Verzich, Suzanne McQuade, Sophie Chin, Denise De Gennaro, Linda Schmidt, Alison Skrabek, John Whitman, Helen Kilcullen, and Heather Lanigan.

DEDICATION

To Chris Warnasch, my editor and dear friend, who has given as much in friendship as in editorial assistance. To my students, who have taught me more about teaching English as a Second Language than any book ever could. To my family and friends, whose patience allowed me to finish this project in a timely manner.

Editor: Chris Warnasch
Production Editor: John Whitman
Production Managers: Helen Kilcullen and Heather Lanigan
Interior Design: Sophie Ye Chin

First Edition

ISBN 1-4000-2088-3

Library of Congress Cataloging-in-Publication Data available upon request.

PRINTED IN THE UNITED STATES OF AMERICA

10 9 8 7

LIVING LANGUAGE®

FLUENT
English

Written by
Barbara Raifsnider

Edited by
Christopher A. Warnasch

Contents

INTRODUCTION

Fluent English is a high intermediate–/advanced–level course in English as a second or foreign language. It is designed to meet the needs of the intermediate-level student in vocabulary, grammar, listening comprehension, idiomatic usage, and pronunciation. It offers a great deal of practice in each of these areas, through both written exercises and recorded materials. The language used in this course is realistic and practical, and the situations in each of its twenty lessons offer a cultural context that will be recognizable and relevant to most intermediate-level students of English.

The course is divided into twenty lessons covering a range of topics from small talk and social situations, to telephones and business meetings, to computers, politics, and the Internet. Each lesson offers essential vocabulary related to its topic, as well as important phrasal verbs and idiomatic expressions that are typically challenging to the intermediate-level student. The lessons are divided into ten sections, each of which focuses on a different English language skill:

- *Say It Clearly!* The first section of each lesson is a recorded pronunciation and intonation warm-up. These sections focus on aspects of pronunciation and intonation that are typically challenging for intermediate students of English — consonant clusters, linking, reduced English, challenging sounds, etc.

- *English at Work.* The second section of each lesson features English in realistic contexts, ranging from dialogues to recorded messages to readings. The English at Work section is the cornerstone of each lesson, where the important grammatical structures and vocabulary are demonstrated. These sections are all recorded, giving the student an opportunity to hear and model native speakers.

- *Build Your Vocabulary.* The vocabulary section of each lesson includes certain vocabulary from the English at Work section as well as other general vocabulary related to the topic of the lesson. Each word or expression is defined in simple English, and an example is given to show realistic usage.

- *English Under the Hood.* Each lesson focuses on three important grammatical structures. Explanations are complete and straightforward, and plenty of examples are given to demonstrate each construction in context. Each grammatical point is also followed by a practice drill, giving the student a chance to practice and check comprehension.

- *Phrasal Verbs.* Each lesson includes a list of important and common phrasal verbs centered either on a common base verb, such as *take* or *get*, or a particular theme. Each phrasal verb is clearly defined, and examples of usage follow each definition.

- *Real English.* Important idiomatic expressions related to the topic or theme of each lesson are included in the Real English section. This section is in the form of a short paragraph, where idiomatic expressions are used in context. The student should be able to understand the meaning of each expression from context, but each idiom is also defined in an appendix at the back of the book.

- *Bring it All Together.* Each lesson also includes five comprehensive review exercises. The first exercise focuses on the vocabulary from the lesson, the next three focus on the grammar and structure, and the last one focuses on the phrasal verbs introduced in that lesson.

- *Listen Up!* Each lesson includes a recorded listening comprehension exercise. The student is directed to listen to a short article or dialogue on a topic related to the lesson, and then to answer questions written in the book. The Listen Up sections are designed to use both vocabulary and idiomatic expressions related to the theme of the lesson.

- *Why Do They Do That?* Each lesson includes a culture note that explains an aspect of American culture related to the lesson's topic. These aspects of culture range from table manners to home ownership to driving habits to proper behavior while being pulled over for speeding. The culture notes are designed to be both interesting and relevant to the student's experiences.

- Answer Key. Each lesson also includes a key to all exercises.

KEY TO SYMBOLS

When you see 🎧, PLAY CD and listen to the examples or exercises on the audio portion of the course.

When you see 📖, PAUSE CD and return to the book until you see the next 🎧.

Fluent English

Lesson 1

ARE YOU READY FOR THE LESSON?

Lesson 1, *How Long Have You Been Here?*, will take you somewhere you may know very well: the INS office. You'll listen in on a conversation between two people waiting in line, which is something people unfortunately do very often, and which is also a situation in which Americans like to make "small talk." Then, you'll learn some vocabulary that will come in handy at the INS or anywhere you have to fill out forms. But that's not all. Lesson 1 also includes:

• The Present Perfect Tense vs. The Simple Past Tense
• Using *for* and *since* with the Present Perfect and
  Simple Past Tenses
• Phrasal Verbs with *pick*
• Idiomatic Expressions for Saying Goodbye

Finally, at the end of the lesson you'll read a culture note about casual greetings and acquaintances. But let's start with a pronunciation warm-up. Ready?

1A   SAY IT CLEARLY!

🎧 Turn on your CD to review the pronunciation of *–ed*, a very important ending in English.

1B   ENGLISH AT WORK

Dialogue: Making Small Talk

📖 Sergei, a Russian immigrant, is waiting in line at the INS. The line is very long, and it's moving very slowly. Peter, an American standing in front of Sergei, turns around and strikes up a conversation. Sergei is surprised by his friendliness.

🎧
    Peter I guess we didn't have anything else to do today, did we?
    Sergei What?
    Peter I said I guess they think that we didn't have anything else to do today. It's just that we've been in this line for a very long time. It seems like we aren't going anywhere very fast.
    Sergei Yeah. I know. I've been here since about 9:30. What about you?
    Peter I think I got here just a few minutes before you did. I decided to pick up a green-card application for my wife. I should've gotten it off the Internet. That way I could have just stayed home. Say, where are you from?
    Sergei Me? I'm from Russia.
    Peter Oh, whereabouts?
    Sergei I lived in Moscow for most of my life, but I moved around a little. I was in the military.

Peter   Interesting. I've never been to Russia, but I've always wanted to visit. It seems like such an interesting country. How long have you lived here?

Sergei   I've lived in San Diego for only a few weeks, but I've been in the U.S. since August.

Peter   Well, welcome to San Diego. I guess the weather must be a bit warmer than where you're from, huh?

Sergei   Yes, that's true. I've gotten used to it.

Peter   Have you visited the zoo or Balboa Park yet?

Sergei   No, but I really want to go to Balboa Park. I've heard about all the flowers and museums that are there.

Clerk   Next!

Peter   Hey. That's me. Gotta go. See you around.

Sergei   Oh. OK. See you.

1C   BUILD YOUR VOCABULARY

Perhaps you need to go to the I. N. S. to fill out some forms. Here are some terms you would see if you were to fill out an application to register for permanent residence. Many of these words have other meanings, but these are the usages you will see on I. N. S. forms and other legal documents.

To be cited. To be summoned to appear in court. *The police could cite you for littering if you throw trash out of your car.*

To be indicted. To be charged with a crime. *Richard Hayward was indicted for espionage when he was caught selling U.S. documents to a foreign government.*

Ordinance. A law or regulation, usually passed by a local government. *The city council passed an ordinance permitting the use of marijuana by cancer patients.*

Beneficiary. A person who is or will be the recipient of something of value from someone who has died. *Harold and Gerry were the sole beneficiaries of their mother's modest estate.*

Rehabilitation. Treatment to help someone return to regular, acceptable, or normal behavior or abilities. Recovery from drug abuse or physical injuries. *It was difficult to convince the governor that Sam had been successfully rehabilitated and was ready to leave jail and return to society.*

Clemency. A lesser penalty than what a court originally suggested. *Thinking that Ralph Smith had suffered enough for the crime he committed, the judge granted him clemency and gave him a shorter prison sentence.*

Amnesty. A pardon given to a large group of individuals. *The government granted amnesty to all illegal immigrants who had come to work in the fields.*

Procure. To obtain, to buy, to take possession of something of value. *Professor Hodges wanted to procure some ancient artifacts before returning from his sabbatical in Africa.*

To engage in. To become involved in something, to do something. *Teresa would never engage in illegal activities, even if she disagreed with a law.*

To induce. To influence someone to do something. *Robbie's older brother induced him to steal money from their parents.*

To conspire. To plan together in secret to do harm. *Kathy and Jane conspired to make Mary look foolish.*

To solicit. To ask for something of value, usually money. *Raymond got a job soliciting money for his political party.*

To sabotage. To destroy or cause to fail. *The lab technician sabotaged the experiment by deliberately mixing up the samples.*

Espionage. Spying. *Espionage was a common practice during the Cold War, and it still is today.*

Affiliated. To be in close connection. *The local television stations are all affiliated with major networks.*

To persecute. To harass, to cause someone to suffer because of a belief. *Many people have come to the United States because they were persecuted in their countries.*

To incite. To move to action, to cause. *The Prime Minister's latest announcement incited the protesting crowd to become violent.*

Fraud. A false claim, trick; a liar or imposter. *Sam Jameson created a false medical license and began practicing medicine until he was exposed as a fraud.*

Waiver. A document that gives up a right or grants unusual permission to someone else. *Juan signed a waiver giving his doctor the right to send his medical records to his insurance company.*

Custody. Having legal guardianship of a child or children, often part of a divorce settlement. *When the Camerons divorced, Mrs. Cameron received custody of both children, and her husband won weekend visitation rights.*

 ENGLISH UNDER THE HOOD

TOPIC 1: The Present Perfect Tense vs. the Simple Past Tense

Let's take a look at the two most common past tenses in English: the present perfect tense and the simple past tense.

Present Perfect	Simple Past
I have spoken	*I spoke*
you have spoken	*you spoke*
he, she, it has spoken	*he, she, it spoke*
we have spoken	*we spoke*
they have spoken	*they spoke*

As you can see, the present perfect tense is formed with the verb *to have* and the past participle of the main verb, in this case, *spoken.* The simple past tense is just the past form of the verb, which in this case is *spoke.* These tenses are used a bit differently. The present perfect tense expresses an event that happened in the past when the exact time is not known, or when there's a result or a connection being made to the present, or when the time reference is still unfinished, as in *so far this week,* or *up to now,* or *during my entire life.* The simple past tense, on the other hand, expresses an action that happened when a specific finished time is given, such as *yesterday* or *last week* or *in 1995*. Sometimes these tenses are interchangeable, depending on what the speaker wishes to emphasize. Here are a few examples.

Julia has returned from her trip. (No specific time is given or is important, and the speaker is emphasizing that Julia is now home.)

Julia returned from her trip. (Perhaps this is part of a longer narration of events in the past.)

I finished reading the novel last night. ("Last night" indicates a specific time in the past.)

Has Pam ever been to New York? ("Ever" means "during her entire life.")

I worked five days last week. ("Last week" is finished time.)

So far this week I've worked three days. ("This week" is unfinished time.)

PRACTICE EXERCISE 1: Complete each of the following sentences with either the present perfect or simple past tense.

1. (drive) Mary _____ her new car to Santa Barbara yesterday.
2. (not try) Sam _____ on his new pants yet.
3. (buy) We _____ a new house last week.
4. (eat) _____ you ever _____ fried bananas?
5. (not go) Mr. and Mrs. Denton _____ out of town last weekend.
6. (see) I _____ never _____ *The Birds*.
7. (not speak) He _____ much English during his trip last April.
8. (miss) _____ you _____ me while I was gone?
9. (dance) _____ you ever _____ the salsa?
10. (get) Richard _____ a new car last week.

TOPIC 2: Verbs with Irregular Forms in the Past and Present Perfect Tenses

A lot of common verbs have irregular simple past and past participial forms. Here are some of the more common ones. You'll also find a list of all of the most important irregular verbs in the appendix on page 211.

Present	Past	Past Participle
be	*was/were*	*been*
begin	*began*	*begun*
bring	*brought*	*brought*
do	*did*	*done*
eat	*ate*	*eaten*
go	*went*	*gone*
have	*had*	*had*
know	*knew*	*known*
see	*saw*	*seen*
sing	*sang*	*sung*
speak	*spoke*	*spoken*

take   *took*   *taken*
write   *wrote*   *written*

PRACTICE EXERCISE 2: Complete each of the following sentences.

1. (sing) Who _____ that last song?
2. (do) Sarah _____ her homework last night.
3. (be) Where _____ you at breakfast?
4. (begin) Madeline _____ already _____ her new job.
5. (know) Henry _____ all of the answers.
6. (write) _____ you _____ that letter yet?
7. (begin) Angel _____ his university education last spring.
8. (sing) She _____ in Las Vegas many times.
9. (see) _____ anyone really ever _____ Big Foot?
10. (take) I had a headache, so I _____ some aspirin.

TOPIC 3: Using *for* and *since* with the Present Perfect and Simple Past Tenses

Use *since* when a specific point in time is given. Use *for* when a period of time, rather than a specific point in time, is given.

Since ...   For ...
yesterday   *one day*
last week   *a week*
last month   *three months*

Richard has lived in Chicago since 1985.

Richard has lived in Chicago for twenty years.

Notice that you can use *for* and *since* with either the simple past tense or the present perfect tense, depending on whether or not the action is still happening.

I've worked for Green Enterprises for three years. (I still work there.)

I worked for Green Enterprises for three years. (Now I work somewhere else.)

PRACTICE EXERCISE 3: Complete each sentence with either *since* or *for*.

1. We've lived in Los Angeles _____ before Barry was born.
2. We've lived in Los Angeles _____ ten years.
3. There's been a roadblock on the freeway _____ three days.
4. I haven't seen you _____ I was in high school.
5. Why haven't you called _____ two weeks?
6. Susan hasn't gone to work _____ last Tuesday.
7. They stayed at this hotel _____ three nights.
8. Roger and Martin have been gone _____ hours!
9. Have you been waiting for me _____ 7:30?
10. She hasn't spoken to me _____ the night we got into an argument.

1E   PHRASAL VERBS WITH *PICK*

Pick up.

a) To take something up off of a surface. *Pick your coat up off the floor.*

b) To meet and collect a person from a specific location. *Who's going to pick Henry up at the airport?*

c) To buy something. *Jordan picked up some milk on the way home.*

*Note that *to pick up a person* can also mean to meet someone, usually at a public place such as a bar or night club, and to become sexually involved with him or her after spending only a short time together.

Pick out.

a) To select, to choose. *Melissa picked out a shirt and brought it to the dressing room.*

b) To separate from. *If you break a wine glass, make sure you pick all of the glass out of the carpet.*

Pick over.

To take the best of something and leave what is not so good. *The shirts have been on sale so long that they've really been picked over.*

Pick on.

To tease. *My sisters and brothers always picked on me because I was the youngest.*

Pick from.

To choose from a group of something. *Mrs. Stefanson picked a new assistant from the group of applicants for the job.*

Pick at.

a) To take only very small amounts of food. *Jessica ate almost everything on her plate, but she only picked at her peas.*

b) To scratch or irritate something, such as a cut or scrape. *Don't pick at that cut! Let it heal.*

Pick up on.

To understand something, especially something that isn't intended to be understood. *They spoke in Spanish in front of Dorothy, so she didn't pick up on what they were talking about.*

*Note that *pick up, pick out, pick from,* and *pick over* are separable. This means the two words can be separated and a pronoun or noun can be inserted between them. *Billy picked out the raisins* or *Billy picked them/the raisins out,* but not *Billy picked out them. Pick on, pick at,* and *pick up on* are not separable. You cannot separate the verbs from the prepositions.

1F   REAL ENGLISH

SEE YOU LATER!

Saying "good-bye!" is only one way to end a conversation. There are a lot of idiomatic expressions that people use when a conversation is over or when they have to leave. Here are some important ones, listed from most to least formal: *Have a good day. Take care. Take it easy. (I'll) See you later. (I'll) See you around. See ya! Catch you later. Gotta go.* Note that these expressions are often preceded with *Well. Well, have a nice day!*

BRING IT ALL TOGETHER

Now let's review everything we've covered in this lesson.

REVIEW EXERCISE 1: Vocabulary

Place the correct vocabulary word in each space. Use each of the following words once: *solicit, beneficiary, indicted, procured, waiver, persecuted, incited, affiliation, espionage, amnesty, conspired, rehabilitation, clemency, sabotage, cited, induce, fraud, custody, ordinance, engaging.*

1. When we found out that Dr. Wells hadn't gone to medical school, we knew he was a
   _____ .

2. Learning new skills is essential to the successful _____ from a life of crime.

3. For some people, working is much harder than _____ in crime.

4. The well-known_____ International is an organization dedicated to encouraging governments to free their political prisoners.

5. Bill Jackson felt_____ because he had received a dishonorable discharge from the army and few employers would hire him.

6. The soldiers sneaked in behind enemy lines to_____ the next shipment of weapons.

7. _____ by jealousy, Roberto accused his wife of having an affair.

8. If you let your dog walk around without a leash, you are violating a city _____.

9. I want to show you some new gems we've recently _____.

10. The senator was forced to resign when his _____ with a racist organization was uncovered.

11. A sixteen-year-old cannot attend adult school without a_____ from high school.

12. Tammy went to several companies to_____ money so that she could afford to travel to the swimming competition.

13. Ralph was_____ for breaking and entering.

14. Mary was _____ for driving with her lights off.

15. The Rangels filed for_____ of their daughter's son.

16. A governor has the power to give_____ to a condemned criminal, commuting a death sentence to life in prison.

17. The boys_____ to scare all the girls in class on Halloween.

18. Wiretaps were placed on the ambassador's phone line in an act of _____.

19. Tony named his wife, Susan, as the_____ on his life insurance policy.

20. The labels of many poisonous products warn not to _____ vomiting in case of accidental ingestion.

REVIEW EXERCISE 2: The Present Perfect Tense vs. the Simple Past Tense

Complete each of the following sentences with the correct form of the verb given in parentheses.

1. (arrive) The plane _____ on time yesterday, but traffic was awful.

2. (be) It _____ a long hot summer, and it's only August 3!

3. (not call) No one can believe he _____ you yet.

4. (put) Who _____ my keys under the couch last night?

5. (eat) We _____ dinner at six.

6. (go) Christian _____ to school already this morning.

7. (visit) We _____ the Metropolitan Museum when we were in New York.

8. (see) I _____ the Eiffel Tower several times, but never in the spring.

REVIEW EXERCISE 3: Irregular Verb Forms

Fill in the spaces with the missing verb forms.

Present	Past	Past Participle
1. _____	was/were	_____
2. do	_____	_____
3. _____	_____	gone
4. _____	gave	_____
5. _____	ate	_____
6. write	_____	_____
7. _____	_____	begun
8. _____	_____	seen

REVIEW EXERCISE 4: *For* and *Since*

Fill in each sentence with *since* or *for*.

1. I don't think I've seen you _____ high school.

2. They didn't speak to each other _____ several weeks.

3. How long has it been _____ you left?

4. We haven't spoken _____ three years!

5. Why did you keep silent _____ so many months?

6. I can't believe you've been in Boston _____ September!

7. I'm not sure why he hasn't called _____ last week.

8. It hasn't rained _____ six months.

REVIEW EXERCISE 5: Phrasal Verbs

Place the correct phrasal verb with *pick* in the blank space in each sentence.

1. What time do you want me to _____ you _____ from the airport?

2. Alex's mother and sister helped her _____ her wedding dress.

3. Look how you _____ your food. You eat like a bird.

4. Johnny, _____ all your toys and put them away.

5. Evelyn _____ the label on her sweater because it irritates her.

6. Mrs. Russell told the class bully not to _____ the younger children.

7. Barry's a pretty smart little boy; he seems to _____ whatever anyone says.

8. I've _____ a beautiful crystal vase for Bill and Cindy's wedding gift.

1H   LISTEN UP!

🎧 Now let's work on your listening comprehension. Turn on your CD and listen to Section 1H. In this exercise, you will hear someone describing a situation. As you listen, choose the phrasal verb that could be used in the situation.

1. _____ pick out, on, up

2. _____ pick over, up, at

3. _____ pick at, on, up on

4. _____ pick up, from, at

5. _____ pick on, up, over

6. _____ pick up on, at, over

1I   WHY DO THEY DO THAT?

Greetings and Small Talk

📖 Have you ever heard a complete stranger say hello to you as you pass him or her on the street? Don't worry. That's not unusual. Americans often greet people they don't even know. They may talk to strangers while waiting in line, or comment on the weather when standing in an elevator, or even strike up a conversation while sitting next to someone at a public event. It's true that this kind of behavior may seem too casual—or even just plain strange—to others, but many Americans consider it friendly. Of course, these little pieces of "small talk" aren't meant to discuss anything very serious or personal or make new friendships. When they end, the participants go their separate ways and rarely commit to any kind of social involvement. This is normal for Americans, who often have a lot of acquaintances—at work, in their neighborhoods, at stores and restaurants, at the gym. But Americans also make an important distinction between casual acquaintances and close friends.

Lesson 1: Answer Key

Practice Exercise 1	1. drove, 2. hasn't tried, 3. bought, 4. Have/eaten, 5. didn't go, 6. have/seen, 7. didn't speak, 8. Did/miss, 9. Have/danced, 10. got
Practice Exercise 2	1. sang, 2. did, 3. were, 4. has/begun, 5. knew, 6. Have/written, 7. began, 8. has sung, 9. Has/seen, 10. took
Practice Exercise 3	1. since, 2. for, 3. for, 4. since, 5. for, 6. since, 7. for, 8. for, 9. since, 10. since
Review Exercise 1	1. fraud, 2. rehabilitation, 3. engaging, 4. Amnesty, 5. persecuted, 6. sabotage, 7. Incited, 8. ordinance, 9. procured, 10. affiliation, 11. waiver, 12. solicit, 13. indicted, 14. cited, 15. custody, 16. clemency, 17. conspired, 18. espionage, 19. beneficiary, 20. induce
Review Exercise 2	1. arrived, 2. has been, 3. hasn't called, 4. put, 5. ate, 6. has gone, 7. visited, 8. have seen

Review Exercise 3	1. be /been, 2. did/done, 3. go/went, 4. give/given, 5. eat/eaten, 6. wrote/written, 7. begin/began, 8. see/saw
Review Exercise 4	1. since, 2. for, 3. since, 4. for, 5. for, 6. since, 7. since, 8. for
Review Exercise 5	1. pick/up, 2. pick out, 3. pick at, 4. pick up, 5. picks at, 6. pick on, 7. pick up on, 8. picked out
Listen Up!	1. out, 2. up, 3. up on, 4. at, 5. on, 6. over

Don't Go Away!

ARE YOU READY FOR THE LESSON?

Lesson 2, *Don't Go Away!*, will take you on that paradise vacation you've been waiting for! You'll read a brochure for a world-class resort hotel and listen to recordings about some exciting vacation spots. Then you'll learn some helpful vocabulary for an exclusive hotel. But there's more. Lesson 2 also includes:

• Helpful Hints for the Present Tense

• Questions and Negatives in the Simple Present Tense

• Phrasal Verbs with *turn*

• Important Idioms for Using the Telephone

We'll finish off Lesson 2 with a culture note discussing why Americans move around so much. But first, let's start with a pronunciation warm-up. Ready?

2A SAY IT CLEARLY!

🎧 Turn on your CD to practice another very important ending, *–s*.

2B ENGLISH AT WORK

Recorded Message: The Hotel Royale

📖 Listen to the following recorded phone message from The Hotel Royale in Florida.

🎧 Hello, and welcome to paradise at The Hotel Royale, Florida, where an exciting adventure beckons. Located near world-famous Disney World in Orlando, Florida, our world-class hotel features well-appointed accommodations designed to pamper you with luxurious amenities. Don't go away. For more information and for rates and reservations, please stay on the line. We'll be right with you.

📖 Now let's take a look at a brochure for The Hotel Royale, Florida on the next page.

2C BUILD YOUR VOCABULARY

Once again, let's take a look at some vocabulary related to the topic of this lesson.

Accommodations. A place to stay, food and services. *Because we were poor college students, we chose inexpensive accommodations for our trip through New Mexico.*

Amenities. Attractive and convenient material comforts. *Whenever Nancy showed the smallest townhouses to her clients, she always pointed out the many wonderful amenities, hoping no one would notice the size.*

Amidst. Among, between. *Meredith found one black gumdrop amidst the many yellow, red, and orange ones.*

FLORIDA'S LEGENDARY HOTEL ROYALE
is the perfect vacation destination.

We are conveniently located just minutes from Disney World, Universal Studios Florida, SeaWorld Adventure Park, and the dazzling Orlando nightlife.

AT THE HOTEL ROYALE, we strive to make your stay memorable. Enjoy a resort atmosphere where you can stroll among the terraced gardens, sip your drink beside the grotto pool, pamper yourself at our luxurious European-style spa, and savor the exceptional cuisine at the Royale Inn.

The Hotel Royale, Florida, features such amenities as:
- Deluxe appointed guest rooms
- A spacious fitness center
- Panoramic views
- A rooftop botanical garden
- Kitchen suites
- Banquet and meeting facilities

Your stay at The Hotel Royale, Florida, will be a fantasy adventure. We simply have everything: an exciting location, beautiful accommodations, and fabulous service. This just might be paradise.

For rates and reservations call 1-800-555-2000.

Appointed. Arranged; furnished, provided with what is needed. *No one could help but notice how tastefully appointed the mansions were.*

Beckon. To call someone or something to come towards you, often with the use of a hand or finger gesture that means "come here." *Mrs. Applebee beckoned Tommy to her desk where they could discuss his mistakes in private.*

Cuisine. Manner or way of preparing food, a tradition of cooking particular to a region or country. *There are so many wonderful restaurants from around the world that it's hard to choose a favorite cuisine.*

Dazzling. Something exciting or beautiful; blinding light. *The local baseball team often puts on a dazzling fireworks display during its games.*

Grotto. A cave or cavern, an artificial structure made to look like a cave. *The zoo had to fashion a variety of grottos for the animals to hide in when they wanted privacy.*

Legendary. Similar to a story handed down from the past; something that is spoken of by many people over many years. *The children love to read stories about legendary heroes, such as Robin Hood or King Arthur.*

Luxurious. Expensive, rich, abundant, magnificent; something that appeals to the senses. *The hotel rooms were luxurious with their king-size beds, whirlpools, and sun decks.*

Nightlife. Places to go and things to see and enjoy at night, e.g., restaurants, theaters, bars, clubs, cafes, movies, etc. *Most people who do a lot of traveling like to sample at least a little of the nightlife in any city they visit.*

Pamper. To give a lot of care and attention to someone. *When Sally is depressed she pampers herself with a shopping spree.*

Panoramic. A view that can be seen from all sides. *The Empire State Building offers a panoramic view of New York City.*

Savor. To find delicious; to taste or smell with pleasure. *Elwin finds Indian food so delicious that he savors every bite.*

Sip. To drink slowly in small amounts. *We sat in the coffee shop and sipped our coffee for hours.*

Spacious. Having a lot of space; very large and open. *Being used to a tiny apartment, Bill found Marie's home quite spacious.*

Strive. To work toward a goal with great effort. *It is difficult to believe that some people never strive to improve.*

Stroll. To walk slowly and in a relaxed way. *Mr. and Mrs. Oglesbee strolled through their garden every evening.*

Terraced. With levels arranged like stair steps. *Villages in mountainous regions have had to raise their crops in terraced gardens.*

World-class. Among the best in the world. *The city council decided to build a world-class stadium in the hopes of attracting a national football team.*

2D ENGLISH UNDER THE HOOD

Many students of English feel that one of the most challenging tenses in English is the present tense. Perhaps this is simply because it's the first tense students learn, or that it has so many different uses. But whatever the reasons, there are three areas that often need to be reviewed:

- The –s ending of the third person singular
- How to form negatives
- How to form questions

TOPIC 1: –s Endings in the Third Person Singular

Only the third person singular, or the he/she/it form, of a verb in the simple present tense has an ending, –s. All other forms are the same as the basic form of the verb: *I speak, you speak, we speak, they speak*, but *he speaks, she speaks, it speaks*.

The –s ending becomes –*ies* if the verb ends in a –*y*: *I fly, you fly, we fly, they fly*, but *he flies, she flies, it flies*.

The –s ending becomes –*es* if the verb ends in one of these letters or letter combinations: –s (*you dress, she dresses*), –*sh* (*I wish, he wishes*), –*ch* (*they touch, it touches*), or –*x* (*you fix, she fixes*). And don't forget that the ending is pronounced –*iz*.

Notice that some verbs end in a silent –*e* in spelling, but have as their last sound a –*j* (*manage, judge*), –*z* (*lose, cruise*), or –*zh* (*massage*). These verbs will only add an –s in spelling, but the ending will be pronounced as an –*iz*: *she manages, he cruises, she massages, it loses*. (You've already seen this in Section A, Say It Clearly!)

PRACTICE EXERCISE 1: Fill in the blanks with the correct form of the verb.

1. (spread) The tree branches _____ over the sidewalk.
2. (begin) When it's very cold, my teeth _____ to chatter.
3. (run) Cedric _____ in a marathon twice a year.
4. (bark) The neighborhood dogs _____ most of the night.
5. (sell) The little girl _____ lemonade on hot Saturday mornings.
6. (take) It _____ a lot of money and good credit to buy a house in some parts of California.
7. (taste) Red apples usually _____ sweet and delicious.
8. (shine) The full moon _____ clear and bright on warm summer nights.
9. (expect) Meredith _____ to have another baby before she is 38 years old.
10. (want) All the employees _____ to take a vacation in August.

TOPIC 2: The Negative Simple Present Tense

As you know, the basic negative simple present tense is formed with *not*. But you also need to use an auxiliary, or "helping," verb with *not*, either *do* or *does*. The pattern is:

subject + auxiliary verb *do* or *does* + *not* + main verb (without –s!) Here are some pairs of examples, first affirmative, and then negative:

I drive a car.	*I do not drive a car.*
She takes the bus to work.	*She does not take the bus to work.*
Mr. Nasser likes this hotel.	*Mr. Nasser does not like this hotel.*
Sabrina has a new car.	*Sabrina does not have a new car.*

The *not* comes between *do* or *does* and the main verb. It's often attached to *do* or *does* in a contraction:

I don't drive a car.

She doesn't take the bus to work.

Mr. Nasser doesn't like this hotel.

Sabrina doesn't have a new car.

Remember that you shouldn't put the –s ending on the main verb in negatives. Also remember that you should use only one negative in English:

I don't speak Spanish. (Not: *I don't speak no Spanish.*)

She doesn't have any money. (Not: *She doesn't have no money.*)

I never walk to work in the rain. (Not: *I don't never walk to work in the rain.*)

And finally, remember that you need *do* or *does* in front of *not* with every verb except *be*:

I am on vacation.	*I am not on vacation.*
They are spending a week at the new resort.	*They aren't spending a week at the new resort.*

PRACTICE EXERCISE 2: Make the following sentences negative.

1. Tammy rides her horse to school.
2. We pay a lot to take the bus.
3. The children do what the teacher says.
4. Most women like to give their clothes away.
5. Darren and Tom care about the rules of good sportsmanship.
6. Maddie gets as much exercise as she used to.
7. It gets better than this!
8. Many flowers bloom all summer long.
9. The yard gets enough water.
10. The mountains have a lot of snow this time of year.

TOPIC 3: Questions in the Present Tense

Questions in the present tense are a lot like negatives, because you always need to use the auxiliary *do* or *does*, except with *be*:

Sandro studies English at the community center.

Does Sandro study English at the community center?

They are in New York this week.

Are they in New York this week?

Remember to begin questions in the simple present tense with *do* or *does*, then the subject, and then the main verb (again, always without an –s ending!).

Does Tom know Mary?

Do the children enjoy reading?

Does Maxime have many friends?

The exception is questions with a main verb *is, am,* or *are*:

Am I wrong?

Are you happy with the meal?

Is Gary at work right now?

PRACTICE EXERCISE 3: Change the following sentences into questions.

1. Harold likes to go bird watching.
2. Carolyn understands Spanish.
3. Mockingbirds sing very early in the morning.
4. You catch the bus at Fourth and Broadway.
5. I write to my mother at least once a week.
6. Tina teaches with the Peace Corps.
7. Minnie hides the cookies from her children.
8. The companies send their products through the U.S. mail.
9. The Smiths hear a catfight in their yard almost every night.
10. Taka's party begins at noon.

2E PHRASAL VERBS WITH *TURN*

Turn around.
To go back in the opposite direction. *Turn around! We just passed the theater.*

Turn down.
a) To lower the power of something, such as lights or volume. *Turn down the TV! It's too loud.*
b) To enter a road, especially a secondary road thought of as leading to a lower place. *You need to turn down this road and continue to the bottom of the hill.*
c) To refuse. *It was a great job offer, but I had to turn it down because it was too much work.*

Turn in.
a) To leave a street or highway and enter a driveway, parking lot, etc. *I think you can turn in here, where the sign says PARK.*
b) To go to bed. *Lawrence usually turns in around 10:00 P.M. because he wakes up so early.*
c) To give an assignment or paperwork to a boss or a teacher; to submit. *Bethany turned in her paper just as the professor was leaving.*
d) To report someone to the police. *When Robert heard about his brother's crimes, he turned him in.*

Turn into.
To become (used with nouns). *Jason got a promotion and turned into a real jerk!*

Turn off.
a) To stop an electronic device. *Turn off the TV, because I can't sleep with it on.*
b) To exit a road or freeway. *I think you should turn off at the next exit.*
c) To be unappealing. *This music is horrible! It really turns me off.*

Turn on.
a) To start an electronic device. *Our show is on in two minutes, so turn on the TV.*
b) To drive onto a street, highway, or freeway. *Why don't we turn on this road and just see where it goes?*

c) To be appealing or exciting. (Also used to mean "sexually stimulating.") *Dancing really turns me on and puts me in a great mood.*

Turn out.
To come to a party, event, etc. *Wow! So many people turned out for your party!*

Turn over.
To reverse the position of something from right-side up to upside down. *Can you turn over my pancake before it burns?*

Turn up.
a) To appear somewhere, to be found. *Don't worry, your earring's not gone forever; it'll turn up.*

b) To increase the power of something, such as lights or volume. *Turn up the lights a bit. It's so dark in here I can't read.*

c) To enter a road, especially a secondary road thought of as leading to a higher place. *Maybe if we turn up this road we'll be able to get to the top of the hill.*

2F REAL ENGLISH

Hold On!
Just about everyone knows that the expressions *hello* and *good-bye* are used to begin and end phone conversations in the United States. Here are some other expressions that are commonly used on the phone.

If you need to leave the phone momentarily but don't want to end the conversation, you can say, *don't go away, hang on, stay on the line, hold on a minute,* or *hold the line.* In business settings, where there is a hold button on the phone, you can say *let me put you on hold, please.* This is often followed with *I'll be right with you.*

If a receptionist is very busy, instead of answering the phone and waiting for a response, he or she may say right away *please hold* or *we'll be right with you.* And then you'll be *put on hold.*

2G BRING IT ALL TOGETHER

REVIEW EXERCISE 1: Vocabulary
Place the correct vocabulary word in each space. Use each of the following words once: *accommodations, amenities, amidst, appointed, beckon, cuisine, dazzling, grottos, legendary, luxurious, nightlife, pampered, panoramic, savor, sips, spacious, strive, strolled, terraced, world-class.*

1. Mr. and Mrs. Bunch _____ to the end of the pier to watch the fisherman.

2. Mrs. Peabody _____ her tea and reads the paper each Sunday afternoon.

3. If you climb to the top of a mountain, you can have a _____ view of the valley below.

4. Many people around the world consider Chinese to be their favorite _____.

5. When Karen got engaged she chose the most _____ diamond ring.

6. I just have to go to Hawaii; the islands _____ me!

7. We drove most of the night to find the cheapest _____.

8. A lot of people _____ to lose weight in a short time.

9. Karen insisted that her wedding reception be held at a _____ hotel.

10. Most English-speaking people know the _____ story of Camelot.

11. Martha has the smallest classroom, and Richard has the most _____ one of all.

12. Little Gloria fell asleep with her head nestled _____ the pillows on the couch.

13. The _____ banks alongside the freeway are planted with flowers.

14. Don't eat so fast. You need to learn to _____ this delicious food.

15. Tom Sawyer's Island at Disneyland has lots of _____ for children to play in.

16. Karen insisted on purchasing the most _____ wedding gown.

17. Las Vegas is known all over the world for its exciting _____.

18. This hotel costs a lot of money per night, but the rooms are very well _____.

19. Greg had the flu, so he left work, went home and _____ himself on the couch all day.

20. We rented a lovely cabin in the mountains that had all the _____ of home.

REVIEW EXERCISE 2: The Simple Present Tense

Fill in the following sentences with the correct form of the verb in the present tense.

1. (burst) The party balloons are cheap, so they _____ easily.

2. (cling) Baby Meredith often _____ to her mother's skirt.

3. (bend) The trees sway and the branches _____ in the cool breeze.

4. (freeze) Oranges and lemons _____ when the temperature drops.

5. (quit) Gerald always _____ before he gets fired.

6. (sweep) Marta _____ her kitchen floor everyday.

7. (stick) This window _____ whenever you try to open it.

8. (rise) Bill and Adriana _____ at 6:00 A.M. to go to work.

REVIEW EXERCISE 3: Negatives in the Present Tense

Make these sentences negative.

1. Our local weathermen forecast the weather correctly.

2. Janey grinds her teeth when she's nervous.

3. The washing machine spins the clothes until they are dry.

4. Terrence winds his wristwatch everyday.

5. The boys spread too much butter on their toast.

6. Gladys and Henry mistake the sugar for the salt.

7. Cats creep up on their prey before they attack.

8. Sharon feeds birds in the park.

REVIEW EXERCISE 4: Questions in the Present Tense

Change the following statements into questions.

1. The leaves fall off the trees every autumn in this city.
2. Joe and Tom split the money for each job they do.
3. Mrs. Warren goes to the store nearly every day.
4. Jenna is part Cherokee.
5. This store has nice things.
6. Edwina's clothes hang neatly in her closet.
7. Jorge sometimes leaves his keys in his car.
8. This bank is open late on Thursdays.

REVIEW EXERCISE 5: Phrasal Verbs

Place the correct phrasal verb with *turn* in the blank space in each sentence.

1. A huge crowd _____ whenever the Rolling Stones play.
2. The next exit is one-and-a-half miles away. Let's _____ there and get something to eat.
3. You have exactly one hour to finish writing and _____ your exams.
4. I'm pretty tired. I think I'll _____ early.
5. Jackie had to _____ the job offer, but she would have made a lot of money.
6. You just missed your exit, so _____ and go back the other way.
7. It's pretty foggy, but I think you can _____ to this parking lot on your left.
8. Hank loses his wallet all the time, but it always _____ in the strangest places.

2H LISTEN UP!

Listen to the recorded telephone recording and answer the following questions.

1. How late does the park stay open?
2. What happens if it rains?
3. How much do daily passes for two adults, one six-year-old child, and one three-year-old child cost?
4. Which pass has the best rate if you want to go to the park twice in one week?
5. What street is the park on?
6. How much does the parking-lot shuttle cost?

2I WHY DO THEY DO THAT?

Americans on the Move

You've probably noticed that Americans tend to move around a great deal during their lives. This begins young, often right after high school, with the first separation from a person's family. It's a tradition for young people to move away from their hometowns to go to college, often going to a college or university on the other side of the country. But even if they decide not to continue their education, young Americans usually get a job and move out of their parents' home after high school graduation. This fast separation and movement is in keeping with the independence and individuality that the American culture fosters. It's also a matter of job opportunity. Americans will often go wherever their jobs take them. This may include moving far away from extended family and friends, and could mean making several different moves from city to city or state to state. It's also common for Americans to live rather far from where they work, commuting hours by car or train to their jobs. All of this is in keeping with a tendency toward movement that many Americans demonstrate.

Lesson 2: Answer Key

Practice Exercise 1	1.spread, 2. begin, 3. runs, 4. bark, 5. sells, 6. takes, 7. taste, 8. shines, 9. expects, 10. want
Practice Exercise 2	1. doesn't ride, 2. don't pay, 3. don't do, 4. don't like, 5. don't care, 6. doesn't get, 7. doesn't get, 8. don't bloom, 9. doesn't get, 10. don't have
Practice Exercise 3	1. Does Harold like . . . ?, 2. Does Carolyn understand . . . ?, 3. Do mockingbirds sing . . . ?, 4. Do you catch . . . ?, 5. Do I write . . . ?, 6. Does Tina teach . . . ?, 7. Does Minnie hide . . . ?, 8. Do the companies send . . . ?, 9.Do the Smiths hear . . . ?, 10. Does Taka's party begin . . . ?
Review Exercise 1	1. strolled, 2. sips, 3. panoramic, 4. cuisine, 5. dazzling, 6. beckon, 7. accommodations, 8. strive, 9. world-class, 10. legendary, 11. spacious, 12. amidst, 13. terraced, 14. savor, 15. grottos, 16. luxurious, 17. nightlife, 18. appointed, 19. pampered, 20. amenities
Review Exercise 2	1. burst, 2. clings, 3. bend, 4. freeze, 5. quits, 6. sweeps, 7. sticks, 8. rise
Review Exercise 3	1. don't forecast, 2. doesn't grind, 3. doesn't spin, 4. doesn't wind, 5. don't spread, 6. don't mistake, 7. don't creep, 8. doesn't feed
Review Exercise 4	1. Do the leaves fall . . . ?, 2. Do Joe and Tom split . . . ?, 3. Does Mrs. Warren go . . . ?, 4. Is Jenna . . . ?, 5. Does this store have . . . ?, 6. Do Edwina's clothes hang . . . ?, 7. Does Jorge sometimes leave . . . ?, 8. Is this bank . . . ?
Review Exercise 5	1. turns out, 2. turn off, 3. turn in, 4. turn in, 5. turn down, 6. turn around, 7. turn in, 8. turns up
Listen Up!	1. 8:00 P.M., 2. The park is closed, 3. $104.85, 4. A five-day pass, 5. Olympia Road, 6. free

Lesson 3

What Would You Like To Do?

ARE YOU READY FOR THE LESSON?

If you're interested in finding a job in the U.S, Lesson 3, *What Would You Like To Do?*, can help. This lesson will take you on a job interview and show you a sample résumé. You'll also learn some important vocabulary for jobs and job hunting, and you'll listen to a job hotline in *Listen Up!* Here are a few more things you will learn in Lesson 3:

- Questions and Negatives in the Simple Past Tense
- Habitual Action in the Past
- Polite Requests
- Phrasal Verbs with *work*
- Idioms for On the Job

We'll finish the lesson by discussing handshakes—for example, when to offer a handshake and the proper handshake technique. But let's begin the lesson by practicing pronunciation in *Say It Clearly!* Ready?

3A SAY IT CLEARLY!

🎧 Turn on your CD to practice some English reductions, which are changes that you make to sounds in natural speech when they're combined. Reductions are an important part of natural-sounding English.

3B ENGLISH AT WORK

DIALOGUE: Would You Mind if I Looked at Your Résumé?

📖 Qing Zhang was trained as a computer programmer in China, so she'd like a job in the same field here in the U.S.A. There's a lot of competition for computer programming positions, but Qing is well qualified. Let's listen to an interview between Qing and the Director of Human Resources at a major telecommunications company.

🎧 **Ms. Peterson** Hello, Ms. Zhang. I'm Marla Peterson. Have a seat, please.

Qing Thank you.

Ms. Peterson Would you like something to drink? Coffee? Tea? Water? . . .

Qing Yes, I'd like some water, please, thank you.

Ms. Peterson Would you mind if I looked at your résumé?

Qing Of course not. Here it is.

Ms. Peterson Well, now. I'd like to know a little bit more about your background. How long have you been here? Where did you study? You do have a green card, don't you? Yes, here it is. I see it here on your résumé. And what would you like to do here at Collcom Communications?

Qing Um, I've been here for about three weeks . . . maybe a little over three weeks. I used to live in Massachusetts before I came here. I was there for a year and a half, I think. And yes, I do have a green card. I studied computer programming at Beijing University. And I would like to be a computer programmer here at Collcom. Collcom is world famous, and I hear you treat your employees very well. So I'd really like to work for such a famous and wonderful company.

Ms. Peterson   Yes, I see you worked at Pellcorp in Massachusetts . . . very impressive. Your résumé looks great, too. You really are well qualified. We need someone to start right away. How soon would you be able to start?

Qing   I could start next week, or maybe sooner. I'd just like a few more days to get a little more settled in my apartment before I start work. But I'm flexible.

Ms. Peterson   All right, Qing. That sounds great. Well, I'll be in touch within the next couple of days.

Qing   Thank you, and it was nice meeting you.

Now take a look at Qing's résumé on the next page.

3C   BUILD YOUR VOCABULARY

Background. Education and work experience. Can also mean family, ethnicity, religion, etc. *The applicant's background was in education; she'd always worked as a teacher.*

Candidate. An applicant for a job or position. *There are nine candidates for the office clerk position.*

Deadline. The date when something is due or must be finished and turned in. *Daniel Dean had only one more week to meet his deadline and turn his manuscript in to the publisher.*

Detail oriented. Capable of paying careful attention to details. *Many positions require that candidates be detail oriented.*

Document. To keep evidence or a written record, such as photocopies, notes, e-mail, etc. *Helen documented every instance of lateness or poor performance by her staff.*

Entrepreneurial spirit. Enthusiasm for business, especially one's own new business. *Linda has great entrepreneurial spirit; she opened her own business and has had a great deal of success.*

Headhunter. An employment scout. A person who matches jobs with applicants. *Debbie was a skilled computer technician, so she went to a headhunter to find a better-paying job.*

Inception. The beginning or start. *This company has had only the finest employees since its inception.*

Interface. To communicate directly, to meet and interact. *One of your responsibilities is to interface with other employees in the company.*

K. One thousand dollars. *The starting salary for this position is 55K.*

Liaison. A person who establishes and maintains communication, a link. *The U.S. Secretary of State acts as a liaison between the President and other governments.*

Qing Zhang
2506 Brighton Manor Road
San Diego, California 92106
(619) 555-2030
q_zhang@xpres.com

OBJECTIVE
Position as computer programmer in a busy, productive office.

QUALIFICATIONS
- Experienced working in demanding office environment with heavy phone traffic
- Proficient in Microsoft SQL Server, Visual Basic, Power Builder, Visual C++/MFC
- Some experience in Java Script, J Script, VB Script, HTML/XML/SGML
- Bilingual Mandarin Chinese (native) and English (fluent)
- Strong research skills
- Detail oriented

EXPERIENCE
July 2002 – February 2005
Pellcorp International, World Center for Communications, Shrewsbury, Massachusetts
Computer Programming Assistant—Compiled code into programs, corrected errors detected in compiling process.

October 2000 – May 2002
International Student Services, Beijing Institute of Technology, Beijing, China
Office Assistant—Prepared documents for mailing, answered phones, provided information to students, filed documents and student files, made photocopies.

June 1998 – August 2000
English Language Institute, Beijing, China
Test Administrator—Gave tests to English as a Second Language students and assessed level, answered phones, performed administrative functions and assisted teachers in office.

EDUCATION
September 1998 – June 2002 Beijng Institute of Technology, Beijing, China
Bachelor of Science in Computer Programming

REFERENCES
Available upon Request

Multitasking. Working on several projects at the same time, usually of different natures. *Brad is great at multitasking, often doing filing, answering the phone, and scheduling appointments for his boss at the same time.*

Pending. Waiting, something not yet decided. *Jordan has a lot of pending projects; he doesn't know if they'll be approved or not.*

Perseverance. The ability to persist in an undertaking. *Even though Natalie isn't the least bit interested in Jack, his perseverance is amazing. He never gives up!*

Prioritize. To organize or accomplish according to importance, to be able to do projects in order of importance. *Sometimes it helps a person's stress level if he or she prioritizes everything that needs to be done and sets aside what is less important.*

Proficient. Thoroughly capable in a skill. *Do you feel proficient in Spanish yet, or are you still learning?*

Prospective. Potential or expected in the future. *I'd like you to meet my prospective assistant. I'd like to know what you think of him before I decide to hire him.*

Recruit. A newcomer to an organization. Someone persuaded or convinced to join an organization. *The army is always looking for new recruits.*

Team player. Someone who works well with others. *Most companies like to hire team players because they know that these individuals will promote a good working environment for everyone.*

Work ethic. Responsible moral philosophy or code of conduct at work. *Elbert was fired because he didn't have a good work ethic. He always got to work late, and he didn't take his duties seriously.*

3D   ENGLISH UNDER THE HOOD

TOPIC 1: Questions and Negatives in The Simple Past Tense

You reviewed the formation and use of the simple past tense in Lesson 1, where you compared it to the present perfect tense. Now let's take a closer look at questions and negatives in the simple past tense. Just like questions and negatives in the simple present tense, questions and negatives in the past tense require a helping verb: *did* instead of *do* or *does*. Let's start with questions. Questions in the simple past tense use *did*, following the same pattern as questions in the simple present tense: *did* + main verb in base form + rest of sentence.

John <u>writes</u> well.	<u>Does</u> John <u>write</u> well?
John <u>wrote</u> well.	<u>Did</u> John <u>write</u> well?

Notice that both *writes* and *wrote* become *write*, the basic form of the verb, in questions. It's up to *does* or *did* to show you whether the question is in the present or past tense.

Greg <u>sailed</u> to Block Island.	<u>Did</u> Greg <u>sail</u> to Block Island?
Federica <u>went</u> to work by train.	<u>Did</u> Federica <u>go</u> to work by train?
They <u>saw</u> a great movie.	<u>Did</u> they <u>see</u> a great movie?

To form a negative in the simple past tense, use the auxiliary verb *did* before the main verb, and insert *not* between the two verbs. The pattern is: subject + *did* + *not (didn't)* + main verb. Again, remember that the main verb is not in the past tense, but reverts to its root or basic form just as in questions.

She <u>talked</u> to him.	She <u>did</u> <u>not</u> <u>talk</u> to him.
I <u>went</u> to the store.	I <u>didn't</u> <u>go</u> to the store.
Kenneth <u>bought</u> a new car.	Kenneth <u>didn't</u> <u>buy</u> a new car.

PRACTICE EXERCISE 1: Change the following statements into questions.

1. Paul studied in the library all last night.
2. Yuri had a beer with his meal.
3. Marilyn left her books at home.
4. Joe and Rich ran a mile and a half to the park.
5. The Jones family lived in Kentucky before moving to Arkansas.

Now make the following sentences negative.

6. We all visited Mother in the hospital last week.
7. They gave me their phone numbers.
8. Tomas withdrew his name from the contest.
9. The phone rang all day long.
10. A bee stung me after the ball game.

TOPIC 2: The Past Habitual: *Used to, Didn't Use to and Would Always*

Used to expresses something about the past that is no longer true, but was once a habit or a regular, repeated action or activity. In this case, the verb *use* does not mean the same as *employ*, but rather has a special meaning in the construction *used to*.

I used to believe in ghosts when I was a kid.

Sandy used to jog along the river every morning.

I used to smoke cigarettes, but I quit three years ago.

The negative of *used to* follows the same rules as any negative past verb. The auxiliary *did* comes after the subject and before the main verb and *not* is inserted between *did* and the main verb (*use*). *Use*, the main verb, will be in the root form. The formula is: subject + *did (didn't)* + *not* + *use to* + verb.

I didn't use to live in L. A. I moved when I was in my twenties.

He didn't use to drink coffee, but now he does all the time.

Questions with *used to* are formed in a similar way. Just put the auxiliary verb *did* in the first position, then the subject, then the basic verb *use*, and finally the rest of the sentence.

Did you use to live in L.A. before you moved to Buffalo?

Did he use to drink so much coffee?

Another way to express the past habitual is to use *would (always)* plus the verb. This construction means the same thing as *used to*, but it can only be used to express a repeated action, and not a specific situation or condition in the past.

I would always sleep with the light on when I was a kid. (Because I used to be afraid of the dark.)

She would go to Prospect Park every day when she lived in Brooklyn. (Because she used to live so close.)

PRACTICE EXERCISE 2: Fill in the blanks with the correct form of *used to* or *didn't use to* plus the verb given.

1. (live) I _____ with my aunt.
2. (call) Marilyn _____ her boyfriend on the phone.
3. (live) Tamara _____ with her boyfriend, but now she does.
4. (be) Local elections _____ so boring, but now they're so boring that few people vote.
5. (be) The radio _____ as important as the television is today.
6. (have) A long time ago, people _____ as much free time as they have today.

Now let's try using *would (always.)*

7. (lie) When Candy was a child, she _____ in the grass and watch the clouds.
8. (ask) I _____ for a doll for every birthday until I was about thirteen.
9. (pick up) When Jacobo was in high school, he _____ his friends and drive them to school.
10. (eat) The Richardson children _____ cereal in front of the TV after school.

TOPIC 3: Making Polite Requests

Would is also used to make polite requests. Here are a few examples:

Would you get me a cup of coffee, please?

Would you please stop by my office at three tomorrow?

Of course, the simple command form in English is: *Get me a cup of coffee* or *Stop by my office at three tomorrow.* But this can sound a bit abrupt or even rude to American ears, so it's common to soften commands by using a polite request construction.

You can also make polite requests using *could* or *can.* These all have the same meaning, but *would* is the most polite. *Could* and *can* imply more familiarity than *would.* Finally, you can form polite requests with *would you mind* + verb + *-ing,* which is also a less formal construction.

Could you get me a cup of coffee, please?

Can you pass me the salt and pepper?

Would you mind getting me a juice glass from the cupboard?

There's another common polite expression with *would you mind* that asks permission rather than makes a request.

Would you mind if I came with you?

Would you mind if Brian borrowed your car?

Notice that the verb in the *if* clause is in the past tense: *came* and *borrowed.*

PRACTICE EXERCISE 3: Complete each of the following sentences with the correct form of the verb given in parentheses.

1. Would you mind (shut) _____ the door?
2. Would you mind if I (close) _____ the window?
3. Could you (get) _____ me an aspirin?
4. Would you mind if I (take) _____ your dictionary for a moment?
5. Would you mind if I (drive) _____ your new car?
6. Would you mind (let) _____ me sit in on the class this afternoon?
7. Can you (fix) _____ me some tea?
8. Could you (take) _____ me to the doctor's office on Tuesday?
9. Would you mind (make) _____ dinner for us?
10. Would you (get) _____ me some bananas, please?

3E PHRASAL VERBS WITH *WORK:*

Work around.
To be flexible. To make adjustments to someone's schedule or needs. *Karen, don't worry about your kids. We can work around your schedule so that you'll be home when they leave school.*

Work at.
To put a lot of effort into something. To pay attention. *The only reason I speak French so well is that I work at it. It doesn't just come naturally.*

Work for.
a) To put effort into achieving something. *In the present day economy, you really have to work for the job you want, because it doesn't just come to you.*
b) To be employed by a person or company. *What company do you work for?*

Work in.
a) To fit into a schedule, especially a busy schedule. *Yes, Mr. Schmitz, it looks like we can work you in at 1:30 today for an appointment.*
b) To blend into or add gradually, especially using your hands. *After you make the dough you have to work in the other ingredients until everything is blended.*
c) To add or introduce, especially a topic in a conversation. *I wanted to talk about the money Dan owed me, but I couldn't work it into the conversation.*

Work on.
To focus on something, to do something attentively. *He just may be up all night working on this report.*

Work out.
a) To work to resolve a problem, especially in cooperation with someone else. *Ray and Jolene are seeing a marriage counselor to try to work out their marital problems.*

b) To exercise, especially at a gym or health club. *You need to work out at least a half hour a day to maintain good health.*

Work toward.
To make an effort to accomplish a long-term goal. *Carl is working toward a degree in medicine so that he can become a doctor.*

Work up.
To work to gain energy or courage to do something. *I didn't use to be able to do any push-ups, but I've worked up to thirty at a time.*

3F   REAL ENGLISH

Put Your Nose to the Grindstone

What do you do? Has anyone ever asked you this question? It means, "what's your job or profession?" Although work can be very fulfilling, it can also be stressful, so as Monday approaches, Americans might say it's *blue Monday*, meaning it's a day to feel depressed because you have to go back to work. After all, on Monday you have to *put your nose to the grindstone*, or *get down to business*. You've got to *stick it out* for the entire week! After your *coffee break*, or rest time, you might say to your coworkers *let's get back to work*. But work also involves socializing and cooperation, so you might ask a coworker to *give you a hand* or *help you out* on a project. Then when Friday finally comes around, everyone's *dressed down* in casual clothes and ready for the weekend, so you might say *TGIF!* or "Thank God it's Friday!"

3G   BRING IT ALL TOGETHER

REVIEW EXERCISE 1: Vocabulary

Fill in the blanks with the following words: *background, candidates, deadlines, detail oriented, document, entrepreneurial spirit, headhunter, inception, interface, K, liaison, multitask, pending, perseverance, prioritize, proficient, prospective, recruits, team player, work ethic.*

1. Jill has a great _____; she's always on time, is never dishonest, and completes her projects flawlessly.

2. If you have legal problems with someone, it's always a good idea to _____ everything they say or do.

3. Nathan has never been able to make his _____. He always turns in his projects a few days late.

4. Can you tell me a little about your _____? What jobs have you held?

5. These concerns have existed since the _____ of this project.

6. There were so many good _____ that it's difficult to choose the best one for the job.

7. Ralph is a real _____. He always does his share of the work and cooperates with his colleagues.

8. A person who works with money really needs to be _____, since making even small mistakes can cause serious problems.

9. I won't take a penny less than 350 _____ for the property!

10. High school students must take an exit exam before they graduate to demonstrate that they are _____ in English and math.

11. Do you think a _____ could help me find a job in my field?

12. Sometimes an _____ seems to be inherited. Successful businesspeople often have parents who are also successful businesspeople.

13. The Pope's _____ met with the Council of American Bishops to try to agree on a plan.

14. It takes a lot of _____ to solve the *New York Times* crossword puzzle.

15. Put all the files that can wait in the "_____" folder until we can resolve the Nelson file.

16. Teachers usually have to do many jobs and often teach several subjects. Therefore an ability to _____ is an important asset for a teacher to have.

17. Which of the new _____ was most eager to join the organization?

18. After Glenn graduated, he had to _____ all the things he had to accomplish because there was so much to do.

19. Donna knows everyone in the company because it's her duty to _____ with all departments.

20. I have many _____ clients, but none that are definite, yet.

REVIEW EXERCISE 2: Questions and Negatives in the Simple Past Tense

Make the following statements negative.

1. I did the dishes last night.

2. Henry brought his books to class.

3. She exaggerated about how hard the test was.

4. Carlton showed me his homework.

5. Sonia took all of the cookies.

Now change the following past statements into questions.

6. The Kelton twins remembered there was a party last Friday night.

7. Jim developed his film at the mall.

8. They drove to Chicago instead of taking the train.

9. Jerry cut his finger.

10. Murphy used all of his sick days for the entire year.

REVIEW EXERCISE 3: The Past Habitual: *Used to, Didn't Use to* and *Would Always*

Fill in the following sentences with *used to* or *didn't use to*.

1. Cindy _____ drive a car, but she does now.

2. We _____ use our imaginations a lot more when we were children.

3. The Nagles _____ live across the street before they moved to Cincinnati.

4. I _____ like to chew gum, but I do now.

5. Jim and Debbie _____ be married, but now they're divorced.

Fill in the following sentences with *would always*.

6. (sleep) We _____ in the car when we took long trips.

7. (chase) The dog _____ the lawn mower, but now she's too old.

8. (buy) Kent _____ old furniture and fix it up.

REVIEW EXERCISE 4: Phrasal Verbs with *work*

Place the correct phrasal verb with *work* in the blank space in each sentence.

1. Even though she was busy, the dentist was able to _____ me _____ yesterday afternoon.

2. If you want to excel at anything, you really have to _____ it.

3. Paul is trying to get in shape, so he's been eating better, running every morning, and _____ several times a week.

4. Sharon is terribly busy because she's _____ her PhD.

5. Kika used to work here, but now she _____ a competitor.

6. Jenny goes to school and has a part-time job, and her boss is understanding enough to _____ her class schedule.

3H LISTEN UP!

🎧 Listen to the recording for the *Great Jobs!* job line and answer the following questions.

1. How many jobs are listed?

2. Do you need experience to apply for all of the jobs?

3. What do you do to listen to the job listings again?

4. Which job would be best for a college student?

5. Which job doesn't involve working with the public?

6. Which position does the caller probably want?

3I WHY DO THEY DO THAT?

Shaking Hands

📖 The handshake is very important in the American business world. When meeting with a customer or prospective client, businesspeople will always hold out their hands for a handshake. This is often true in purely social situations as well — when two strangers are introduced through a mutual friend, for example. Americans read a lot into the quality of a handshake. If it is limp and weak, Americans may assume that the person is weak-willed, insecure, or indecisive. For this reason, it is important to make your handshake firm and strong, without being painful or aggressively firm, because this will also send the wrong message! When shaking hands, grasp the other's hand and firmly pump it up and down once or twice, and then let go. In situations where there is a closer relationship the handshake may last for several seconds longer. Some people even clasp the other person's forearm with their free hand. For a more tender touch, the hand of one's friend may be held by both hands and gently shaken.

Lesson 3: Answer Key

Practice Exercise 1	1. Did Paul study … ?, 2. Did Yuri have … ?, 3. Did Marilyn leave … ?, 4. Did Joe and Rich run … ?, 5. Did the Jones family live … ?, 6. didn't visit, 7. didn't give, 8. didn't withdraw, 9. didn't ring, 10. didn't sting
Practice Exercise 2	used to live, 2. used to call, 3. didn't use to live, 4. didn't use to be, 5. used to be, 6. didn't use to have, 7. would always lie, 8. would always ask, 9. would always pick up, 10. would always eat
Practice Exercise 3	1. shutting, 2. closed, 3. get, 4. took, 5. drove, 6. letting, 7. fix, 8. take, 9. making, 10. get
Review Exercise 1	1. work ethic, 2. document, 3. deadlines, 4. background, 5. inception, 6. candidates, 7. team player, 8. detail oriented, 9. K, 10. proficient, 11. headhunter, 12. entrepreneurial spirit, 13. liaison, 14. perseverance, 15. pending, 16. multitask, 17. recruits, 18. prioritize, 19. interface, 20. prospective
Review Exercise 2	1. didn't do, 2. didn't bring, 3. didn't exaggerate, 4. didn't show, 5. didn't take, 6. Did the Kelton twins remember … ? 7. Did Jim develop … ? 8. Did they drive … ? 9. Did Jerry cut … ? 10. Did Murphy use … ?
Review Exercise 3	1. didn't use to, 2. used to, 3. used to, 4. didn't use to, 5. used to, 6. would always sleep, 7. would always chase, 8. would always buy
Review Exercise 4	1. work … in, 2. work at it, 3. working out, 4. working towards, 5. works for, 6. work around
Listen Up!	1. There are three jobs listed. 2. No, not for the health information clerk, 3. Press 9 to return to the main menu. 4. The health information clerk, 5. Number 3, the graphic artist, 6. Number 3.

Lesson 4

Laughing All the Way to the Bank

ARE YOU READY FOR THE LESSON?

In Lesson 4, *Laughing All the Way to the Bank,* you'll read about electronic banking, and you'll listen to some information comparing banks and credit unions. You'll learn some essential banking vocabulary and phrasal verbs with *pay.* But there's more. You'll also learn about:

- The Simple Future and the Immediate Future
- The Present Continuous and Simple Present to Express the Future
- The Simple Present Tense with Prepositions of Time
- Idioms about Money and Finance

But first, let's listen to the "y-vowel link" in *Say It Clearly!* Ready?

4A SAY IT CLEARLY!

Just like reductions, linking is an important part of natural-sounding English. Linking means joining words or sounds together, and there are actually several different types of linking in English. In this lesson, you'll practice what's called the "y-vowel link."

4B ENGLISH AT WORK

Read and listen to the following passage, which as you can guess is all about banking.

Not too long ago, U.S. banks were offering incentives to entice clients into using ATM machines. No one wanted to use them though, because machines lack the warmth and personal touch of a human teller. But today, of course, nearly everyone uses ATM machines to get cash, deposit money, or transfer funds. And that's not the only banking innovation. There are other banking services that are rapidly becoming more and more useful to busy people who do not have the time to go to a bank in person and wait in line to see a teller. Banking by phone allows you as an account holder to check on your balances, make transfers, listen to transaction histories, and much more, all by using your touch-tone phone. You can of course do all of this after the bank has closed, including weekends. Online banking offers you the same services by accessing an account online. E-banking, or electronic banking, can be done without cash or checks. Your paycheck can be deposited automatically through direct deposit, and your bills can be paid by transferring funds electronically out of your account. You don't have to write a single check or mail a single statement. Managing your money is simple, too. All you have to do is check your e-statement, daily if you like. Isn't it hard to remember the time when you had to go to a bank and stand in line to do all of this? So who needs cash? You've already got your debit card!

BUILD YOUR VOCABULARY

Access Code. A code or personal identification number. *I can't get into my account because I don't remember my access code.*

ATM. Automatic Teller Machine. A machine that dispenses money and debits a bank account. *If you need to get cash or make a deposit, there's an ATM just down the block.*

Assets. Property. Everything of value owned by an individual or organization. (Assets can be used to secure loans by ensuring repayment through their sale.) *My uncle's assets are going to be distributed equally among his heirs.*

Balance. The total amount of money in an account. The amount due on a bill. *It's important to know the balance of your checkbook each month.*

Cleared Checks. Checks that have gone through the banking system and been paid in full. *You can call your bank's phone express service to find out about your cleared checks.*

Deposit. To put money into a bank account. *Madeleine's savings account has grown because she has deposited a lot of money this month.*

Dividends. Cash that is paid for the use of money. The sharing of a profit. Money that has been divided and distributed. *Credit unions pay a dividend into their members' checking and savings accounts.*

E-Statements. Bank statements that can be accessed online through one's bank. *It's a good idea to check your e-statement online at least once a month.*

Identity Theft. The use of someone else's social security number, name, address, phone number, etc., to gain illegal access to credit. *Sam was a victim of identity theft; someone opened a credit card account in his name and made several online purchases.*

Interest. The charge or payment for borrowed money. *The new interest rate on my mortgage will only be 6.125 percent.*

Member Number. A person's account number for an organization such as a credit union. *Be ready to give your member number when you call your credit union.*

Portfolio. Securities or evidence of ownership of stock, etc., held by an investor. *Financial planners always recommend that you diversify your portfolio so that you have a variety of ways to earn money for your retirement.*

Surcharge. Additional cost or tax. *Be prepared to pay a surcharge when you use an ATM machine from a bank other than your own.*

Transaction. A withdrawal, transfer or deposit of funds. *Check your e-statement to see which transactions have occurred this month.*

Transfer. To move funds from one account to another. *I'm transferring $1000 from my savings to my checking account.*

Volatile Market. A stock market that changes erratically; an unstable stock market. *Investors are worried because it's been such a volatile market.*

Waive. To set aside, to choose not to apply a penalty, a right, etc. *If you forget to make a payment on time, some companies will waive the penalty if it is the first occurrence.*

Withdraw. To take funds from an account. *You can withdraw money at ATMs everywhere nowadays.*

4D ENGLISH UNDER THE HOOD

TOPIC 1: Simple Future vs. Immediate Future

The simple future (*will*) and the immediate future (*going to . . .*) are the two most common forms of the future tense.

We will eat later.   *We are going to eat later.*
It'll rain tomorrow.   *It's going to rain tomorrow.*

As you can see, these two tenses can be interchangeable. But in general, *going to* is less emphatic and more neutral than *will*, especially for events in the near future.

I'm going to buy a new car. (I've decided to buy a new car, and I'll do it soon.)

I will buy a new car. (More emphatic and insisting. A stronger intention.)

When you want to make a promise or describe an intention or willingness to do something, use *will* + verb.

Don't worry. I promise I'll call you when I get home.

I'll be there, no doubt about it.

Also note that *will* is used for events or activities in the more-distant future.

Jane will retire in twenty years.

Someday the sun will burn out and explode.

*Note that *shall* is also used with verbs to indicate the future, but it's rare in American English.

PRACTICE EXERCISE 1: Choose *be going to* or *will* + verb. Note that in some cases both answers are correct.

1. I promise I (come) _____ to see you in the hospital.
2. Do you think it (rain) _____ ?
3. She's having a caesarian so the baby (be) _____ on August 15th.
4. Teddy says he (study) _____ medicine next fall.
5. You (stand) _____ to the right of the bride.
6. Rob said that he (pass) _____ his test no matter what.
7. Jean (apply) _____ to several universities.
8. I think Jerome and Cindy (get) _____ married within a year.
9. August (be) _____ extremely hot this year.
10. I'm driving to town later so I (get) _____ some oranges.

TOPIC 2: The Present Continuous and Simple Present to Express the Future

The present continuous tense, *be* + verb + *ing*, can also be used to express the future. It is used mostly to talk about planned events. *I'm going to school after work. We're studying in the library at 10:00 tomorrow.*

The simple present tense can be used to mean the future for scheduled or planned events as well. Notice that these sentences usually include future-time words, such as dates. *Classes begin in September. We leave next Wednesday for Puerto Rico.*

PRACTICE EXERCISE 2: Rewrite each of the following sentences using the tense indicated in parentheses.

1. The budget committee will be in session all next week. (simple present)
2. I am going to take Spanish next semester. (present continuous)
3. Linda is going to start her new job next week. (simple present)
4. Tomorrow we will begin a new lesson. (simple present)
5. The shuttle bus will arrive at 8:45. (simple present)
6. We are going to have a party Friday night. (present continuous)
7. Jay is going to have band practice this afternoon. (simple present)
8. The bookstore will open at 10:00 tomorrow. (simple present)
9. Your favorite TV show will begin in a few minutes. (present continuous)
10. Anita will take the bus to work all next week. (present continuous)

TOPIC 3: The Simple Present Tense with Prepositions of Time

The simple present tense is used to express future events in clauses that begin with conjunctions such as *when, as soon as, before, after, unless,* or *until*. Note that even though these conjunctions introduce future events or action, the verbs after them are in the simple present tense. The verbs in the main clause, though, can be in a future tense.

As soon as I get home, I'm going to make dinner.

I'll answer the phone when it rings.

PRACTICE EXERCISE 3: Use the simple future and the simple present in each sentence.

1. I (call) _____ when I (get) _____ there.
2. I (finish) _____ this report before I (fix) _____ dinner.
3. The meeting (begin) _____ after the boss (arrive) _____.
4. She (be able) _____ not _____ to get to work unless she (take) _____ the bus.
5. The fireworks (begin) _____ after the sun (go) _____ down.
6. Barry (do) _____ not _____ anything about it unless you (ask) _____ him to.
7. The flowers (open) _____ after the clouds (clear) _____ away.

8. The VCR (record) _____ only_____ a TV show after you (program) _____ it.

9. The trees are so dry that they (catch) _____ on fire when lightning (strike) _____ them.

10. Your attitude (change) _____ after you (learn) _____ the truth.

4E   PHRASAL VERBS WITH *PAY*

Pay back.

a) To pay someone money that is owed. *Don't I always pay you back when I borrow money from you?*

b) To get revenge for something. *Hannah finally paid her brother back for a joke he'd played on her ten years earlier.*

Pay down.

a) To pay money in order to decrease a debt. *It takes a long time to pay down the interest on credit card debt.*

b) To pay a portion of the total price at the time of a purchase and to agree to pay the rest in installments. (Also: *put down.*) *We'll have to pay $1500 down on a new car and then make payments for five years.*

Pay off.

a) To pay a debt in full. *Tom paid off his student loans after 15 years.*

b) To bribe someone. *Mr. Fallows is paying off the building inspectors so they overlook the violations they find.*

Pay out.

To distribute money or wages. *Your insurance plan will pay out if you are injured on the job.*

Pay up.

To pay money owed, as for a bet or a bill. *Ok, you lost. Pay up!*

4F   REAL ENGLISH

In the Black

During the dot.com era, stocks *skyrocketed* in a *bull market,* making a lot of people *filthy rich. Money making* was so easy and people had so much *dough* that they were *laughing all the way to the bank*! But a short time later, the bubble burst and the *bull market* became a *bear market.* Companies were *priced right out of the market* and began to go *bust.* Suddenly a lot of people were *down on their luck* because their companies *went broke* and couldn't afford to keep them on. It got so bad that some people could only get jobs where they were paid *under the table* so that their employers didn't have to pay the extra *bucks* in taxes. Everyone was *in the red.*

4G BRING IT ALL TOGETHER

REVIEW 1: Vocabulary

Place the correct vocabulary word in each space. Use each of the following words once:

access code, ATM, assets, balance, cleared checks, deposits, dividends, e-statement, identity theft, interest, member number, portfolio, surcharge, transactions, transfer, volatile market, waive, withdrawal.

1. The _____ on a home loan is the largest part of a mortgage payment for many years.

2. We made a $750 _____ for our vacation from our savings account.

3. Jack was a victim of _____; someone else used his social security number.

4. If you want to know which checks have been cashed, go online to check your _____. It will show you all your _____.

5. Joyce always forgets her _____ and can't get into her account.

6. Jerry had to list his _____ when he applied for a loan.

7. Stockholders get very nervous during a _____ because things are so unpredictable and a lot of money can be lost.

8. You get a _____ when you join a credit union.

9. Could you please _____ $500 from my savings account to my son's checking account?

10. _____ paid into your account each month are often small, but they add up over time.

11. If you need cash, let's stop at an _____.

12. Tell me the _____ on your credit card statement.

13. Kerry never goes to the bank to cash her checks because she has automatic _____.

14. A judge will often _____ the fine if you go to court for your first traffic ticket.

15. The bill was much more than we expected because there was a _____.

16. I checked on my most recent _____ to see if the check had cleared.

17. Would you like to add a utility stock to your _____?

REVIEW 2: Simple Future vs. Immediate Future

Fill in the blanks with the simple future or immediate future form of the verb in parentheses.

1. Jim promises he (take) _____ you home.

2. Alex (have) _____ a dinner party this Friday.

3. You definitely (need) _____ a textbook for this class.

4. We (charge) _____ a $3.50 late fee each day.

5. Someone (get) _____ hurt if you're not careful.

6. The play (begin) _____ on time, even if you're late.

7. The bank (not cash) _____ your check if it isn't signed and endorsed.
8. Who (go) _____ to the store for me?

REVIEW 3: The Present Continuous and Simple Present to Express the Future

Fill in the blanks in the following sentences with both the present continuous and the simple present tenses to express the future.

1. The plane (leave) _____ in ten minutes.
2. The meeting (start) _____ at 10:30.
3. The new bank branch (have) _____ its grand opening next month.
4. The movie (begin) _____ very soon.
5. Vincent's vacation (end) _____ on Friday.
6. We (go) _____ to Mexico next month.
7. The Logans (arrive) _____ on March 13.
8. Jennifer and Tom (return) _____ from their honeymoon on Sunday.

REVIEW 4: The Simple Present Tense with Prepositions of Time

Fill in the blanks with either the simple present or future tense.

1. When you (understand) _____ it, it (be) _____ easy.
2. Katy (try on) _____ the dress tomorrow, before she (decide) _____ to buy it.
3. You (not be able) _____ to go to the movies unless you (clean) _____ your room.
4. There (be) _____ a new business here when you (come) _____ back.
5. As soon as David (arrive) _____, we (leave) _____.
6. It (be) _____ 5:00 before anything (get) _____ done.
7. Unless you (tell) _____ me, I (not know) _____ how you feel.
8. The birds (move) _____ as soon as you (get) _____ close.

REVIEW 5: Phrasal Verbs with *pay*

Place the correct phrasal verb with *pay* in the blank space in each sentence.

1. The land developers _____ a few local politicians so they would be able to build on the old farmland.
2. You can _____ your credit cards a lot faster if you double your monthly payments.
3. I'll _____ you _____ on Friday when I get paid.
4. Doug swore that he would _____ John _____ for betraying his friendship.
5. I want the money you owe me. You'd better _____ !
6. You'll save a lot of money if you _____ your car early.
7. After Jason scratched his neighbor's car with his bike, he _____ them _____ for the damages by doing work around their house.
8. When she was hurt in an accident, Natalie's insurance policy _____ thousands of dollars.

LISTEN UP!

Listen to the article on credit unions and banks, and then respond to the following statements with *true, false,* or *I don't know.*

1. Credit unions do not have checking account services.
2. You can become a member of a credit union.
3. Banks pay dividends on both checking and savings accounts.
4. It is usually cheaper to use a bank than to use a credit union.
5. Credit unions' ATMs are usually free to members.
6. A credit union member can make deposits at any ATM.

4I   WHY DO THEY DO THAT?

Debt

If you drive down any street in a typical middle-class American neighborhood on a Saturday afternoon, you're likely to see at least two cars in every driveway. You're also likely to see people landscaping their yards, or painting, repairing, or otherwise upgrading their homes. Inside, you're likely to find two or more TVs, a phone in each bedroom, computers, video games, DVD players, sound systems, all sorts of home appliances, and many other pieces of material wealth that so many Americans seem unable to do without. All of these consumer products come with a price tag, of course, and if you have a hard time imagining how most Americans can afford so many luxury items, the answer is technically that many of them can't — many people buy on credit. Americans are very comfortable buying on credit, which means that Americans are also comfortable living with debt. Credit card payments are a large portion of many Americans' monthly expenses, but credit card debt is of course just one kind of debt. There are also mortgages, car loans, student loans ... and the list can go on. For some people, debt is just an expected part of life in this country, along with all of the stress and other negative effects being in debt can cause.

Lesson 4: Answer Key

Practice Exercise 1	1. I'll come, 2. will rain/ is going to rain, 3. will be born, 4. is going to study/will study, 5. are going to stand/will stand, 6. will pass, 7. is going to apply/will apply, 8. are going to get/will get, 9. is going to/will be 10. I'll get
Practice Exercise 2	1. is, 2. am taking, 3. starts, 4. begin, 5. arrives, 6. are having, 7. has 8. opens 9. is beginning, 10. is taking
Practice Exercise 3	1. will call/get, 2. will finish/fix, 3. will begin/arrives, 4. will be able/takes, 5. will begin/goes, 6. will do/ask, 7. will open/clear, 8. will/record/program, 9. will catch/strikes, 10. will change/learn
Review 1	1. interest, 2. withdrawal, 3. identity theft, 4. e-statement, cleared checks, 5. access code, 6. assets, 7. volatile market, 8. member number, 9. transfer, 10. dividends, 11. ATM, 12. balance, 13. deposits, 14. waive, 15. surcharge, 16. transactions, 17. portfolio
Review 2	1. will take, 2. is going to have, 3. will need, 4. will charge, 5. is going to get/will get, 6. will begin, 7. won't cash, 8. is going to go
Review 3	1. is leaving/leaves, 2. is starting/starts, 3. is having/has, 4. is beginning/begins, 5. is ending/ends, 6. are going/go, 7. are arriving/arrive, 8. are returning/return

Review 4

1. understand/will be, 2. will try on/decides, 3. won't be able/clean, 4. will be/come, 5. arrives/will leave, 6. will be/gets, 7. tell/won't know, 8. will move/get

Review 5

1. paid off, 2. pay down/pay off, 3. pay . . . back, 4. pay . . . back, 5. pay up, 6. pay off, 7. pay . . . back, 8. paid out

Listen Up!

1. False 2. True 3. False 4. False 5. True 6. I don't know

Lesson 5

The Customer's Always Right!

ARE YOU READY FOR THE LESSON?

In Lesson 5, *The Customer's Always Right!*, you'll read a dialogue about returning items to a store, and later you'll listen to what happens to someone who's waiting for a home delivery. In this lesson you'll also learn some important vocabulary and phrasal verbs for shopping. But there's more. You'll also focus on:

- Prepositions of Time, Motion, and Location
- Adjectives Followed by Prepositions
- Verbs Followed by Prepositions
- Phrasal Verbs for Shopping
- American Business Culture

But let's begin by listening to the "w-vowel link" in *Say It Clearly!* Ready?

5A SAY IT CLEARLY!

🎧 In this lesson you'll practice another kind of link, the "w-vowel link." Turn on your CD now.

5B ENGLISH AT WORK

Dialogue: Did You Need Some Help?

📖 Tracy has recently bought a new dining set at a local department store, but when it was delivered she noticed some scratches on the tabletop. She's very unhappy because she paid a lot of money for the table and would like to exchange it.

🎧

Clerk	Did you need some help?
Tracy	Yes. I bought a dining room table and chairs here two weeks ago. It was delivered yesterday, but there are two big gashes on the surface. I've bought furniture from you before and I've always been satisfied with the quality and the service. But now I just don't know.
Clerk	Oh, I'm sorry ma'am. But did you notice whether the scratches were there when the table arrived?
Tracy	Um, actually, no. I wasn't home when they brought them in.
Clerk	Who signed for the delivery?
Tracy	My husband. But he's not very observant. He wouldn't have noticed. But I saw the gashes right away.
Clerk	Well, ma'am, we have a policy. That's why you sign for the delivery. You are acknowledging that the product is delivered in good condition.
Tracy	So you're saying you can't do anything?
Clerk	I'm afraid we can't.

Tracy   Well, look. I'm really disappointed about this. I'm a good customer. I've bought several pieces of furniture from you before.... Can I speak to the manager?

Clerk   Sure.... One minute.

Manager   Hello, I'm Bob Mack, the department manager. What can I do for you?

Tracy   Hi. I'm Tracy Bell. Well, as I was saying to the clerk, I'm a regular customer. I've bought furniture from you before, and I've always been satisfied with the quality of your products and the service. But I bought a table from you that was delivered yesterday. My husband signed for it, but he never notices anything, and when I got home yesterday, I saw two big gashes on the tabletop.

Manager   No problem, ma'am. We can send out another one and pick up the damaged one. Let's see. Let me check the delivery schedule. OK, we can deliver your replacement table next week, next Friday. How's that? Are the chairs OK?

Tracy   Oh, thank you so much. I really appreciate this! Yes, the chairs are fine.

Manager   Good, so we'll just send out a new table.... We really appreciate your business, Ms. Bell. I'm very sorry for the inconvenience. Just have that table ready for pickup on Friday the 21st between 9:00 and noon, and we'll bring the new one at the same time.

Tracy   Thanks. It'll be in my dining room waiting for you.

5C   BUILD YOUR VOCABULARY

 Let's take a look at some vocabulary that will come in handy for shopping.

Brand name. A product produced by a major company and carrying that company's name on its label. *Many people believe that brand name products are better than ones produced by companies they aren't familiar with.*

Bulk. Products that can be bought in very large quantities. *Health food stores usually sells grains, nuts, dried fruit and cereals in bulk.*

Clearance. Products that are no longer in style or in demand and that are sold at the lowest possible price to be cleared from the store. *If you wait long enough, you can sometimes buy exactly what you want at clearance prices.*

Closeout. The disposal of a product by selling it at the lowest possible price. The store will not stock any more of that product. *Look at this beautiful jacket I just bought on closeout!*

Co-op. A store that sells products at a discounted price because the customers are also the owners. Members pay an annual fee and buy products at a discount. *If you want to join a food co-op you'll have to pay a membership fee, but you'll spend much less on food than you would elsewhere.*

Coupon. A piece of paper found in magazines or newspapers that offers a discount on a product. *I got a 25 percent discount on these cans of soup because I had a coupon.*

Discount card. A card offered by some stores or other businesses to certain groups, such as students or senior citizens, for special discounts on products. *If you're a student, you can get a discount card at the theater.*

Generic products. Products that do not have a brand name and that are not advertised. *The generic tomato sauce is much cheaper than the brand name product.*

Gift certificate. A piece of paper from a specific store that's worth a certain value and can be used to make a purchase for that amount in the store. *Since we don't know what Isabel wants, let's just get her a gift certificate so she can buy what she prefers.*

Grandopening. A celebration at the opening of a store, often with special gifts and/or food for the customers. *Did you see the balloons at the grandopening for the new car dealership?*

Layaway. A way to purchase a product by paying a portion of its price as a deposit, and then making payments until the entire price is paid in full. The store holds the product until it is paid for in full. *Yoko wanted to buy an expensive coat, but she didn't have enough money, so she put it on layaway for two months.*

Limited quantities. Products that are available only in small numbers, and usually sold at a higher price for that reason. *The silkscreen artist knew that she should produce and sell only a limited quantity of the signed paintings.*

Money-back guarantee. The option to return a product for a refund during a certain period of time. *Jolene felt safe buying the diet pills because they had a money-back guarantee.*

Promotion. A product selected to have special advertisement, with samples or discount coupons made available to potential buyers. *The best time to shop is the weekend, when all the stores are giving out promotions to advertise their products.*

Rebate. A product discount in the form of money returned from the company after a rebate form is filled out and mailed in to that company. *Sal paid $120 for his cell phone, but he got a rebate for $70 after signing a service contract.*

Special purchase. A product bought and made available specifically for a sale, usually with a considerable discount. *These computers are on sale for $499 this week because they were a special purchase.*

Stock. Products available in a store, including products on the shelves and in the storeroom. *The store's entire stock was destroyed in the fire.*

In stock. Currently available for purchase. *Just a minute, I'll check to see if we have that color in stock for you.*

Storewide. Throughout the entire store, in all departments. *The clearance sale was storewide, so we got all kinds of different products on sale in various departments.*

 5D ENGLISH UNDER THE HOOD

TOPIC 1: Prepositions of Time, Motion, and Location

Here are some common prepositions, listed alphabetically:

about, above, across, across from, after, against, along, among, around, as, at, before, behind, below, beneath, beside, besides, between, beyond, by, down, during, for, from, in, inside, into, like, near, of, off, off of, on, onto, opposite, out, out of, outside, over, since, through, to, toward, towards, under, underneath, until, up, upon, with, within, without.

Prepositions can show time, location, motion, or some other type of relationship.

Time:

We leave <u>in</u> one hour.

The Robertsons stayed in Mexico <u>for</u> two weeks.

Have you been waiting <u>since</u> 1:00?

Location:

Jeanne lives <u>in</u> France.

The dog is sleeping <u>under</u> the table.

The bank is <u>across from</u> the library, <u>between</u> the post office and the police station.

Motion:

We are going <u>to</u> the movies tonight.

The students are all returning <u>from</u> spring break.

The plane is descending <u>toward</u> the airport.

Other Relationships:

There's a letter <u>for</u> you.

Are you <u>for</u> or <u>against</u> gun control?

The director is speaking <u>with</u> a candidate for the new position.

Often, common prepositions can fall into more than one category.

The new computer is <u>in</u> my office. (location)

The students went <u>in</u> the classroom. (motion)

I'm leaving <u>in</u> five minutes. (time)

PRACTICE EXERCISE 1: Fill in the sentences with prepositions from the list above:

1. The ball rolled _____ the desk _____ the living room.
2. Jeremy traveled _____ London _____ Paris _____ one week.
3. The ball fell _____ the hole.
4. Sit _____ me so I can see you.
5. Can you stay and watch Jamie _____ I get back?
6. Go _____ that door and turn to your left.
7. Wow! We haven't seen each other _____ high school.
8. I think the note I left you is _____ the newspaper. I see the corner sticking out.
9. We'd better go _____ the house. It's raining.
10. I think the book you want is _____ the dictionary and the atlas.

TOPIC 2: Adjectives Followed by Prepositions

Some adjectives in English are followed by certain prepositions. Sometimes there's a logical connection between the adjective and the preposition, but usually you simply have to memorize which prepositions are used with which adjectives. Here is a list of some common adjectives and the prepositions that often follow them.

accused of, afraid of, amazed at, angry at/with, bored with, capable of, concerned about, devoted to, disappointed in, disgusted by, divorced from, excited about, exhausted from, familiar with, frightened at/by, interested in, jealous of, known for, made of, married to, nervous about, pleased with, polite to, prepared for, proud of, qualified for, related to, responsible for, saddened by, satisfied with, sorry for/about, tired of, upset with, worried about.

I am <u>tired of</u> cooking every night.

He is <u>frustrated by/with</u> his job.

She is <u>surprised at/by</u> the intensity of her emotions.

We are <u>bored with/by</u> each other.

They are <u>interested in</u> buying a new car.

Turn to the appendix for a longer list of common adjectives followed by prepositions.

PRACTICE EXERCISE 2: Complete each sentence with the correct preposition.

1. Are you bored_____ this town?
2. Sarah is jealous _____ her younger sister.
3. Jason's mother is proud _____ his good grades!
4. This blouse is made_____ cotton.
5. I hope she's capable _____ reaching her goal.
6. How long have you been married _____ your husband?
7. Don't be nervous_____ your date tonight!
8. I'm sorry _____ hurting your feelings.
9. Susan is related _____ the mayor.
10. I'm worried _____ paying the bills.

TOPIC 3: Verbs Followed by Prepositions

Some verbs in English are followed by certain prepositions. Again, you usually have to memorize which preposition to use with which verb. Here is a list of some of the more common ones.

agree with, apologize for, apply to/for, approve of, argue with/about, believe in, blame for, care about, compare to, complain about, contribute to, cover with, decide (up)on, depend (up)on, dream of/about, escape from, excuse for, feel like, forget about, hope for, insist (up) on, object to, prevent from, protect from, respond to, stop from, subscribe to, take care of, thank for, vote for

I don't always <u>agree with</u> the president.

Does anyone <u>object to</u> my driving tonight?

Whatever you do, don't <u>forget about</u> us.

Turn to the appendix for a longer list.

PRACTICE EXERCISE 3: Fill in the sentences with the correct preposition.

1. Parents try to protect their children _____ danger.
2. You need to insist _____ getting a pay raise.
3. Most homeowners subscribe _____ a newspaper.
4. Don't try to blame me _____ your mistakes.
5. People always complain _____ the noise in this building.
6. I'd like to apologize _____ bumping into you.
7. It's nice to dream _____ winning the lottery.
8. No one objected _____ the suggestion I made.
9. Vote _____ change if you want to improve things around here.
10. A lot of politicians say they care _____ the environment.

5E   PHRASAL VERBS FOR SHOPPING:

Buy out.
To buy all of an available product. *The new computer game is so popular that the customers buy it out as soon as it goes on the shelf.*

Buy up.
To purchase a lot of a product. *Buy up as many boxes of paper towels as you can when you go to the discount warehouse.*

Give away.
a) To give products as a gift. *The cosmetics counter is giving away samples of perfume today.*

b) To give something you no longer use to another person or organization. *I gave my old word processor away to a friend who needed one.*

c) To tell something unintentionally, such as a secret or an answer. *Benny gave my secret away to Debbie, and now she knows how I feel.*

Sell out.
a) To sell all of a product before a new order comes in. *We'd better get to the store before they sell out of that new computer game.*

b) To switch loyalties or act against a principle; to betray trust. *Did you hear that Barry sold out to another team because they offered to pay him twice as much as he's getting now?*

Trade in.
To turn a product in to get a discount on a newer or more expensive model. *Most car dealerships will let you trade in your old car for a new model.*

Try on.
To put clothes on in a store to see if they fit and look good before buying them. *Gina tried on the dress in the store before she bought it.*

Try out.
To use a product before deciding to purchase it. *You are welcome to try out the new computer game right here in the store.*

5F REAL ENGLISH

Shop Till You Drop!

You know? I'm a confirmed *shopaholic*. I shop at *bargain basements* and buy clothes off the *bargain rack* because I can save so much money. Wow! Look at this dress! Only $35! *It's a steal*. I just have to have it. It's so cheap.

I usually try to stay out of the *high-end* departments though. If I see something I like, *I want it in the worst way*. I can't resist buying it even though I think the prices they charge are *highway robbery*.

Some days I wake up in the morning and just have to go on a *shopping spree*. I even love to go to *vintage stores*. They have really cute clothes from the '60s, and even earlier. Sometimes I even shop at *secondhand stores*. In fact, the other day I was in one and I saw a dress I'd given away last month. It was only 50 cents! So I bought it back. It was so cheap, they were practically *giving it away*! *What a deal!*

5G BRING IT ALL TOGETHER

REVIEW EXERCISE 1: Vocabulary

Place the correct vocabulary word in each space. Use each of the following words once: brand-name, bulk, clearance, co-op, coupon, discount card, generic, gift certificate, grand opening, layaway, limited quantities, money-back guarantee, promotion, rebate, special purchase, stock, in stock, storewide.

1. Can I put this dress on _____ and pick it up in two weeks?

2. Did you see the signs for the _____ of that new store on Broadway?

3. It's cheaper to buy products in _____, but you need to have storage space.

4. If you're a student, you should get a _____, and your ticket will be cheaper.

5. We're having a big sale on Saturday, so we need to have enough _____ of the most popular items.

6. Department stores usually put their clothes on _____ when they are out of season. That way they sell them off faster.

7. If you want to save money, you can buy _____ products instead of brand-name.

8. I'm more comfortable buying _____ products that I'm familiar with.

9. Often companies will sell popular products to stores in _____ so they can keep the price high and ensure good sales.

10. Did you know there was a great _____ on campus? If you're a member you pay very little.

11. When you order products through the mail, it's important to be sure that they have a _____. That way you will not lose your money if you don't like the product once you see it.

12. A customer wanted to buy four boxes of a particular kind of tea, but the store only had three _____.

13. When I bought my computer, I was supposed to get a _____. I sent them the form, the receipt and the UPC label, but I still haven't gotten the money.

14. We just got a whole shipment of these jackets. They were a _____ for the sale tomorrow.

15. This box of cereal is 15 percent off if you have a _____.

16. There's a _____ sale this weekend, with discounts in every department.

17. Ray has very unique tastes in clothes, so we got him a _____ for his birthday.

18. The bookstore is having a _____ for the new book by my favorite author. She'll be doing a book signing on Friday.

REVIEW EXERCISE 2: Prepositions

Fill in the blanks using the following prepositions once: *back, across, inside, in, through, along, up, down*.

1. How about taking a trip _____ the Southwest?

2. You could start somewhere _____ Northern California.

3. Then you could drive _____ into the mountains to King's Canyon National Park to see the giant sequoias.

4. After that, drive _____ to Las Vegas to catch a few shows.

5. You could travel _____ Arizona to the Grand Canyon.

6. Try riding a mule _____ the rim of the canyon to get to the bottom.

7. Then, you could go to New Mexico and see what it's like _____ Carlsbad Caverns.

8. Then you could head _____ to California for a trip to Disneyland.

REVIEW EXERCISE 3: Adjectives Followed by Prepositions

Fill in the sentences with the correct preposition.

1. I'm concerned _____ the test I have to take tomorrow.

2. Why do you have to be angry _____ me about this?

3. Jim isn't afraid _____ anyone.

4. Let me know if you're interested _____ going to a movie this weekend.

5. It's important to be polite _____ everyone.

6. Janie's really tired _____ being told what to do.

7. We're all responsible _____ one another.

8. Peter Sellers is known _____ his role as Inspector Clouseau.

REVIEW EXERCISE 4: Verbs Followed by Prepositions

Fill in the sentences with the correct preposition.

1. Don't blame me _____ someone else's mistake!

2. Does anybody feel _____ going in the pool?

3. Helen only applied _____ one company and got a great job.

4. Let's cover this wall _____ wallpaper.

5. You don't need to apologize _____ anything. It doesn't bother me at all.

6. What time will you arrive _____ Atlanta?

7. I think a lot of people believe _____ ghosts.

8. Bart doesn't want to depend _____ his parents once he graduates from college.

REVIEW EXERCISE 5: Phrasal Verbs

Fill in the blanks of the following sentences with: *bought out, gave away, sold out, trade in, try on, try out.*

1. I'm going to _____ my old car for a newer model.

2. Would you like to _____ the new model before you buy it?

3. That book is so popular that customers _____ every single copy in the bookstore.

4. We cleaned out our closets and _____ all the things we don't need.

5. Here's a size 10. Go _____ it _____ and see how it fits.

6. I didn't make it to the store on time, and they _____ of all the shirts that I wanted.

5H LISTEN UP!

🎧 Now turn on your CD to practice listening comprehension. Listen to the story and then answer the following questions.

1. Why did Tracy get up early?

   a) She wanted to go to the new department store in Southcrest.

   b) She wanted to be ready for her new table.

   c) She had to go to the dentist.

2. What time did Lucy call Tracy?

   a) 10:05   b) 2:00   c) 2:15

3. How many phone calls did Tracy get that day?

   a) 1   b) 2   c) 3

4. Why did Tracy think it was important for her to be at home when the new table arrived?

   a) She was excited about getting her new table.

   b) Her husband wouldn't be home.

   c) She wanted to be sure the table was in good condition.

5. What time will the table arrive?

   a) Around 2:00   b) At 11:45   c) Between 9:00 and noon.

6. Where will Tracy be when the table arrives?

   a) At home

   b) At the dentist

   c) At the Southcrest Mall

51 WHY DO THEY DO THAT?

Service with a Smile

 You may have noticed that store clerks in the U.S. are generally friendly and helpful. American businesses encourage "service with a smile," and that is exactly what customers expect from the businesses they patronize. In fact, a person's job may depend on his or her ability to interact with customers in a friendly and respectful way, always trying to satisfy a customer's needs. For example, if a customer complains about a product, it is often the store clerk's job to replace the product or refund the cost of the product with no questions asked. Naturally, a customer may be irate when returning a product, but the clerk must remain courteous at all times. If a customer complains about the service received, the responsible clerk may be informed about the complaint and warned to treat the customers with more respect in the future, or else... To American businesses, good service means accepting a customer's complaint with a smile, and maintaining good customer relations is more important than being right, because this is the best way to develop a solid and loyal customer base. This attitude explains the common saying, *the customer is always right*.

Lesson 5: Answer Key

Practice Exercise 1	1. under, in, 2. from, to, in, 3. down/into, 4. opposite/across from, 5. until, 6. through/out, 7. since, 8. under/underneath, 9. in/inside/into, 10. between
Practice Exercise 2	1. with/by, 2. of, 3. of, 4. of, 5. of, 6. to, 7. about, 8. for/about, 9. to, 10. about
Practice Exercise 3	1. from, 2. (up)on, 3. to, 4. for, 5. about, 6. for, 7. of/about, 8. to, 9. for, 10. about
Review Exercise 1	1. layaway, 2. grand opening, 3. bulk, 4. discount card, 5. stock, 6. clearance, 7. generic, 8. brand name, 9. limited quantities, 10. co-op, 11. money-back guarantee, 12. in stock, 13. rebate, 14. special purchase, 15. coupon, 16. storewide, 17. gift certificate, 18. promotion
Review Exercise 2	1. across, 2. in, 3. up, 4. down, 5. through, 6. along, 7. inside, 8. back
Review Exercise 3	1. about, 2. with/at, 3. of, 4. in, 5. to, 6. of, 7. for, 8. for
Review Exercise 4	1. for, 2. like, 3. to, 4. with, 5. for, 6. in, 7. in, 8. on
Review Exercise 5	1. trade in, 2. try out, 3. bought out, 4. gave away, 5. try ... on, 6. sold out
Listen Up!	1. b, 2. a, 3. b, 4. c, 5. a, 6. b

I Have Got to Have a New Car!

ARE YOU READY FOR THE LESSON?

If you've been thinking about how to get around in the United States, Lesson 6: *I Have Got to Have a New Car!*, might give you some tips. In this lesson, you'll listen in as two friends discuss a new car that one of them has just bought. You'll learn some useful vocabulary and idioms for cars and driving, and you'll also listen to a car commercial in *Listen Up!* Here are a few more things you will learn in Lesson 6:

• Modals of Necessity: *must, have to,* and *have got to*
• Modals of Advisability: *should, ought to,* and *had better*
• Negative Modals
• Phrasal Verbs with *come*

We'll finish off the lesson with some important insights into American car culture—such as what cars represent to Americans. But let's begin the lesson by practicing pronunciation in *Say It Clearly!* Ready?

6A SAY IT CLEARLY!

In this lesson you'll practice the consonant-vowel link. Turn on your CD.

6B ENGLISH AT WORK

DIALOGUE: Let's Go Look at My New Car.

Alida and Suzette have known each other for years, and they keep in touch by getting together once every few months for coffee. Let's listen in as they're about to say good-bye.

Alida   Well, it was great to catch up with you, but I'd better go. I have to pick my mom up and drive her to a doctor's appointment. I'd better leave now if I want to avoid the traffic.

Suzette   Yeah, me too. It'll be bumper-to-bumper soon. Oh, and say hello to your mom. I haven't seen her in ages. How is she doing, by the way?

Alida   She's doing really well for her age. She still walks every day, but she doesn't drive much anymore. Which reminds me, you haven't seen my new car.

Suzette   You got a new car?

Alida   Yeah. Two weeks ago. I just love it!

Suzette   Where is it?

Alida   It's parked over there. C'mon, let's take a quick look before we leave.

Suzette   Which one is it?

Alida   It's the little gray EXS, parked next to the SUV.

Suzette   Oh, it's beautiful. I love it. Look! It even has a spoiler. Is it an automatic?

Alida   No. It's a standard. And it has power windows, brakes, power
          everything. It even has chrome alloy wheels. And I had the
          windows tinted.
Suzette   Does it get good mileage?
Alida   Much better than that gas-guzzler I used to have.
Suzette   Can I ask how much you paid for it?
Alida   Oh, I don't mind. It was $21,000.
Suzette   Did you lease or buy?
Alida   I bought it. The payments are about $380 a month. I put a couple
          thousand down and traded in my old car for another $1000.
Suzette   Oh, Alida. It's fantastic. I'm so jealous.
Alida   Well, you'll just have to get one, too.
Suzette   I was going to try to get another year or so out of my old one, but now I
          don't know. I think I've got to have a new car right away!

6C BUILD YOUR VOCABULARY

ABS. Anti-lock brake system. A system that allows the brakes to automatically adjust
pressure to avoid skidding when a sudden stop is necessary. *We added brake fluid to
ensure that your ABS works properly whenever you need your brakes.*

Automatic. Automatic transmission. A transmission system where the engine
automatically shifts gears as needed, without use of a stick shift. *I prefer to buy an
automatic because I don't know how to drive a stick shift.*

Bucket seats. Two front seats that are individual rather than a bench, with or without
a console separating them. They are slightly scooped out in the middle like a bucket.
Some people prefer the look and comfort of bucket seats.

Chrome alloy wheels. Wheels with chrome alloy plating on the interior hub of the
tires. *When Terrence bought his car, he asked for chrome alloy wheels because he
thought they looked so great.*

Cruise control. A system that maintains speed without the need for the driver to push
on the accelerator. *Cruise control is a great feature when you drive for long distances,
because it allows your foot to rest.*

Cylinders. The part of the engine where fuel is burned (combusted). Four is the
standard number, but some engines have more cylinders, and therefore more power,
but also use more gas. *With the price of gas these days, we'd better get a four-
cylinder car.*

Dashboard. (Also called "dash.") The inside front of the car where the instruments are
located. *As you can see, the dash is fully illuminated so that at night you can read your
instruments.*

Horsepower. Power equivalent to the power a horse exerts in pulling. A measure of a
car's power. *What's the horsepower on that engine?*

Moon roof. A window on the roof of the car that does not open, usually tinted and
offered as an extra feature. *It's such a pleasure to look up at the stars through the
moon roof on the car.*

MPH. Miles per hour, the number of miles that can be traveled in one hour. *The speed limit on most freeways in the U.S. is 65 MPH.*

Power windows. Windows that are opened at the touch of a button rather than hand cranked. (Anything automatic is called power: power brakes, power steering, etc.) *Only the highest-quality cars have extra features like power windows.*

Spoiler. A long narrow plate across the back of a car that deflects air to keep the car from lifting off the road at high speeds. *Look at the spoiler on that little sports car! I wonder how fast it can go.*

Standard. A transmission that has gears that need to be shifted by hand; a stick shift, opposite of an automatic. *If you want to save on gas, buy a standard. They use less gas than automatics.*

Sunroof. A glass window on the roof of a car that can be opened up. *Selena opened up her sunroof and flew down the freeway with her hair flying.*

Tilt wheel. A steering wheel that can be adjusted by tilting to fit the driver's body angle or style of driving. *Because Bill's so tall he says he'll never buy a car without tilt wheel steering again.*

 ENGLISH UNDER THE HOOD

TOPIC 1: Modals of Necessity

Modals are auxiliary verbs used before other verbs to express a distinct shade of meaning. There are many kinds of modals. The modals of necessity are *must, have to* and *have got to.* In meaning, they are all basically the same, but *must* expresses absolute necessity. In spoken American English, *must* is usually only used with extra emphasis. When you use *have to* and *have got to,* the necessity is less strong.

My car is broken, so I <u>must buy</u> a new car!

I've got to leave work early because I <u>have to catch</u> a train.

Note that these modals are often used for exaggeration.

I can't live without that car. I <u>have got to have</u> it.

Oh, I <u>have to eat</u> that slice of chocolate cake!

PRACTICE EXERCISE 1: Fill in the following sentences with the correct form of the verb in parentheses, and select a main verb from the following:

read, work, get, go, be, finish, see

1. (have to) If you live in the country, you _____ a car.
2. (have got to) A person _____ hard in order to live well.
3. (must) If you like horses, you _____ that movie.
4. (have got to) We _____ this project by noon!
5. (have to) I just _____ that movie star's autobiography.
6. (must) Cindy _____ at the office by 7:00 tomorrow.

7. (have to) The dog _____ for a walk every night.

Now select the correct modal for each sentence. Use *have to, have got to* and *must* one time each.

8. You just _____ get this dress! It's perfect for you.

9. We _____ get to the store before it closes or we won't have anything to eat for breakfast.

10. You received a subpoena for jury duty? Unless you have a good excuse, you _____ go.

TOPIC 2: Modals of Advisability

The modals of advisability are *should, ought to* and *had better.* These three modals are used when offering advice. *Should* is used when offering advice with an implication of rules, morals, ethics, experience, etc. *Ought to* is used when the giver of the advice feels strongly that the advice should be taken, and *had better* is used when the giver believes a failure to follow the advice might result in harm or some other ill effect.

You <u>should</u> quit smoking and then you <u>should</u> join a gym to get in shape!

You <u>ought to</u> buy a house, because you're paying too much in rent.

<u>You'd better</u> tell your boss the truth, because she'll find out anyway and you'll be in trouble.

PRACTICE EXERCISE 2: Fill in each blank with the correct form of the verb in parentheses and select a main verb listed here for each sentence.

go, bring, eat, tell, get, buy, cut

1. (should) What do I think? Hmmm. Yeah, you _____ your hair.

2. (ought) You _____ the car to the mechanic before your trip.

3. (should) We _____ together before you leave.

4. (had better) You _____ to the dentist before your tooth gets worse.

5. (should) Don't you think you _____ him you've met someone else?

6. (ought) Sam _____ a new suit before his interview.

7. (had better) Joe _____ before he goes to the game or he'll be hungry!

Now select the correct modal for each sentence. Use *should, ought to,* and *had better* one time each.

8. You _____ know your job by now, since you've been here for two months!

9. You _____ take some aspirin for that headache.

10. We _____ bring the patio furniture inside, because it looks like rain.

TOPIC 3: Negative Modals

Some of the negative forms of these modals do not always mean the same thing as the positive forms.

Must not expresses a prohibition or rule. *You must not leave your engine running while filling up at a gas station.*

Must not can also express a logical assumption. *It must not be raining yet, since no one has a wet coat or an umbrella.*

Don't have to has the opposite meaning as its positive form. *Don't have to* means there is *no* obligation or necessity to do something. *You don't have to go to school today if you're not feeling well.*

The negative form of *have got to* is not used. Use *don't have to* in its place.

Shouldn't means the opposite of *should. You should get up early everyday; you shouldn't sleep late.*

The negative of *ought to* is not used often in American English; *shouldn't* usually replaces it.

Had better not is a strong prohibition. *You had better not stay out late tonight if you have to work tomorrow!*

PRACTICE EXERCISE 3: Choose the correct negative modal to fill in the blank in each sentence.

1. Don't worry. You _____ pick me up. David said he'd do it.
2. You _____ know anyone here since you're sitting by yourself.
3. We _____ do anything until we talk to the boss.
4. You _____ drive across the border without car insurance.
5. You _____ buy anything else with your credit card, because the balance is so high.
6. Julie _____ be in yet, since her office door is closed.
7. You _____ make dinner for me. I'll probably pick something up on the way.
8. Please don't buy me anything. You _____ spend your money on me.
9. I _____ eat any more ice cream or I'll get fat.
10. We _____ leave those boxes out here. It might rain.

6E PHRASAL VERBS WITH *COME*:

Come across.
a) To seem, to be considered, to be perceived. *Nathan comes across as rude, but he's really just shy.*
b) To find, especially in an unexpected way. *I was cleaning out the closet when I came across this old photo album.*

Come along.
To accompany. *You can come along. We'd love to have you join us.*

Come around.
a) To visit or frequent a place. *Ever since Josh broke up with Mary, he doesn't come around anymore.*
b) To change one's mind or attitude in a positive or favorable way. *Don't worry about Greg; he'll come around soon enough and agree with you.*

Come back.
To return. *Bring your family when you come back.*

Come by.
a) To visit for a short time. *Come by when you're in the neighborhood.*
b) To receive, to get something, usually of value. *How did you come by that expensive car?*

Come down.
a) To decrease, such as a price. *The price on that house has come down a lot. They were asking about $45,000 more.*
b) To visit an area considered geographically lower or further south. *I'll be in New York that week, but I'll see if I can come down to Philadelphia.*

Come down on.
To punish severely. Used with "hard." *When her parents caught Jessica smoking, they really came down hard on her.*

Come in.
a) To enter. *The door's open, so just come in.*
b) To be received as a signal, as in a television, radio, or cell phone. *I love this station, but it doesn't come in very well outside the city.*

Come into.
To receive something valuable, especially inherited money. *Kevin came into some money, so he paid off all of his debts.*

Come on.
To request that someone do something, often pronounced *c'mon*. *Come on. I'd really like you to come to the movie with me.*

Come out.
To divulge something about oneself or one's identity, especially sexual orientation. *None of Dan's friends was surprised when he came out; they knew he was gay.*

Come through.
To help or perform something according to expectation. *I wasn't sure if he'd be able to lend me the money, but Jack really came through for me.*

Come to.
a) To arrive at. (Used with "conclusion," "realization," etc.) *I've just come to the conclusion that I'd like to go to school.*
b) To awaken after having been unconscious. *When Mary came to, she discovered that someone had moved her to the sofa.*

Come up.
a) To visit an area considered geographically higher or further north. *I'll come up and visit you when you go to the mountains this summer.*
b) To rise socially, economically, or professionally. *Bob's really come up since he became the president of the company.*

Come up with.
a) To get an idea. (Used with "idea," "solution," "proposal," etc.) *Where did you come up with the idea that the director was quitting?*

b) To obtain or acquire, especially money. *If you can come up with enough money for the down payment, the car is yours.*

 6F REAL ENGLISH

I Need Some New Wheels!

You just have to have a car, don't you? Well, so does everyone else. Whatever you do, be sure to *check* each car *out* carefully before you decide to buy one. If you don't, you could be lucky enough to find a *good catch* at a great price, but you also might get a *lemon*. If you get a *lemon*, you'll have to *pay through the nose* for repairs, so it's not *worth it*.

If you go to a used car lot you may get a salesman who'll *rip* you *off* because he's such a *smooth operator*. He'll *sweet talk* you into buying a car you don't want at a price you can't afford.

Take my advice, go to the *Blue Book* to find out how much a car is worth and check out the consumer reports to find out which are the *best and worst rated* cars. But be careful, because once you've *done all your homework* you may find yourself *getting into* a used car instead of *breaking in* a new one.

6G BRING IT ALL TOGETHER

REVIEW EXERCISE 1: Vocabulary

Match each vocabulary item with its description.

1. ___ ABS	a.	These make your drive more comfortable.
2. ___ automatic	b.	You don't have to keep your foot on the accelerator with this.
3. ___ bucket seats	c.	Sports cars have these on the back.
4. ___ chrome alloy wheels	d.	This is a measure of speed.
5. ___ cruise control	e.	All of the car's instruments can be read here.
6. ___ dash	f.	You don't have to change gears while driving with this.
7. ___ cylinders	g.	Your hair may get messed up when you open this.
8. ___ horsepower	h.	These look great on tires.
9. ___ moon roof	i.	This helps you if you have long legs.
10. ___ MPH	j.	You can see the stars on a clear night with this.
11. ___ power windows	k.	These help you control your car when you stop suddenly.
12. ___ spoiler	l.	These are the parts of the engine where the power is created.

13. ___ standard

14. ___ sunroof

15. ___ tilt wheel

m. How much your car needs depends on the car's weight.

n. You can open these at the touch of a button.

o. You change gears with your hand.

REVIEW EXERCISE 2: Modals of Necessity

Fill in the blank with the modal in parentheses and choose the best main verb from the following list.

turn in, get, save, fix, go, dress, walk, wear

1. (have to) She _____ to work everyday, doesn't she?
2. (have got to) Since you broke the window, you _____ it.
3. (must) If you want to go on a trip, you _____ money.
4. (have to) If he _____ everywhere, he'll lose weight.
5. (have to) When do you _____ your term paper?
6. (must) It's too cold outside. You _____ a coat.
7. (have got to) You don't make enough money; you _____ get another job.
8. (have got to) When you're a teenager, you feel like you _____ like everyone else.

REVIEW EXERCISE 3: Modals of Advisability

Fill in the blank with the modal in parentheses and choose the best main verb from the following list.

call, rest, hurry, ask, stay, go, tell, be able

1. (should) I think you _____. You look tired.
2. (ought to) We _____ to find a new apartment by the first of the month.
3. (had better) I guess we _____ home tonight since you don't feel well.
4. (should) Who do you think I _____ for help on this project?
5. (had better) We _____ or we'll be late.
6. (should) Will you be at home tonight? What time _____ I _____ you?
7. (ought to) Do you think I _____ him the truth?
8. (had better) You have a very high fever. You _____ to bed.

REVIEW EXERCISE 4: Negative Modals

Fill in the blank with the verb in parentheses and choose the best main verb from the following list.

work, study, call, send, eat, wash, put, watch

1. (had better not) You _____ in sick again today!
2. (shouldn't) You _____ ever _____ your finger in a light socket.
3. (do not have to) I _____ today because it's a holiday.
4. (must not) No! You _____ that letter. You don't know what the consequences might be.

5. (shouldn't) If you're allergic to strawberries, then you _____ them.

6. (had better not) You _____ that movie. It's too disturbing.

7. (do not have to) Sandra's really smart. She _____ as hard as we do.

8. (shouldn't) You _____ white clothes with dark clothes unless you like wearing gray.

REVIEW EXERCISE 5: Phrasal Verbs

Fill in the blanks with one of the following phrasal verbs.

come around, come along, came back, come into, come down, come in, come on, come over, came to, come up, come up with

1. How much money were you able to _____ for your down payment?

2. The price of that car has really _____ a lot since it first came out.

3. I haven't seen him in ages! He doesn't _____ here anymore.

4. Why don't you _____ and visit me today?

5. If you like Thai food, you should _____ with us for dinner tonight.

6. I'm not sure how you _____ that conclusion, but it's wrong.

7. Jordan _____ to his office to get a file he'd forgotten.

8. You bought a new house? You must have _____ some money!

9. _____! You can do it. Try a little harder.

10. Please _____! It's freezing outside.

6H LISTEN UP!

Turn on your CD to listen to a car commercial, and then answer the following questions.

1. Who is Lucky Joe?

2. What does he want you to do?

3. How much is the Titan?

4. How old is the pick-up?

5. How much is the Mac-X?

6. What street is Lucky Motors on?

6I WHY DO THEY DO THAT?

Americans and Their Cars

Americans are hopelessly in love with their cars. There are over 135 million cars on the roads of the United States each day. Just to buy a new car, the average American spends roughly half of his or her annual income. The average American family owns two or three cars, each logging approximately 15,000 miles a year. In fact, there are more registered vehicles than there are licensed drivers. Clearly, Americans have a unique relationship with their cars, to say the least.

Outside of a few major cities, not having a car is simply unthinkable to most Americans. This dependence on automobiles starts young. To American teenagers, for example, getting a driver's license is a crucial milestone in their lives. It's a rite of passage that brings the freedom and independence young people crave and associate with adulthood. Being able to drive represents not only personal freedom, but also mobility and individuality, and this association is carried into adulthood.

This notion is so strong that its influence can be seen everywhere in the U.S., from the layout of cities to the choices of how people spend free time. While most of the rest of the world relies heavily upon public transportation, Americans refuse to give up their car keys. Vast winding freeways are unmistakable characteristics of most American cities, along with wide boulevards, car-lined side streets, parking lots, and strip malls. American behavior is also shaped by cars. Americans use their cars to drive to work, to shop, to take their kids to school and even to rock their babies to sleep at night. On weekends, they like to jump in their cars just to go for a drive. Americans spend several hours a day in their cars, turning their cars into substitute homes and offices. It's common to see drivers talking on cell phones and eating, but it's not unheard of even to see them brushing their teeth, shaving, putting on makeup or even watching TV while driving. In fact, it's been necessary to pass laws prohibiting dangerously distracting behavior while driving.

Given the importance of cars in American culture, it's not surprising that some people believe that a lot can be learned about drivers' personalities based on their cars. For example, some cars are known to be safe and reliable; others are flashy and ostentatious. Some are shallow status symbols of wealth or (presumed) taste. Still others are considered unnecessarily large, obnoxious, and wasteful of fuel. Certain makes of cars are considered boxy and ungraceful, but solid and fortress-like, while others are sleek and nimble. It's tempting to extend these perceptions to drivers! No matter how much truth there is to any of that, it's certain that the car has been shaping America for years. Clearly, that engine is still running strong!

Lesson 6: Answer Key

Practice Exercise	1. have to get, 2. has got to work, 3. must see, 4. have got to finish, 5. have to read, 6. must be, 7. has to go, 8. have to, 9. have got to, 10. must
Practice Exercise 2	1. should cut, 2. ought to bring, 3. should get, 4. had better go, 5. should tell, 6. ought to buy, 7. had better eat, 8. ought to, 9. should, 10. had better
Practice Exercise 3	1. don't have to, 2. must not, 3. shouldn't, 4. shouldn't/ mustn't/ had better not, 5. had better not/ shouldn't, 6. must not, 7. don't have to, 8. shouldn't, 9. had better not, 10. shouldn't/ had better not
Review Exercise 1	1. k, 2. f, 3. a, 4. h, 5. b, 6. e, 7. l, 8. m, 9. j, 10. d, 11. n, 12. c, 13. o, 14. g, 15. i
Review Exercise 2	1. has to go, 2. have got to fix, 3. must save, 4. has to walk, 5. have to turn in, 6. must wear, 7. have got to get, 8. have got to dress
Review Exercise 3	1. should rest, 2. ought to be able, 3. had better stay, 4. should ask, 5. had better hurry, 6. should . . . call, 7. ought to tell, 8. had better go
Review Exercise 4	1. had better not call, 2. shouldn't . . . put, 3. don't have to work, 4. must not send, 5. shouldn't eat, 6. had better not watch, 7. doesn't have to study, 8. shouldn't wash
Review Exercise 5	1. come up with, 2. come down, 3. come around, 4. come over, 5. come along, 6. came to, 7. came back, 8. come into, 9. Come on, 10. come in
Listen Up!	1. A car salesman. 2. Come to his car lot and buy a car from him. 3. $5999, 4. $7000. 5. $2900, 6. El Camino Blvd.

Pushing the Envelope

ARE YOU READY FOR THE LESSON?

In Lesson 7, *Pushing the Envelope*, you'll read about the history of mail delivery in the U.S., and you'll listen in on a game show to test your memory of post office tunes. You'll learn some essential vocabulary for the post office as well as phrasal verbs for giving and receiving. But there's more. You'll also learn about:

- Degrees of Certainty in the Present Tense
- Degrees of Certainty in the Past Tense
- Degrees of Certainty in the Future Tense
- Phrasal Verbs for Giving and Getting

We'll finish off the lesson by discussing the American work ethic and how it shapes the character of the United States. Let's begin the lesson by practicing pronunciation in *Say It Clearly!* Ready?

7A SAY IT CLEARLY!

🎧 Turn on your CD to practice how to link words that end in one consonant sound to words that begin with the same consonant sound.

7B ENGLISH AT WORK

📖 READING: A Brief History of Mail Delivery in the U.S.A.

Read and listen to the following passage about the history of the postal service in the United States.

🎧 Mail delivery was something very different during colonial times from what it is today. In the early 1600s, overseas mail service used a tavern in Boston as the drop-off point for mail received from and sent to England. From there, it was delivered to other cities in the thirteen colonies. The first official post office was established in Pennsylvania in 1683.

In 1737, Benjamin Franklin was appointed the postmaster of Philadelphia. He was only 31 at the time, but this was where the young Franklin began to make his mark in the New World. He immediately began inspecting post offices throughout the British territories and established new and shorter routes between cities. For the first time, the postal service in the colonies began to make money for the British government, and mail service began to operate regularly. Later, Franklin was dismissed from his position as postmaster because of his sympathies for the independence movement in the colonies. However, by the time of his departure there were 30 post offices operating in the colonies.

After the revolution, almost every mode of transportation was tried for improving mail delivery service in the U.S., including even balloons. Naturally, as the size of the new country grew, so did the challenges facing mail delivery. Mail service to California first followed the Butterfield Express, a stage line that began in Missouri and ended—2800 miles later—in San Francisco. Mail delivery took between 24 days and several months. Later, the Pony Express delivered mail to California by horseback. A rider covered between 75 and 100 miles a day, rapidly changing horses at relay stations set about 10 to 15 miles apart. This method of mail delivery took about 10 1/2 days from St. Joseph, Missouri to Sacramento, California. This legendary mail delivery service lasted only a little over a year, until completion of the transcontinental telegraph line in late 1861.

About forty years later, the automobile began to play a role in mail delivery, and other technological advances in transportation would follow. Today, mail is delivered from city to city in the U.S. by truck, train or airplane. Within cities, mail is hand delivered by mail carriers who walk their routes. In many areas, mail carriers drive cars with steering wheels on the right so they can pull up beside mailboxes set along main roads and highways and deliver the mail without getting out of the car. The Internet is, of course, another means of delivering much of the kind of mail that was once sent as letters.

Mail delivery in the U.S. has undergone many changes during its history. Some of these changes have been significant in helping to establish different modes of transportation. Others have disappeared almost completely into legend. So the next time you mail a letter, remember how far things have come since that tavern in Boston!

7C   BUILD YOUR VOCABULARY

Addressee. The person or group to whom a piece of mail is addressed. *This package has my address but it's to a different addressee; it's not mine.*

Bulk mail. A large and inexpensive way of sending mail, often used by advertisers to a targeted group of people. *Jerrod just went to apply for a bulk-mail permit so he can send fliers advertising his new business.*

Certified mail. Regular first-class mail, with proof of delivery or signature required. *Since it's so important that the addressee receive this letter, I'd like to send it certified mail.*

COD. Cash on delivery. Purchase made through the mail where a customer agrees to pay on delivery. Uncommon today. *Martha, do you have $20? The mail carrier has a COD package for you.*

Direct mail. Advertising sent directly to the addressee's name rather than being addressed to "occupant." *They say we'll get better results if we send these flyers directly to the customer, so let's go with direct mail.*

Forward. To send mail from one address to another, usually used when moving. *I'm moving next week, so I have to have the post office forward my mail to my new address.*

Junk mail. Unsolicited mail, usually advertising. *Jack's mailbox is always full, but it's usually just junk mail.*

Postmark. Post office mark over the stamp in the right upper corner of a letter, including date sent and originating post office zip code. *Some people like to collect unusual stamps, but Melissa likes to collect letters with unusual postmarks.*

Parcel post. A mail service that handles packages. *All packages have to be brought directly to the post office and sent parcel post.*

Priority mail. Mail guaranteed to be delivered in two to three days. *Jay ordered a CD and priority mail delivered it in two days.*

Registered mail. Mail that is recorded at every point along the route to its destination for tracking. *If you send your application by registered mail, you can track it until it's delivered.*

Route. Service area or path assigned to a mail carrier to deliver mail in an eight-hour day. *This route is a mail carrier's nightmare, because there's a dog in every other yard and it's all uphill!*

Special delivery. Mail delivered faster than normal for a higher fee. *If you want it to arrive tomorrow, you'd better send it special delivery.*

Surface mail. Mail that travels by truck, train, or boat, but not by airplane. *Don't bother buying airmail stamps if you're just sending this in the U.S., because it'll go surface mail anyway.*

Zip code. A five-digit code that identifies a particular post office. *Do you know the zip code for Helena, Montana?*

 7D **ENGLISH UNDER THE HOOD**

TOPIC 1: Degrees of Certainty in the Present Tense

When you are absolutely certain of something, use the present tense form of the verb.

Bob is a student at the city college.

Terry has curly brown hair.

When you think you know something, but you're not completely sure, express that uncertainty by using *must* + verb.

That must be David. (Someone told you what David looks like, and you think you recognize him.)

Sarah must be hungry. (You know that she hasn't eaten for a long time.)

If you feel less than 50 percent certain about something, you can use *may* + verb, *might* + verb, or *could* + verb.

Hank may be home now. (But traffic is often bad.)

We might be at the right address. (But I can't read the house number.)

To express a negative certainty, use the present-tense negative form of the verb when you are 100 percent certain.

Catherine doesn't have blue eyes.

Delia isn't a teacher.

If you are very close to sure about something, use *couldn't* + verb or *can't* + verb.

Sam couldn't be old enough to drive yet. (He seems too young.)

The grass can't be dry. (It just rained last night.)

If you are a little less certain, then use *must not* + verb.

Troy must not be at work today. (He was out sick yesterday, and his office is empty.)

When you are less than 50 percent sure of something, use *may not* + verb or *might not* + verb.

Frederic may not be available on Tuesday afternoons. (I don't know his schedule.)

Jessica might not be a member of my gym. (I haven't seen her there.)

PRACTICE EXERCISE 1: Fill in each blank with the verb form that expresses the appropriate amount of certainty. First use the positive form. (In some cases, there may be more than one correct answer.)

1. George (like) _____ coffee, because he always has a cup in his hand.
2. Billy (be) _____ asleep, because it's after midnight and he went to bed three hours ago.
3. Anne (be) _____ outside working in the garden, but I'm really not sure.
4. If you feel awful but don't have a cold, you (have) _____ allergies.
5. That animal looks like a dog, but it's not; it (be) _____ a coyote.

   Now use the negative form.

6. Danny (be) _____ hungry; I asked him to eat with us if he wanted to.
7. The museum (be) _____ closed. It closes at 5:00 and it's only 4:30.
8. He only moved here a week ago, so he (know) _____ anyone yet.
9. Bob gets off work at 5:00, so 6:00 (be) _____ too early for dinner.
10. Thirty minutes (be) _____ enough time to get there; it takes at least 40 minutes.

TOPIC 2: Degrees of Certainty in the Past Tense

Use the simple past-tense form when you are 100 percent certain.

Terrence was home last night. (I called him and talked to him.)

Dennis ate a big salad for lunch. (I saw him eat it.)

Use *must have* + participle when you are almost certain.

Karen must have been hungry. (She ate three eggs for breakfast.)

You must have had a good time. (You look happy.)

When you are less than 50 percent certain, use *may have* + participle, *might have* + participle or *could have* + participle.

Ken may have been at work yesterday. (He wasn't at home, but it's possible he was somewhere else.)

June might have taken the bus to work. (She didn't take her car, but maybe she walked.)

Leslie could have driven June to work. (It's possible that she did.)

To express a negative certainty in the past tense, use the negative past tense.

Terrence wasn't at home last night. (I saw him at the baseball game.)

Use *couldn't have* + participle or *can't have* + participle when you are very close to sure.

Karen couldn't have been hungry. (She ate very little.)

Denny can't have had a good time last night. (He was sick all night and looked miserable.)

For less than 50 percent certainty use *may not have* + participle or *might not have* + participle.

They may not have eaten before they left. (There's a lot of food left over, and no dishes.)

He might not have arrived yet. (The bus he takes is often late.)

PRACTICE EXERCISE 2: Fill in each blank with the verb form that expresses the appropriate amount of certainty in the past. First use the positive.

1. I know my son (be) _____ in school yesterday because I took him there.
2. Bill (leave) _____ work early because no one saw him in the meeting at 3:30.
3. John and Frank (be) _____ at the beach yesterday, but I'm not sure.
4. That movie (be) _____ awful, but I haven't read any reviews yet.
5. Henry (spent) _____ the day taking photographs, since that's his hobby.

Now use the negative.

6. David (be) _____ at the party; no one saw him there at all.
7. They (run) _____ in the park this morning, since the weather was so awful.
8. Janet (get) _____ the letter yet, since we haven't heard from her.
9. Larry (felt) _____ better, because he ate almost none of his dinner.
10. The Roundtrees (leave) _____ for vacation, because their car is still here.

TOPIC 3: Degrees of Certainty in the Future Tense

When you are absolutely certain that something will happen, use the simple future tense.

Ralph will finish his PhD next June. (There is no reason to doubt it.)

If you are a little less certain, use *should* + verb or *ought to* + verb.

Ralph should finish his PhD next June. (Unless something interferes.)

Venus ought to win first place. (I think her painting is the best, but someone else may disagree.)

When you are much less certain, use *may* + verb, *might* + verb or *could* + verb.

Kevin may take off from work tomorrow. (If he thinks he can afford to do that.)

Calixte and Jay might go to the beach tomorrow. (If it's sunny.)

Arend could get a job with National Geographic. (If they like his work.)

To express a negative certainty in the future, use the negative future tense.

Harold won't be home until after 10:00 tonight.

Sophie will not be at work tomorrow.

Many other expressions of negative certainty in the future look very similar to the present tense.

Keith couldn't be getting out of the hospital tomorrow. (He still seems too weak.)

Troy must not be coming to work today. (He was out sick yesterday, and his office is empty.)

Frederic may not be available next Tuesday. (I don't know his schedule.)

Jessica might not be coming to the party tonight. (She said she wasn't feeling well.)

PRACTICE EXERCISE 3: Fill in each blank with the verb form that expresses the appropriate amount of certainty in the future. In some cases you will need to use the negative form.

1. The delivery (arrive) _____ tomorrow, because I had it sent overnight.
2. It's beginning to clear up; it (rain) _____ later today after all.
3. We (get) _____ some ice cream after dinner if everyone is still hungry.
4. I (speak) _____ Spanish well after my month-long trip to Costa Rica.
5. I (visit) _____ you next time I come to your city, without fail.
6. We (have) _____ to call the plumber if we can't fix the drain ourselves.
7. If you don't study hard enough, you (do) _____ well on your test.
8. I (call) _____ you as soon as I get home, I promise.
9. We (win) _____ win tomorrow, because the other team is very good.
10. I (stop) _____ by and pick you up after work tomorrow, but I'm not sure it's possible yet.

7E PHRASAL VERBS FOR GIVING AND GETTING

Drop off.
To deliver something or someone to a specific location. *Can you drop this package off at the post office?*

Get back.
To receive again. *I got back the message I sent Kevin, so he must have gotten a new e-mail address.*

Get back to.
To return a call or respond to a message. *Sorry, I can't talk now. I'll get back to you later.*

Get out.
To put something in the mail. *Did you get that package out yet? It needs to be in the mail by 5:00 PM.*

Get to.
To arrive somewhere. *I'm just calling to see if the letter I sent has gotten to you yet.*

Give out.
To issue, to give something to many people at the same time. *Meredith is giving out invitations to her birthday party.*

Go out.
To leave, as by mail. *Has the mail gone out yet?*

Hand out.
To distribute something by hand. *I'll hand out the tests after you put all your books away.*

Mail out.
To put something in the mail. *Have you mailed out the bills yet?*

Pass out.
To distribute to many people at the same time, similar to *hand out*. *Look at this book they passed out to everyone at the last workshop I went to.*

Pick up.
a) To get or obtain something. *You can come and pick up your new security ID after Tuesday.*

b) To become infected by something. *Walt must have picked up a cold or something at work, because he feels awful today.*

c) To get something from a store, to buy. *Can you pick up a few things from the grocery store on the way home from school?*

d) To learn, to absorb knowledge. *Isn't it amazing the way children pick up languages?*

Pick up on.
To understand. *Terry's young, but she picks up on everything, so be careful what you say in front of her.*

Send off for.
To order through the mail. *Oh, I like this skirt. I'm going to send off for it as soon as I get paid.*

Send out for.
To (call and) request a delivery, usually food. *Since we have to work late, we'd better send out for some dinner.*

7F **REAL ENGLISH**

Keeping in Touch with Friendly Advice

I could really use a friend's advice now. I'm feeling really *boxed in* at work right now, like I have no choice, and I may need to quit my job. I know that work and stress are often a *package deal*, but things are really getting tough, and I think I may *go postal* if I don't *sort* things *out* soon! I've got a new boss, and it's not like I need a *stamp of approval* for everything I do, but with this guy, it seems like nothing is right! I mean, *rain or shine*, there's something I do that he complains about every day. Just the other day I made a suggestion in a meeting, and I thought I was really *pushing the envelope*, but he just looked at me like I was crazy. I don't want to *go over his head* and complain to the general manager, but I might have to. Well, anyway, *drop me a line* when you get a chance and let me know what you'd do. Let's *keep in touch*. I can always use your advice!

7G   BRING IT ALL TOGETHER

REVIEW EXERCISE 1: Vocabulary

Try to match each of the following words with the clues.

addressee, bulk mail, certified mail, COD, direct mail, forward, junk mail, postmark, parcel post, registered mail, route, special delivery, surface mail, zip code.

1. _____ The advertiser has your name and address and sends you an ad that is addressed to you.
2. _____ You get a package and the mail carrier tells you to pay for it or you can't have it.
3. _____ The person to whom the letter is addressed.
4. _____ The mark on the upper right side of the envelope.
5. _____ Your mail carrier follows this every day.
6. _____ You must sign for it when it arrives.
7. _____ You need this if you want to send a package through the mail.
8. _____ You need to send the same information to a large group of people.
9. _____ You've moved, and you want your mail to be sent to the new address.
10. _____ This mail is tracked from the first post office to the last post office.
11. _____ You pay extra to have the mail sent to someone faster.
12. _____ This mail does not travel by airplane.
13. _____ You recycle this kind of mail, because you don't want it.
14. _____ Don't forget to put this on the address!

REVIEW EXERCISE 2: Degree of Certainty in the Present Tense

Fill in the blank with the correct form of the verb. (There may be more than one correct answer.)

1. You (not be) _____ hungry. You've just eaten.
2. Don't worry. It (not be) _____ time to go yet. We leave in half an hour.
3. Bill (be) _____ in his room. I saw him go in there a few minutes ago.
4. Don't wait for me. I (be) _____ late, but I'm not sure.
5. Terry (not take) _____ the same bus as I do—I never see her on it.
6. Debbie (be) _____ tired. She was up all night with the baby.
7. Jack (like) _____ you. He calls you all the time.
8. We (be) _____ the next champions if we practice hard all season.

REVIEW EXERCISE 3: Degree of Certainty in the Past Tense

Fill in the blank with the correct form of the verb.

1. You (not understand) _____ what I said. I said you looked *lovely,* not ugly!

2. They (return) _____ from their trip last night. I think I heard their car.

3. Joe (stay) _____ at work late tonight; he said he'd call when he got home.

4. The kids (be) _____ too tired to do anything earlier this morning, because they got to bed so late last night.

5. Randy (be) _____ too sick to go to the party last night, because he wasn't feeling well when I talked to him yesterday afternoon.

6. Tony (call) _____ me last night, but my answering machine was turned off.

REVIEW EXERCISE 4: Degree of Certainty Future Tense

Fill in each blank with the correct form of the verb.

1. Dena gets off work at 3:00, and it takes 45 minutes to get here, so she definitely (be) _____ by about 4:00.

2. We've been making such good time on this project that we (finish) _____ ahead of schedule.

3. Everyone's been doing so well this semester that they all (get) _____ A's or B's.

4. If she starts working much harder, Nina (become) _____ a very good manager.

5. He's such a smart child that he (do) _____ very well in this school.

6. If you feed the stray cats, they (come) _____ to your house.

7. I (buy) _____ a new car before the year's end, but it depends on how much I can save.

8. Ralph (do) _____ very well in culinary school, because he seems to have a natural talent for cooking.

REVIEW EXERCISE 5: Phrasal Verbs

Fill in the sentences with one of the following phrasal verbs.

drop off, getting back, get out, gets to, give out, hand out, gone out, mailing out, passing out, pick up, send off, send out

1. I'm sorry I was so late _____ to you, but I've been very busy.

2. The mail's already _____ this morning, so you'll have to wait till tomorrow.

3. If you want to be certain this package _____ its destination, you should send it by registered mail.

4. Don't you get tired of all these companies _____ their advertisements?

5. Did Emmy Lou _____ all the perfume samples to the customers?

6. How long ago did you _____ for your rebate? It usually takes several months to get it.

7. I can _____ that letter _____ at the post office on my way home.

8. If I _____ this _____ today, you'll get it by Monday for sure.

9. Let's _____ for lunch. I'm starving!

10. If you'd all please form one line, we'll start _____ applications on a first-come, first-serve basis.

11. Oh, I don't feel very well. I hope I didn't _____ something over the weekend.

12. When you're done with your lesson, could you please _____ these papers to the rest of the class?

7H LISTEN UP!

🎧 Listen in to see how Jesse Porter does on the game show "What's That Song?", and then answer the following questions.

1. What is Jesse's profession?
2. Where is Jesse from?
3. Stevie Wonder's song is called "Signed, Sealed . . . "?
4. The Marvelettes sang which song in 1961?
5. What rock-and-roll legend sang "Return to Sender?"

7I WHY DO THEY DO THAT?

Benjamin Franklin and the American Work Ethic

📖 In this lesson's reading you learned that Benjamin Franklin was once postmaster of Philadelphia. But many people know him better as a great statesman, inventor, and the person who penned the words "Early to bed, early to rise makes a man healthy, wealthy and wise." In fact, the man whose face is seen on the $100 bill has had a profound effect on the character of the United States, and to many Americans Benjamin Franklin embodies the qualities that they admire and strive for in their own lives. Above all, perhaps, is the notion that Franklin exemplifies the American work ethic. Born in 1706 into a working-class family in Boston, Massachusetts, Franklin was one of seventeen children. He began working diligently from a very young age, ultimately becoming successful in many fields as well as achieving worldwide fame. His example of dedicating himself to work and striving to succeed has made him one of the fathers of the American work ethic, and he is often thought of as proof that individuals can achieve lofty goals no matter what their origins may be.

Success, perhaps on a scale less visible than that of Benjamin Franklin, is the promise behind the American work ethic. There is a simple belief that if a person works hard enough, success can and will follow naturally. This notion has been a part of the American landscape since the country's birth. The promise of hard work and sacrifice in order to create a kind of heaven on earth captured the imagination of many people in the early history of this country, and this opportunity was in fact exactly what motivated so many to leave their homelands and settle in America. This ideal survives today, seen as the model for success in any area of life—in education, in any profession, in sports, or in any skill. Perhaps Benjamin Franklin's words "Early to bed, early to rise makes a man healthy, wealthy, and wise" may sound like a bit of an oversimplification, but they do capture a lot of the spirit of the American work ethic. And that ethic, along with its promise of success, has helped people from all over the world build this country together.

Lesson 7: Answer Key

Practice Exercise 1	1. likes/ must like, 2. is/ must be, 3. may/ could/ might be, 4. may/ could/ might have, 5. may/ could/ might be, 6. isn't/ must not be, 7. isn't/ must not be, 8. doesn't know/ must not know/ couldn't know/ can't know, 9. may/ might not be, 10. isn't/ can't be
Practice Exercise 2	1. was, 2. must have left, 3. may/ might/ could have been, 4. may/ might/ could have been, 5. may/ might/ could have spent, 6. wasn't, 7. must not have run, 8. must not/ could not/ cannot have gotten, 9. must not have felt, 10. must not have left
Practice Exercise 3	1. should/ ought to arrive, 2. may not/ might not rain, 3. may/ might/ could get, 4. ought to/should speak, 5. will visit, 6. will have, 7. won't do, 8. will call, 9. may not/ might not win, 10. may/ might/ could stop by
Review Exercise 1	1. direct mail, 2. COD, 3. addressee, 4. postmark, 5. route, 6. certified mail, 7. parcel post, 8. bulk mail, 9. forward, 10. registered mail, 11. special delivery, 12. surface mail, 13. junk mail, 14. zip code
Review Exercise 2	1. aren't/ must not be/ can't be/ couldn't be, 2. isn't, 3. is/ must be, 4. may/ might be, 5. must not take, 6. must be, 7. must like, 8. may/ might/ could be
Review Exercise 3	1. didn't understand/ must not have understood, 2. may have/ might have/ could have returned, 3. may have/ might have/ could have stayed, 4. must have been, 5. may have/ might have/ could have been, 6. may have/ might have/ could have called
Review Exercise 4	1. will be, 2. should/ ought to finish, 3. may/ might/ could get, 4. may/ might/ could become, 5. should/ ought to do, 6. will come, 7. may/ might/ could buy, 8. should/ ought to do
Review Exercise 5	1. getting back, 2. gone out, 3. gets to, 4. mailing out, 5. give out, 6. send off, 7. drop . . . off, 8. get . . . out, 9. send out, 10. passing out, 11. pick up, 12. hand out
Listen Up!	1. teacher, 2. Anchorage, Alaska, 3. Delivered, 4. "Please, Please Mr. Postman", 5. Elvis Presley

Your Rights and Responsibilities

ARE YOU READY FOR THE LESSON?

In Lesson 8, *Your Rights and Responsibilities,* you'll listen in as a driver is pulled over for speeding, and later you'll hear some tips about what you need to know if you get stopped by a highway patrol officer. Then you'll learn some vocabulary and phrasal verbs about crime and the law. But there's more. You'll also learn about:

- The Passive Voice in the Simple Present and Present Continuous Tenses
- The Passive Voice in the Simple Past and Present Perfect Tenses
- The Passive Voice in the Simple Future and Immediate Future Tenses
- Idioms for a traffic stop and phrasal verbs related to the law

But first, let's listen to how to link words with similar consonants in *Say It Clearly!* Ready?

8A SAY IT CLEARLY!

🎧 Turn on your CD to practice another common type of linking that you'll often hear in relaxed or rapidly spoken English.

8B ENGLISH AT WORK

DIALOGUE: Do You Know Why I Pulled You Over?

📖 Anyone who lives in the United States has certain basic rights and responsibilities. One of those responsibilities is knowing traffic laws and following them when you drive. Listen to the following dialogue about a driver who failed to pay attention to the speed limit.

🎧
Officer	Good morning, ma'am.
Kathrine	Good morning, officer. What's the problem?
Officer	May I have your license and registration, please?
Kathrine	Of course. Could I ask why you stopped me?
Officer	Well, ma'am, do you know what the speed limit is?
Kathrine	It's 45, officer. I wasn't speeding. I know I was doing just under 45.
Officer	Do you know that this is a school zone?
Kathrine	I'm sorry, what?
Officer	This is a school zone, ma'am. The speed limit is 25, not 45.
Kathrine	But I just saw a sign. It said 45.
Officer	That was several blocks back, ma'am. This is a school zone, and the speed limit is 25.
Kathrine	A school zone? What do you mean?

Officer   A school zone is any street that borders the grounds of a school, or where kids usually cross the street on their way to school. There are signs all over.

Kathrine   I'm sorry, but I didn't see them. I don't normally drive this way, and I don't understand how I could have known that there was a school here.

Officer   I understand that, ma'am, but it's every driver's responsibility to know the traffic laws. Now, if you'll just give me a minute, I'll be right back with your license and registration.

A few minutes later . . .

Officer   Okay, ma'am, I'm going to give you a citation for speeding in a school zone.

Kathrine   But officer, I already explained that I didn't know it was . . .

Officer   Ma'am, I'm sorry about that, but you really need to pay closer attention to the signs, especially in areas you're not familiar with. I clocked you at 43, and the speed limit is 25. Luckily the kids are in class now, but . . .

Kathrine   Officer, this isn't fair! I . . .

Officer   Ma'am, I'm going to ask you nicely not to argue with me. I noticed that you're also missing a headlight, and you don't have your seat belt on either. I can give you a ticket for those violations or just a warning.

Kathrine   Oh . . . Um . . . I'm sorry, officer. I don't mean to argue.

Officer   If you disagree with this citation, it's your right to fight it in court. All of that information is on the ticket. You can also call the number listed there.

Kathrine   Okay, um, thank you, officer.

Officer   Have a nice day, and please, ma'am, be more careful about the speed limit. If there were children around, it could have been much worse than just a ticket.

Kathrine   Okay. Thank you, officer.

8C   BUILD YOUR VOCABULARY

Arrest. To place someone in custody legally, to capture. *You are allowed only one phone call when you are arrested.*

Bribe. Money or something of value used to try to influence another person. *The officer was offered a bribe of one hundred dollars in exchange for not writing a speeding ticket.*

Citation. An official summons to appear in court, a ticket. *Mr. Timms received a traffic citation for exceeding the speed limit.*

Code compliance. Adherence to a system of rules that citizens are expected to follow in certain situations, such as building construction. *A building inspector came out to check on the code compliance of our new bathroom addition.*

Convict. To find or prove guilty in a court of law. (Stress on second syllable.) *The burglar was convicted of breaking and entering.*

Convict. A person who has been sentenced to a prison term. (Stress on first syllable.) *In many prisons, convicts may receive special rewards or privileges for good behavior.*

Custody. Control or responsibility by an authority. *Minors under eighteen are in the custody of their parents or legal guardians.*

Exception. A case where a rule does not apply. *Although the sign says "no dogs allowed," seeing-eye dogs are an exception.*

Felony. A serious crime, a crime declared a felony by statute, or a crime punishable by imprisonment for more than one year. *Dean was convicted of a felony—armed robbery—and sent to prison.*

Fine. Money paid as a penalty for breaking the law. *It's a $500 fine for throwing litter out your car window.*

Handicapped zone. The parking space or spaces reserved for handicapped drivers. *You can be fined over $1000 for parking illegally in the handicapped zone.*

Infraction. A violation, breaking the law. *Driving without a seat belt is a minor infraction, but you could still get a ticket.*

Misdemeanor. A minor offense, a crime that is less serious than a felony. *Running a stop sign is a misdemeanor, but it's dangerous.*

Municipal. Referring to a local government, such as a city or town. *The municipal building is in the center of town, and city government offices are there.*

Noise abatement. Rules regarding the controlling of noise. *Dog barking, construction, or heavy-machinery operation may all be violations of noise abatement ordinances.*

Peace officer. A police officer, a civil officer whose duty it is to keep the peace. *Miguel Garcia loves his job as a peace officer because it allows him to help people in his neighborhood.*

Record. A record kept on the legal conduct of an individual. *Well! Now that Jimmy has three traffic tickets, he has a record!*

Regulation. A rule adopted by a regulatory agency that implements or makes specific the law. *The regulations state that a front-yard fence must be six inches from the sidewalk.*

Subpoena. A notice commanding the recipient to appear in court or be punished. *George finally got a subpoena for not paying his parking tickets, so he has to appear in court next Tuesday.*

Statute. Laws or rules passed by the legislature. Regulations receive power from statutes. *Some states have a statute against nude sunbathing.*

8D ENGLISH UNDER THE HOOD

Lesson 8 focuses on the passive voice. Most of the verbs you've seen in this course—and probably most of the verbs that you hear or use in general—are in the active voice. The passive voice is formed with the verb *to be* and the past participle, and it is used most frequently in a few situations:

When it's not important to know who or what does an action:

The trash is collected twice a week, but recyclables are taken away only once a week.

When it's not known who or what does an action:

My wallet has been stolen!

When the speaker wants to focus on an action rather than on who or what does the action:

If the proposition is passed, everyone will be affected.

When a general statement is made about an action:

Crimes are often not reported in this neighborhood.

It is possible to mention the "agent" of a passive sentence, introduced by the preposition *by*:

If the proposition is passed by the town council, everyone will be affected by the new law.

Crimes are often not reported in this neighborhood by citizens who don't trust the police.

Now let's look at the passive voice in a few particular tenses.

TOPIC 1: The Passive Voice in the Simple Present and Present Continuous Tenses

Remember that you can change the active present to the passive present by making the object of the active sentence the subject of the passive. Use a form of *to be* and the past participle of the main verb. If you want to mention the agent, use *by* right before it.

Active	Passive
Police officers write citations.	*Citations are written by police officers.*
That man is stealing my car!	*My car is being stolen (by that man)!*

PRACTICE EXERCISE 1: Change these active sentences into the passive. Do not include the agent.

1. Bartenders do not serve alcoholic beverages to people under twenty-one.
2. Sam keeps the door open when it's hot during the day.
3. People in this town do not break the law.
4. Everyone trusts and respects that police officer.
5. A security system protects most of the houses in this neighborhood.
6. A thief is stealing that woman's purse.
7. A highway patrolman is pulling over the sports car we saw earlier.
8. The townspeople are debating the proposal for a new shopping center.

TOPIC 2: The Passive Voice in the Present Perfect and Simple Past Tenses

The present perfect tense of the passive voice uses *have/has been* + past participle, and the past tense of the passive voice uses *was/were* + past participle.

Active	Passive
Someone has stolen Lucy's watch.	*Lucy's watch has been stolen.*
They vandalized the school last night!	*The school was vandalized last night!*

PRACTICE EXERCISE 2: Change these active sentences into the passive. Again, do not include an agent.

1. A thief took my wallet out of my back pocket.
2. Someone assaulted John in the park last night.
3. The police officer has warned James about fixing his taillights.
4. They have written a new report about crime rates in this city.
5. The people in this town have established a citizen's patrol association.

6. The voters defeated two proposals to build new shopping centers.

7. The reform candidate has beaten the mayor.

8. Someone saw the suspect leaving his house at 8:30 last night.

TOPIC 3: The Passive Voice in the Simple Future and Immediate Future Tenses

The future tense of the passive voice uses *will be* + past participle, and the immediate future tense of the passive voice uses *is/are going to be* + past participle.

Active	Passive
The police will write a lot of tickets this weekend.	*A lot of tickets will be written this weekend.*
People are not going to notice the traffic sign.	*The traffic sign isn't going to be noticed.*

PRACTICE EXERCISE 3: Change these active sentences into the passive. Do not use an agent.

1. Someone is going to challenge that new law as unconstitutional.

2. The authorities will prosecute all violators.

3. A tow-truck driver will tow illegally parked vehicles away.

4. They are going to raise the speed limit next year.

5. Someone is going to install a new security system at the museum.

6. The judge will dismiss the charges against the city council member.

7. The people in town are going to consider the proposal.

8. The arresting officer will read the suspect's rights.

8E   PHRASAL VERBS FOR CRIMINAL ACTS

Break into.
To enter a house illegally, usually by breaking a window or door. *Someone broke into Mary and Ted's house last night and stole their television, VCR, and jewelry.*

Break out.
To get out of prison through force or stealth. *A prisoner broke out of state prison late last night and is still at large.*

Break up.
To disorganize, to cause to stop. *Police broke up a stolen car ring after a long undercover investigation.*

Get away with.
a) To do something wrong without being caught or punished for it. *The thief is going to get away with his crimes because they don't have enough evidence against him.*

b) To steal and escape with. *The bank robbers got away with $10,000.*

Get even.
To harm someone in some way to make them pay for a perceived injustice. *Jenny's flirting with Elizabeth's boyfriend because she wants to get even with her.*

Get off.

To be found not guilty of a crime. *Jerry got off on a technicality, even though everyone knows he's guilty.*

Lock up.

To put in prison, to incarcerate. *Most people think murderers should be locked up for a long time.*

Make off with.

To steal and escape with. *The thieves made off with a painting from the museum.*

Pay off.

To bribe, to give money to someone in exchange for something illegal. *The landlord was paying off the building inspector for years, so no one knew how dangerous the building was.*

Pin (something) on (someone).

To create evidence to make it look like an innocent person committed a crime. *Everyone knows that Jim didn't rob the liquor store. The Jones brothers pinned it on him.*

Take (someone) for.

To take advantage of someone, usually for money. *I heard that a scam artist took Mrs. Higgins for $50,000!*

Take a look at.

To study something carefully. *Take a look at these mug shots, Ms. Jones, and see if you can pick out the guy that attacked you.*

Watch out for.

To guard someone or something. (Also *look out for.*) *Julian's job was to watch out for the police while the others were in the bank.*

Throw the book at.

To prosecute someone to the full extent of the law. (*The book* means the law.) *If Gary is ever arrested again, they're going to throw the book at him.*

8F REAL ENGLISH

YOU'RE BUSTED!

Have you ever gotten a *ticket*? I don't just mean a parking ticket. I mean a real driving citation. If you have, then you know how it feels. You're driving down the freeway, feeling good, *cruising along*, when *out of nowhere* you see that black-and-white sedan in your rear view mirror. *Your heart sinks to your feet.* "Is it me? Is he after me?" You start *sweating buckets* as you try to lift that *lead foot* off the accelerator to slow down. Then your suspicions grow because you see that red light flashing. You might as well start *pulling over* because next you're going to hear that big bullhorn telling you to "PULL OVER. PULL OVER TO THE SIDE OF THE ROAD. PULL OVER, NOW!" So you pull over, *breaking* two or three more traffic laws as you cross the freeway to get to the other side.

What is it about police officers that *freaks us out*? Could it be their *build*? Maybe it's the uniforms, or the *shades*, or maybe it's the gun they're *packing*. Or maybe it's just an encounter with the *long arm of the law*. Whatever it is, it's difficult to *look* the officer *in the eye* and say, "did I do something wrong, officer?" in a clear, strong voice. Once you've *squeaked out* that you've never had a ticket before, he looks at you and says, "can I see your license and registration, please?" Then it's so hard to pull your license out of your wallet, because you're *all thumbs*.

Once it's *all over with* and the *cop* has *thrown the book at you* in the form of a $500 ticket and told you to *straighten up*, he tells you that you can go. You try to wait until the officer *leaves the scene of the crime* first, but he usually has paperwork to do. So, ever so carefully, you *ease back onto* the freeway, *feeling about two inches shorter* and driving at least 20 MPH slower than before.

8G   BRING IT ALL TOGETHER

REVIEW EXERCISE 1: Vocabulary

Place the correct vocabulary word in each space. Use each of the following words once: *arrested, bribe, citation, code compliant, convicted, custody, exceptions, felony, fine, handicapped zones, infraction, misdemeanor, municipal, noise abatement, peace officer, records, regulations, subpoena, statutes.*

1. The city's _____ water district office is at Fourth and C.
2. The police officers _____ the thief before he could get away.
3. John's neighbor's accused him of breaking _____ laws when he had such a loud party.
4. If you receive a _____ to go to court, the law says you must show up.
5. Most people only have a few traffic tickets on their _____.
6. The extra-large parking spaces marked by blue lines are the _____.
7. If you are found guilty of a _____, you may not have to go to jail.
8. If you are found guilty of a _____, you will probably spend at least a year in jail.
9. When the neighbors built an apartment less than three feet from my fence, they were not _____.
10. When the county clerk accepted $50 and put it in his pocket, he was taking a _____.
11. Joe got a _____ for speeding in a residential zone.
12. "_____" is another word for a violation.
13. A person who is charged with keeping the peace is a _____.
14. If you pay your _____ and go to traffic school, you can put the whole mess behind you—and drive more carefully!
15. In most states, a person cannot vote if he or she is _____ of a felony.
16. There are a lot of _____ you need to know if you want to build an addition to your house.
17. When a child's parents are found guilty of a crime and jailed, the state takes _____ of the child until a family can be found to take him or her.
18. The governor signed twelve new _____ that will go into effect on January 1.

REVIEW EXERCISE 2: The Passive Voice in the Simple Present and Present Continuous Tenses

Rewrite each of the following sentences in the passive voice. Use the agent this time.

1. The captain praises the officers in the department.
2. The mechanic is repairing the car right now.
3. Our neighbors are breaking the law.
4. People all over town hear the music from the concert.
5. The wind is blowing trash across the highway.
6. The legislature passes several new laws each year.

REVIEW EXERCISE 3: The Passive Voice in the Present Perfect and Simple Past Tenses

Rewrite each of the following sentences in the passive voice. Use the agent this time.

1. The couple has returned the car to the dealership.
2. One of the students stole money from the teacher's purse.
3. Someone has vandalized the library.
4. A civil-rights group challenged the new law.
5. Many journalists have reported the crime statistics from this city.
6. The government raised the speed limit on interstate highways.

REVIEW EXERCISE 4: The Passive Voice in the Simple Future and Immediate Future Tenses

Rewrite each of the following sentences in the passive voice. Use the agent this time.

1. The police will escort the car to the hospital.
2. The city is going to repair those streetlights.
3. The city council will debate the issue tomorrow night.
4. The police will eventually catch the criminal.
5. The suspect's lawyers are going to call a press conference tonight.
6. The people of the community will protest the new law.

REVIEW EXERCISE 5: Phrasal Verbs for Criminal Acts

Place the correct vocabulary word in each space. Use each of the following words once: *broke into, break up, got away with, get even, got off, made off with, locked up, pinned (something) on (someone), take (someone) for, take a look at, watch out for, threw the book at.*

1. The judge was so angry at what the criminal had done that he _____ him.
2. Jeremy wanted to _____ with Susan for telling the teacher that he cheated on his test.
3. Someone _____ their house last night and stole their computer equipment.
4. Be careful of telephone scams. They could _____ you _____ a lot!

5. The thieves stole the diamond and _____ the crime _____ the museum curator.

6. Since the crime was committed fifteen years ago and no one was ever caught, I guess they _____ it.

7. The police asked the victim to _____ some photos of known criminals.

8. If you walk through the park at night, _____ muggers!

9. When the F. B. I. got the intelligence they needed they were able to _____ a major terrorist cell.

10. The defendant hired a good lawyer and _____ on a technicality.

11. The art thieves _____ a Van Gogh and a Renoir!

12. If you're found guilty of a felony, you'll get _____!

8H   LISTEN UP!

Listen to the article and then decide whether the following statements are true or false.

1. If you're on the highway and see a police officer's flashing light in your rearview mirror, drive to the nearest police station.

2. Roll down your passenger's side window to speak to the officer.

3. You must have your driver's license and your passport.

4. If you think the officer is wrong, argue with him or her.

5. Go to court if you think the officer was wrong and let the judge decide.

6. You should never try to bribe a police officer.

8I   WHY DO THEY DO THAT?

SOME IMPORTANT DRIVER'S RESPONSIBILITIES

Here are a few responsibilities for anyone driving on the streets and highways of the United States that you may not know about.

EMERGENCY VEHICLES

You may have noticed that when they hear a siren, Americans immediately pull their cars over to the right and stop and wait until the emergency vehicle passes before pulling out again. This is because the siren tells drivers that the ambulance, fire engine, or police car is on its way to an emergency. You can be ticketed for not pulling over, so be sure that nothing obstructs your hearing and that you also pull over immediately. Everyone stops at an intersection until the emergency vehicle has passed. If the emergency vehicle is behind you when you are at a traffic light and you are blocking the street, even though the light is red you may need to proceed through the intersection with caution until you can safely pull over. The object is to get out of the way of the ambulance, police car, or fire truck as soon as possible.

LITTERING

If you are driving along eating a hamburger or drinking a can of soda, keep the wrapper or can in your car until you can stop and throw them away. Do not throw anything out of the window of your car onto the road. Littering is considered very offensive to many Americans, and it is also illegal. If you are caught you may have to pay a fine of $1,000 or more depending upon the state laws on littering.

NOISE POLLUTION

It may also be illegal to turn your radio or CD player up so loud that other drivers can hear it. There are laws in many cities or states against noise pollution, whether you are in your home or in your car. You must be aware that other people do not enjoy the same music that you do, and if someone complains, you may be fined for noise pollution.

HANDICAPPED PARKING

Most states have special parking places designated for handicapped drivers. In order to park in handicapped zones you must get a permit from the state to hang in your window or put on your dashboard. If you are not certified to park in handicapped zones you can be fined as much as $1,000 in some states.

Lesson 8: Answer Key

Practice Exercise 1
1. Alcoholic beverages are not served to people under twenty-one. 2. The door is kept open when it's hot during the day. 3. The law is not broken in this town. 4. That police officer is trusted and respected. 5. Most of the houses in this neighborhood are protected. 6. That woman's purse is being stolen. 7. The sports car we saw earlier is being pulled over. 8. The proposal for a new shopping center is being debated.

Practice Exercise 2
1. My wallet was taken out of my back pocket. 2. John was assaulted in the park last night. 3. James has been warned about fixing his taillights. 4. A new report about crime rates in this city has been written. 5. A citizen's patrol association has been established. 6. Two proposals to build new shopping centers were defeated. 7. The mayor has been beaten. 8. The suspect was seen leaving his house at 8:30 last night.

Practice Exercise 3
1. That new law is going to be challenged as unconstitutional. 2. All violators will be prosecuted. 3. Illegally parked vehicles will be towed away. 4. The speed limit is going to be raised next year. 5. A new security system is going to be installed at the museum. 6. The charges against the city council member will be dismissed. 7. The proposal is going to be considered. 8. The suspect's rights will be read.

Review Exercise 1
1. municipal 2. arrested 3. noise abatement 4. subpoena 5. records 6. handicapped zones 7. misdemeanor 8. felony 9. code compliant 10. bribe 11. citation 12. Infraction 13. peace officer 14. fine 15. convicted 16. regulations 17. custody 18. statutes

Review Exercise 2
1. The officers in the department are praised by the captain. 2. The car is being repaired by the mechanic right now. 3. The law is being broken by our neighbors. 4. The music from the concert is heard by people all over town. 5. Trash is being blown across the highway by the wind. 6. Several new laws are passed each year by the legislature.

Review Exercise 3
1. The car has been returned to the dealership by the couple. 2. Money from the teacher's purse was stolen by one of the students. 3. The library has been vandalized by someone. 4. The new law was challenged by a civil-rights group. 5. The crime statistics from this city have been reported by many journalists. 6. The speed limit on interstate highways has been raised by the government.

Review Exercise 4
1. The car will be escorted to the hospital by the police. 2. Those streetlights are going to be repaired by the city. 3. The issue will be debated by the city council tomorrow night. 4. The criminal will eventually be caught by the police. 5. A press conference is going to be called tonight by the suspect's lawyers. 6. The new law will be protested by the people of the community.

Review Exercise 5
1. threw the book at, 2. get even, 3. broke into, 4. take … for, 5. pinned … on, 6. got away with, 7. take a look at, 8. watch out for, 9. break up, 10. got off, 11. made off with, 12. locked up

Listen Up!
1. False. 2. True. 3. False. 4. False. 5. True. 6. True

Lesson 9

This Is Paradise, Isn't It?

ARE YOU READY FOR THE LESSON?

Do you like to travel? Well, good, because in this lesson you'll read a letter about a Hawaiian vacation and listen to two friends discuss their vacations over the phone. Then you'll learn some idioms about travel and one of the reasons why we travel: work stress. But there's more! You'll also learn about:

• Tag questions
• Negative questions
• Sentences that begin with negative adverbs
• Phrasal verbs with *look*

We'll finish up the lesson by learning some American travel customs. But first, let's get started on the intonation of tag endings in *Say It Clearly!*

9A SAY IT CLEARLY!

🎧 Listen to your CD to practice the two different types of intonation used for tag questions.

9B ENGLISH AT WORK

Reading: Aloha from Hawaii!

📖 Meredith is on vacation in Hawaii, and she's taking a moment to write an e-mail message to her friend, Kathy, who's not on vacation.

Dear Kathy,

Hey! Don't think I'm mean for sending you an e-mail while I'm sitting next to a pool in the sun sipping one of those big tropical drinks while you're sitting at your computer in your office back in Minneapolis! I'm just trying to send you some sun!

What a trip this has been! You remember how much I was looking forward to coming here, don't you? Well, practically as soon as I arrived I began to catch a cold. What a bummer! Anyway, I missed the hiking expedition we had planned. I had to stay in bed the whole day, but David went and told me all about it when he got back. He said it was unbelievable, so picturesque. They got to walk near the summit of a volcano! David said the tour guide told them that the flora and fauna were relatively undisturbed and that the area was reminiscent of what Hawaii used to look like before the tourists took it over.

I felt better the next day and was ready to start my adventures. Since we had more than one and a half weeks left we decided I should go slowly; so we went for a cruise in a glass-bottom boat. It was absolutely spectacular! The colors of the tropical fish and the coral formations were just amazing. But I was still a bit sick, and I was pretty exhausted after the cruise, so I just hung around the hotel for the rest of the day and read while David went off and looked into some other things for us to do.

We spent a couple of days just walking around looking at the shops and lying on the beach. When I started to feel like myself again, we decided to take an ecotour. We were able to see how Hawaii has some amazingly different terrain. One of the things we saw was a Hawaiian temple on a bluff above Waimea Bay. The panoramic view overlooking the ocean from there was incredible. We also went to a bird sanctuary where we looked through a telescope to enhance our view. Then we got to go for a walk on this absolutely pristine beach where we saw plants, birds, dolphins, whales, and even a sea turtle.

I leave in a few days, but one of the last things I want to do here is visit Hawaii's lush rainforest. You know all those commercials you see with the beautiful swaying coconut trees, the white sand, and the turquoise-colored ocean, don't you? Well they're all true. I can't wait to see the rainforest.

I hope you get to come to Hawaii someday soon. You'd just love it here, and it sure beats January in Minneapolis.

See you real soon,

Meredith

9C BUILD YOUR VOCABULARY

Bluff. A high, steep bank; a cliff; a land mass that rises steeply and is flat on top. *The hotel stood on a bluff overlooking the ocean.*

Coral formations. Shapes made of coral. *The Great Barrier Reef in Australia has a lot of beautiful coral formations.*

Cruise. A vacation on a boat, often an ocean liner. *The Swifts took a cruise to the Bahamas for their second honeymoon.*

Ecotour. A tour of a natural habitat conducted in a manner that minimizes ecological impact. *Jim prefers ecotours because he is an environmentalist at heart.*

Enhance. To heighten, increase or improve the quality of something. *The caramel sauce enhanced the flavor of the crepes.*

Exhausted. To be completely tired, to be drained of energy. *We were completely exhausted after our three-day trip to Chicago and back.*

Expedition. A long journey taken for a specific reason; the group taking such a trip. *Ed Rumswell and George Clark planned an expedition to the top of Mt. Whitney.*

Flora and fauna. Plant and animal life, respectively. *The flora and fauna of remote islands are often very unique.*

Hiking. A long walk taken for pleasure or exercise, usually in a forested or mountainous area. *There are some wonderful hiking trails on Mt. Palomar.*

Lush. Very rich in plant life, very green. *Houses look best with lush plant life around them.*

Picturesque. A scene so perfect that it looks like a picture; a very charming scene. *The quaint mountain cabin nestled among the hills and the trees looked quite picturesque.*

Pristine. Fresh, clean, not polluted, in original condition. *It's rare to find a truly pristine beach anywhere in the world.*

Reminiscent. Suggestive of a memory, similar to something remembered. *Catalina Island is reminiscent of San Francisco with its hills and houses perched in high places.*

Sanctuary. A safe haven, a holy place; the room where worshipping takes place in a church. *Ned regarded his mountain home as a sanctuary that kept him safe from big city life.*

Shimmering. Softly shining with a quivering effect, as the sun on water. *It's so beautiful to watch the sun setting over the ocean with its lingering, shimmering glow.*

Spectacular. Sensational, striking, visually stunning. *The fireworks over the ocean were spectacular last night!*

Summit. The top of a mountain, the highest point of something. *Since Sir Edmond Hillary reached the summit of Mt. Everest, many others have also accomplished this feat.*

Terrain. A geographical area, often used to describe the environment or physical features of an area. *The terrain of the Midwest is completely different from that of the western region of the United States.*

Tropical. With a climate like the area near the equator. *People on the West Coast like to simulate a tropical environment in their yards, even though tropical plants use a lot of water.*

Turquoise. Light greenish blue; a mineral of the same name. *Come see the shimmering turquoise waters of the Florida Keys.*

 9D ENGLISH UNDER THE HOOD

TOPIC 1: Tag Questions

Use tag questions when you want to be sure that you are correct or when you want to seek agreement. Tag questions are composed of a statement followed by a helping verb and a pronoun in inverted order like a question. A negative tag question follows affirmative statements. The negative ending is usually a contraction.

You like to take ecotours to Costa Rica, don't you?

A positive tag ending follows negative statements.

You're not taking vacation this month, are you?

The helping verb on the tag ending must agree with the tense of the statement it is attached to.

You travel to Nova Scotia every year, don't you?

You didn't take the train to Cincinnati, did you?

They're coming tomorrow, aren't they?

You've been to Greece before, haven't you?

This is paradise, isn't it?

If the statement contains *can, could, would, should,* or *must,* repeat it in the tag ending.

You can't speak Arabic, can you?

I shouldn't take a vacation this month, should I?

If the statement contains *have to, has to, need(s) to,* or *want(s) to,* use *do* or *does* in the tag ending.

We have to leave first thing tomorrow morning, don't we?

She doesn't want to take the tour, does she?

Knowing what pronoun to use in the tag ending isn't always easy. Here are a few hints to help you make the decision.

If the subject is *this* or *that,* use *it* in the tag ending.

This is your passport, isn't it?

That isn't an American passport, is it?

If the subject is *these* or *those,* use *they* in the tag ending.

Those are your bags, aren't they?

These aren't very good seats, are they?

Use *it* for indefinite pronouns that refer to things, such as *everything, something,* or *anything.* Use *they* for indefinite pronouns that refer to people, such as *everybody, everyone, someone,* or *anyone.*

Everything is okay here, isn't it?

Everyone on this flight has checked luggage, haven't they?

If the subject of the statement is a negative word such as *nothing* or *no one,* or if *never* is used in the sentence, follow it with a positive tag ending.

No one lives here, do they?

Nothing is going right on this trip, is it?

Follow *I am* in the statement portion with *aren't I* in the tag ending. The formal ending is *am I not,* but this is rarely used and may sound stilted.

I'm in the aisle seat, aren't I?

Remember that the negative contraction for *will* is *won't.*

She'll be there, won't she?

PRACTICE EXERCISE 1: Finish each sentence with the correct tag ending.

1. You have to pick up your kids at the airport, _____?
2. There were too many babies on the flight, _____?
3. You never eat before going skiing, _____?
4. We can't go to Spain for vacation, _____?
5. The bus will be late, _____?
6. This isn't your boarding pass, _____?
7. Your boss won't be back from Hawaii tomorrow, _____?
8. Mary hasn't ever been to Italy, _____?

9. This seat isn't yours, _____ ?
10. No one liked the restaurant, _____ ?

TOPIC 2: Negative Questions

Negative questions are used when the speaker has a strong expectation or assumption of a positive answer. They can express a range of emotions from uncertainty, surprise, or shock to anger or suspicion, depending on the tone of voice used.

Don't you have to work today? (I'm surprised that you're not at work.)

Don't you have anything to do? (I'm annoyed or angry that you're here.)

Doesn't it ever rain here? (I'm surprised because it's so dry.)

Don't they know any better? (I'm shocked that they would do something so stupid.)

When beginning sentences with negatives, use contractions.

Isn't it cold? Don't you want to bring a sweater?

The non-contracted "is it not cold" or "do you not want" are rarely used and sound very formal.

The responses to negative questions can be confusing. Take the example: *Aren't you supposed to be at work?* The response, *Yes, I am* means you are supposed to be at work. But if it is a holiday or you took the day off, the response is *No, I'm not*, meaning: *No, I'm not supposed to be at work*.

PRACTICE EXERCISE 2: Fill in the blanks with the appropriate negative questions.

1. Why didn't you eat your lunch? _____ you hungry?
2. Why is it so dry here? _____ it ever rain in this city?
3. You can't be tired! _____ you sleep on the flight?
4. They're taking a cruise to Alaska? _____ that too expensive?
5. He's traveling by train? _____ that take too long?
6. Jordan is going back to Brazil? _____ he go there last year?
7. The plane is landing already? _____ it running late earlier?
8. You're checking your e-mail? _____ you supposed to be on vacation?

TOPIC 3: Beginning Sentences with Negative Adverbs

In order to make a more emphatic statement, you can begin a sentence with a negative adverb such as *never, rarely, not once, hardly ever, seldom*, or *scarcely*. Sentences that begin in this way invert the order of subject and verb.

Rarely had I seen him so angry as when the airline lost his luggage.

Never would I have agreed to such a thing if I had known the truth!

Notice that these statements are the emphatic equivalents of "I had rarely seen him ..." and "I would never have agreed ..." In both cases, there is an auxiliary verb—*had* and *would*. To make an emphatic statement out of a sentence that doesn't contain an auxiliary verb, such as "I seldom hear such good news" or "Jim never slept so deeply as on vacation," you have to add an auxiliary:

Seldom do I hear such good news!

Never did Jim sleep so deeply as on vacation!

Notice that this word order can be used not only for emphasis, but also for a dramatic or even poetic quality.

Never had she felt so lost and alone.

Rarely had the night seemed so long and lonely.

PRACTICE EXERCISE 3: Rewrite the following sentences so that they begin with negative adverbs.

1. We had never seen such beautiful mountains.
2. Paul had scarcely left the house when the blizzard hit.
3. Jim had rarely spoken with such sincerity.
4. We seldom take such relaxing trips.
5. The Harding family hardly ever went on vacation.
6. Tony rarely goes to bed before midnight.
7. I had never seen such clear water as during our trip to Curaçao.
8. The sky had never looked so ominous.

9E PHRASAL VERBS WITH *LOOK*:

Look after.
To watch carefully, as in babysitting. *Could you look after my kids for about a half hour so I can run to the store?*

Look around for.
To search for something. *If you don't find the plane tickets on the table, look around for them.*

Look at.
To watch or study; to consider. *Look at that beautiful waterfall. It's spectacular!*

Look away.
To stop looking at something, to turn one's eyes away. *Look away from the sun or you'll hurt your eyes!*

Look for.
To hunt for something lost or misplaced. *Jake looked for his keys for twenty minutes before finally finding them.*

Look forward to.
To anticipate with pleasure. *Are you looking forward to your trip to Hawaii?*

Look in on.
To check on, to see if someone is okay. *Joe always looks in on his kids right before he goes to bed.*

Look into.
To research; to find information. *The human resources department should always look into prospective employees' backgrounds.*

Look on.
To watch or observe in order to gain knowledge or information. *If you're doing a new procedure, do you mind if I look on to see how it's done?*

Look out for.
a) To watch or wait for. *Look out for the waiter and ask him for some water if he comes by.*
b) To be careful of. *Look out for that icy patch on the road!*

Look out on/over.
To be above a view. *Our hotel balcony looked out on/over a beautiful bay.*

Look over.
To inspect or examine. *Class, be sure to look over your papers before turning them in.*

Look (someone) up.
a) To make contact with, especially during a visit to another city. *If I'm ever in Montreal, I'll be sure to look you up so we can have dinner.*

Look (something) up.
b) To find, as in an answer or a definition. *If you don't know a word, look it up in your dictionary.*

Look up.
c) To seem to be improving. *The weather's looking up, so we can finally spend time on the beach tomorrow.*

Look up to.
To view someone with respect and admiration. *Jenny had always looked up to her father and tried to follow his example.*

9F   REAL ENGLISH

YOUR ISLAND *GETAWAY*

If you're *all stressed out* because you've *got your nose to the grindstone* and you're *up to your ears* in work, don't *have a nervous breakdown*. Why not *break away*? Take a trip to an island paradise. You can *take it easy* while *living it up*. You'll find the water warm and soothing, and the views will absolutely *take your breath away*. So come on, why not *check it out*? See you there.

9G   BRING IT ALL TOGETHER

REVIEW EXERCISE 1: Vocabulary

Fill in the blanks with the words below.

bluff, coral formations, cruise, ecotour, enhances, exhausted, expedition, flora and fauna, hiking, lush, picturesque, pristine, reminiscent, sanctuary, shimmering, spectacular, summit, terrain, tropical, turquoise

1. Bob's favorite form of exercise is _____ in the mountains.
2. We went scuba diving so that we could see the _____ up close.

3. Dina's _____ after her busy three-day trip to San Francisco.
4. All the _____ plant life makes your garden look like a jungle!
5. Is the _____ hilly, flat, or mountainous in your country?
6. If you're concerned about the environment, try an _____ for your next vacation.
7. The moon's reflection was _____ on the lake.
8. While at Big Sur, Jim and Mary sat on a high _____ overlooking the Pacific Ocean below.
9. What a _____ scene, with all the pine trees surrounding the clear blue lake!
10. You look great in _____; it's one of your best colors.
11. Your new haircut _____ the best features in your face.
12. The image on the new plasma TV is _____.
13. _____ to an island getaway are the most romantic vacations.
14. The national park preserves hundreds of square miles of _____ wilderness.
15. Joe fantasizes about being at a _____ beach, sitting under palm trees with a tall, cool drink in his hand.
16. Charles Darwin was fascinated by the _____ of the Galapagos.
17. Penny regarded her bedroom as her _____ away from the difficulties of school.
18. Take a picture of the valley below when you reach the _____.
19. The writer's fans found her latest book _____ of her much earlier novels.
20. The _____ to King Tut's tomb was interesting and exciting.

REVIEW EXERCISE 2: Tag Questions
Supply the correct tag ending.

1. You look tired. You aren't sick, _____?
2. Kevin's lost a lot of weight. You don't think he looks too thin, _____?
3. The streets were wet this morning. It didn't rain, _____?
4. I'm sitting next to you on the plane, _____?
5. You can postpone your vacation one week, _____?
6. She's been to the Caribbean before, _____?
7. Ann hasn't left for the excursion yet, _____?
8. You'll come with us, _____?

REVIEW EXERCISE 3: Negative Questions
Complete the following negative questions by supplying the proper auxiliary.

1. _____ you ever been to California before?
2. _____ you just love to sit on the beach and relax when you're on vacation?
3. _____ you remember to pack you passport last night?
4. _____ I taking the same flight as you?
5. _____ the guided tour that we took of the chateau fascinating?
6. _____ Thai cuisine one of the most delicious in the world?

7. _____ that guy take the same flight as we did?

8. _____ you at least try to learn some Arabic before your trip to Cairo next month?

REVIEW EXERCISE 4: Beginning Sentences with Negative Adverbs

Rewrite each of the following sentences so that they begin with negative adverbs.

1. Murray has never taken such a long vacation.
2. I seldom have the opportunity to meet such interesting people.
3. Janet hardly ever leaves the office before 6:30 in the evening.
4. I had never felt so frightened on a flight.
5. We had scarcely arrived at the beach when the weather turned ugly.
6. The kids have never swum in such warm water.
7. The flowers have never looked so stunning.
8. The children hardly ever take an interest in museums.

REVIEW EXERCISE 5: Phrasal Verbs with *look*

Fill in the sentences with the following phrasal verbs.

look after, look at, looking for, looking forward to, look into, look out, looked out on, look over, look up, look up to

1. We need to _____ the new charter school before we decide where Jamie should go to school.
2. I'm _____ cheap flights on the Internet.
3. _____ for the sharp turns in the mountain roads.
4. Would you please _____ these plans _____ before we get started?
5. Most children _____ one or both of their parents.
6. Could you _____ our house while we're away?
7. The Carlson's have been _____ their cruise for months.
8. The houses in the hills all _____ the valley below.
9. _____ this brochure about hiking trails in the national park.
10. It's easy to _____ information on the Internet.

9H LISTEN UP!

🎧 Turn on your recording and listen in as Meredith and Kathy talk about a trip that Kathy took while Meredith was in Hawaii. Then answer the following questions.

1. What country was Kathy's vacation in?
2. What did Kathy learn to do while she was there?
3. What do cliff divers hold in their hands?
4. What type of jewelry does Kathy show Meredith?
5. Did Kathy like the food she ate there?
6. What was Kathy doing when she met someone?

91   WHY DO THEY DO THAT?

Travel in America

Americans travel a lot. And, as you read in an earlier lesson, Americans also love their cars. So it's not surprising to know that Americans' favorite mode of transportation to take a trip is the automobile. According to a study of 80,000 households in 1995, over 80 percent of all trips were taken in personal vehicles. Even for long trips between 500 and 1,000 miles, Americans chose to drive 75 percent of the time. That is compared to only 15.6 percent who traveled by plane. And most of these trips were for long distances, too. According to the same study, the average American traveled over 3,000 miles on long-distance trips. Most of this travel took place within the United States. Only about 4 percent of the long distance trips were to other countries.

What does all this say about the American character? Once again, personal freedom is the primary reason why Americans choose cars over all other types of transportation. Americans want to be in control of what they see, where they go, what they do, and when they do it. There's something special about getting in a car and just driving off. But why are the long-distance trips primarily confined to the U.S.? There could be a few reasons for that. It could be economics, or it could be a symptom of an isolationist mentality some people associate with Americans. Or it could be simple geography— the U.S. is a vast country, so it's possible to travel distances here that would take a person through two or more countries in some other parts of the world. Whatever the reason, there's a lot to see and a lot of people and places to visit, so it's no wonder that the "road trip" is a beloved part of American culture.

Statistics taken from *Americans Prefer Cars for Long Trips*, by Scott Bowles, Cincinnati.com, Sept. 3, 2003

Lesson 9: Answer Key

Practice Exercise 1	1. don't you 2. weren't there 3. do you 4. can we 5. won't it 6. is it 7. will he/she 8. has she 9. is it 10. did they
Practice Exercise 2	1. Aren't/Weren't, 2. Doesn't, 3. Didn't, 4. Isn't, 5. Doesn't/Won't, 6. Didn't, 7. Wasn't, 8. Aren't
Practice Exercise 3	1. Never had we seen such beautiful mountains. 2. Scarcely had Paul left the house when the blizzard hit. 3. Rarely had Jim spoken with such sincerity. 4. Seldom do we take such relaxing trips. 5. Hardly ever did the Harding family go on vacation. 6. Rarely does Tony go to bed before midnight. 7. Never had I seen such clear water as during our trip to Curaçao. 8. Never had the sky looked so ominous.
Review Exercise 1	1. hiking, 2. coral formations, 3. exhausted, 4. lush, 5. terrain, 6. ecotour, 7. shimmering, 8. bluff, 9. picturesque, 10. turquoise, 11. enhances, 12. spectacular, 13. Cruises, 14. pristine, 15. tropical, 16. flora and fauna, 17. sanctuary, 18. summit, 19. reminiscent, 20. expedition
Review Exercise 2	1. are you 2. do you 3. did it 4. aren't I 5. can't you 6. hasn't she 7. has she 8. won't you
Review Exercise 3	1. Haven't, 2. Don't / Won't, 3. Didn't, 4. Aren't 5. Wasn't, 6. Isn't 7. Didn't 8. Won't
Review Exercise 4	1. Never has Murray taken such a long vacation. 2. Seldom do I have the opportunity to meet such interesting people. 3. Hardly ever does Janet leave the office before 6:30 in the evening. 4. Never had I felt so frightened on a flight. 5. Scarcely had we arrived the beach when the weather turned ugly. 6. Never have the kids swum in such warm water. 7. Never have the flowers looked so stunning. 8. Hardly ever do the children take an interest in museums.
Review Exercise 5	1. look into, 2. looking for, 3. look out, 4. look . . . over, 5. look up to, 6. look after, 7. looking forward to, 8. looked out on, 9. Look at, 10. look up
Listen Up!	1. Mexico, 2. Dance the salsa, 3. Torches, 4. A silver bracelet, 5. Yes, 6. Dancing

Take Me Out to the Ball Game!

ARE YOU READY FOR THE LESSON?

Do you enjoy watching sports for entertainment? If you do, then Lesson 10, *Take Me Out to the Ball Game!*, will tell you everything you want to know about sports in America. You'll hear some TV announcers talking about baseball playoffs in *English at Work*. Then you'll hear the final results for the playoffs *Listen Up!* If you're wondering what America's favorite sport is, you'll find out in *Why Do They Do That?* You'll also learn:

• Reported Speech in the Past, Present, and Future
• Reported Speech Using Modals
• Questions in Statement Form
• Baseball Vocabulary
• Phrasal Verbs with *keep*

In *Real English* you'll learn some "entertaining" idioms, but that's not all. So let's get started with *Say It Clearly!*

10A SAY IT CLEARLY!

🎧 Turn on your recordings to practice a very typical kind of question used in natural spoken English.

10B ENGLISH AT WORK

Dialogue: It's a Great Day for Baseball!

📖 The Bisons and the Mud Hens both finished in first place in their divisions. Now they'll meet in the playoffs to determine which team will go to the League Championship Series. Channel 10 News is reporting.

🎧 **Ted Thompson** Well folks, it looks like we're going to have great weather for the playoffs. Let's go down to the stadium where Kevin Brenten is covering the games this weekend. Kevin . . . ?

Kevin Brenten Good afternoon, Ted. It's a great day for baseball! Our own Bisons will be taking on the Mud Hens here in about thirty minutes. It looks good for our team. They have to win four out of seven to go on to the League Championship Series, and the first two games are at home, so our guys have the home-field advantage.

The Bisons lineup has all the best hitters going out there first, and they're starting with Jed Buck, one of the best pitchers in the league. I spoke to a few of the players earlier today, and they're really excited and confident about the playoffs. Jed said his arm had never felt better. First baseman, Marty Bevins, said his arm was healed up and ready to play. Coach Carl Lyons said that although this would be his second chance for the League Championship Series, he's much more confident that they're going for the gold this time.

Ted Thompson   Hey, that's great. Say, what kind of a crowd do you have out there, Kevin?

Kevin Brenten   Well, the stadium's getting pretty full. The folks out here seem real excited. I see a lot of Mud Hens fans, too. You can tell there are Mud Hens fans because of all the orange out here! But our fans are here, too, and they're really worked up. There are more tailgate parties out in the parking lot than usual.

Ted Thompson   Wow, that sounds great, Kevin. I wish I were there.

Kevin Brenten   I think the whole city wants to be here today. I hear traffic's really bad from all sides getting to the stadium.

Ted Thompson   Yeah, I heard the same thing. Well, thanks Kevin. And of course, Kevin will give a full report on the game later on tonight. But now let's turn back to local news . . .

10C BUILD YOUR VOCABULARY

Base. Any one of three stations on a baseball field that runners must stop on or touch as they pass by to reach home plate (the starting point, also called home base.) *There were runners on all three bases when Rick came up to bat.*

Bunt. A light tap with the baseball bat on a pitched ball, making the ball roll only a short distance. *Some pitchers can't hit a baseball very far, so they often bunt.*

Catcher. The player who stands behind home plate to catch the ball that's pitched to a hitter on the opposing team. *The catcher put his mask on and signaled that he was ready to play ball.*

Concessionaire. The owner or operator of a concession stand (a small shop) at a recreation center. *The concessionaires had a meeting to discuss price changes before the big game.*

Diamond. The part of the playing field that is outlined by three bases and home plate and is in the shape of a diamond. *"It's a homerun! Willy's running the whole diamond."*

Fly ball. A ball hit very high into the air, usually making it easy for someone to catch it. *John hit a fly ball into left field and got the third out of the inning.*

Foul ball. A ball that is hit outside the base lines, out of bounds to the right or the left of the diamond. *Timmy caught a foul ball when he was sitting on the sidelines.*

Hit. A baseball hit that is within the sidelines of the diamond. *After three foul balls, Edgar finally got a hit and made it to first base.*

Home run. A ball that is hit beyond the playing field allowing the hitter to run all three bases and return to home base, scoring one point. *There is always a contest to see who can hit the most home runs in one season.*

Infield. The part of the playing field that is outlined by a line connecting the three bases and home plate. *I think that ball was hit just inside the infield. Let's see what the umpire says.*

Innings. The period that both teams have to hit the ball before they each get three outs. An inning can last from a few minutes to an hour. There are nine innings per game, but if there is a tie, additional innings are added. *It's the bottom of the eighth inning and the Carps are ahead by two runs.*

Mound. A small hill built up in the middle of the infield where the pitcher stands and pitches the ball. *The pitcher kicked the dirt up on the mound as he wound up for the throw.*

Out. When a batter gets three strikes, a ball is caught before it hits the ground, or when a runner is tagged while running from one base to another. There are three outs for each team per inning. *The runner was tagged out just before he got to second base.*

Outfield. The playing field outside of the diamond or infield. *The two players ran into each other in the outfield as they raced to catch the ball.*

Pitcher. The player who throws the ball for the batter to attempt to hit. *Tom Lankey's one of the best pitchers in the league.*

R. B. I. The average of Runs Batted In. When a player hits the ball bringing a runner or runners to home base. *Gerald Teague has such a good R. B. I. He's really one of the most valuable players.*

Roster. A listing of the team's players in their batting order. *Pitchers usually can't hit well, so coaches put them at the end of the roster.*

Sacrifice fly. A ball that is intentionally hit high in the air to be caught before it hits the ground, giving a runner on third base time to run to home base. *McDermott saw that his team had a chance to get another run, so he hit a sacrifice fly.*

Slugger. A batter that hits the ball harder than most players. *McDermott's such a good slugger. He can really hit that ball harder than just about anyone.*

Strike. When the batter swings and misses the ball, or does not swing at a ball that was within the batting zone. *"Here comes the ball. He swings . . . and he misses the ball! Strike one."*

Umpire. A sports official who makes decisions about plays made during a game. *"Oh, the fans did not like that call. They're yelling at the umpire. It looked to me like it was a bad decision, too."*

 ENGLISH UNDER THE HOOD

TOPIC 1: Reported Speech: Past, Present, and Future

Reported speech is speech that reports what someone else said, but it is not a direct quotation. For example:

Direct quotation: *"It's a foul ball! You're out!"*
Reported Speech: *The umpire said that it was a foul ball and I was out.*

Notice that the verb in the reported speech (*was*) changes tense from the direct quotation (*is* or *are*) and that the pronoun changes logically (*you* became *I*). Also notice that the reported speech is introduced by *said* in the case of statements, as in the example above, but *asked* in the case of questions or requests, or *told* in the case of commands. Let's take a look at some other examples of the past, present, and future tenses, and compare direct quotes to reported speech. Pay careful attention to the verbs.

"I <u>study</u> English every day."	He said (that) he <u>studied</u> English every day.
"I <u>am studying</u> English."	She said (that) she <u>was studying</u> English.
"Thierry <u>has left</u> for the game."	Nora said (that) Thierry <u>had left</u> for the game.
"I <u>played</u> baseball on Saturday."	The student said (that) she <u>had played</u> baseball on Saturday.
"We <u>will win</u> the game."	They said (that) they <u>would win</u> the game.
"We <u>are going to practice</u> tonight."	They said that they <u>were going to practice</u> tonight.

Here are a few examples of reported questions. Use *ask* to report questions and add *if* to the beginning of the reported portion.

"<u>Do</u> you <u>like</u> basketball?"	Sarah asked me if I <u>liked</u> basketball.
"<u>Are</u> you <u>watching</u> the game?"	He asked if I <u>was watching</u> the game.

Ask is also used to report requests or polite commands. Notice that the requested verb is put into an infinitive form.

"<u>Could</u> you please <u>turn</u> down the TV?"	He asked me <u>to turn</u> down the TV.
"<u>Would</u> you <u>mind sitting</u> down?"	She asked me <u>to sit</u> down.

Use *tell* for commands, and again change the verb into an infinitive.

"<u>Pass</u> me the ball!"	He told me <u>to pass</u> him the ball.
"<u>Hit</u> the ball!"	The coach told the player <u>to hit</u> the ball.

PRACTICE EXERCISE 1: Change the following direct quotes into reported speech.

1. John: "I'm going to play hockey this weekend."
2. Sarah: "I will practice every day after school."
3. The players: "We are tired of losing!"
4. Coach Silver: "You are not trying hard enough."
5. The reporter: "It is one of the most exciting games ever."
6. Gary: "We lost the game."
7. Betty: "I played soccer when I was a girl."
8. The woman: "Where is the stadium?"
9. Keith: "Give me the ball!"
10. Mary: "Do you prefer hockey or basketball?"

TOPIC 2: Using Modals in Reported Speech

When using the modals *may, might, can, should, have to, ought to,* or *must* in reported speech, make the following replacements in the reported portion of the sentence: *may* and *might* both become *might, can* becomes *could, should* remains *should, ought to* remains *ought to,* and *have to* and *must* both become *had to.*

"I <u>may</u> buy season tickets."	He said he <u>might</u> buy season tickets.
"Dawn <u>might</u> come to the stadium."	He said that Dawn <u>might</u> come to the stadium.

"Gerard _can_ play the best."	She said that Gerard _could_ play the best.
"I _should_ join the swim team."	Doug said that he _should_ join the swim team.
"Johan _ought to_ win easily."	Lucia said that Johan _ought to_ win easily.
"We _must_ win tomorrow!"	The coach said that we _had to_ win tomorrow.
"I _have to_ work harder."	Paul said that he _had to_ work harder.

PRACTICE EXERCISE 2: Rewrite the following direct quotes into reported speech.

1. Enrique: "I have to get some sleep for the big game tomorrow."
2. Adrian: "Each player must play as well as possible."
3. Harry: "That player may need the team doctor!"
4. Jane: "Bill ought to be at soccer practice right now."
5. The coach: "Can all of you come an hour early tomorrow?"
6. Daniel: "We might be tired after the workout."
7. Derrick: "Should we go to the game tonight?"
8. Lucy: "You must work out four or five times a week."
9. Lawrence: "We can see the whole ballpark from our seats!"
10. Reporter: "It has to be a hard decision for Coach Matthews."

TOPIC 3: Questions in Statement Form

As you heard in the _Say It Clearly!_ section of this lesson, questions can have the same word order and form as statements. This type of question often shows surprise, disbelief, or uncertainty, but depending on the intonation used, just about any question can take this form, especially in informal or spoken English. Here are a few examples in context.

You're tired today? But you slept for ten hours last night!

It's Tuesday already? I thought it was Monday.

They lost the game? But they've been winning for weeks!

Tomorrow is the championship? I thought it wasn't for a few weeks.

PRACTICE EXERCISE 3: Rewrite each of the following questions in statement form. Practice saying them aloud with high intonation.

1. Are you a fan of the Tigers?
2. Is Mark Sommer pitching tonight?
3. Did you join the wrestling team?
4. Are you going to buy season tickets?
5. Do you agree with the umpire?
6. Is Sarah planning on quitting the team?
7. Is the game tied?
8. Has the game gone into extra innings?

10E PHRASAL VERBS WITH *KEEP*:

Keep an eye on.
To watch carefully. *Sam, can you keep an eye on my books while I go get another cup of coffee?*

Keep away from.
a) To avoid something or someone. *Kids, keep away from the street!*

b) To prevent someone from getting something. *Keep those peanuts away from Judy. She's allergic.*

Keep in mind.
To think about or remember while making a decision. *Always keep in mind how important this project is.*

Keep in touch.
To continue to communicate with someone. *They worked together years ago, but they still keep in touch.*

Keep off.
To avoid, stay off of something, not to touch. *Keep off the field! They just seeded it.*

Keep on.
To continue to do something. *Class, keep on working on your papers.*

Keep out.
Not to enter, not to allow to enter. *Keep out of the abandoned house. It's dangerous.*

Keep time.
To function well, said of a clock or watch. *I have to buy a new watch. Mine doesn't keep time anymore.*

Keep track of.
To maintain a record of something, to watch carefully. *Keep track of how much you spend so that you can get your money back.*

Keep up with.
a) To remain on the same level as someone else. *Sarah can't keep up with the class because she never studies.*

b) To be able to understand something that is fast or confusing. *He talks so fast that it's hard to keep up with him.*

10F REAL ENGLISH

A Day at the Races

Have you ever been to the horse races? Well, I have, and it's *a blast*! But watching the people can be more fun than watching the horses. A lot of people go *dressed to kill! Man*, they *look like a million dollars*. On opening day, they actually compete to see who can wear the most interesting or *craziest* hat. And if you've *got stars in your eyes*, here's one place you might see some *stars* . . . movie stars, that is. Seeing a star there *could make your day*. Oh, and if you like watching fast horses, those horses will *take your breath* away. If you're careful and don't bet too much money on the horses, going to the races can be a fun and entertaining experience that won't *cost you an arm and a leg*. So go on, *live it up*! Go *check out* the horse races!

10G BRING IT ALL TOGETHER

REVIEW EXERCISE 1: Vocabulary

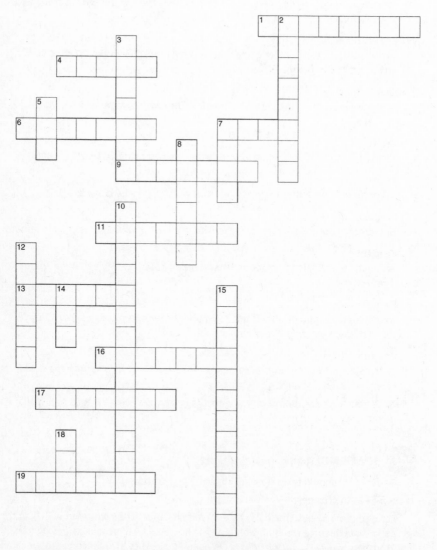

Across

1. A hit outside the lines
4. The small hill where the pitcher stands
6. A hard hitter
7. A runner steps on this as he runs by.
9. The shape made by the four bases

11. A hit that goes beyond the playing field

13. When you can't hit the ball it's a

    _____.

16. The one who throws the ball to the batter

17. There are nine of these.

19. The person standing behind the batter

Down

2. The field beyond the diamond

3. Inside the diamond

5. A ball hit high in the air and then caught

7. A hit that rolls a short distance

8. The person who decides if a play is good or not

10. Person who sells snacks or other items at a game

12. A list of players

14. Runs batted in

15. This hit is used to help a runner come home.

18. When a player doesn't make it home, he or she is _____.

REVIEW EXERCISE 2: Reported Speech: Past, Present, and Future

Rewrite the following direct quotes as reported speech.

1. Jaime: "Are you hungry?"

2. Meredith: "Is Kevin going to the zoo or the swimming pool?"

3. Stuart: "Give me a hand with the net, Joe."

4. Raul: "Will you be here tomorrow?"

5. Randy: "The washing machine was repaired this morning."

6. Tammy: "It's going to be a great game!"

7. The reporter: "The fans have been having a great time all day!"

8. Mack: "Have you every seen a hockey game before?"

9. The umpire: "Play ball, team."

10. Coach Jordan: "Will you be able to play with your injured leg, Kelly?"

REVIEW EXERCISE 3: Using Modals in Reported Speech

Rewrite the following direct quotes as reported speech.

1. Robin: "Can you pick me up at 10:00?"

2. Jennifer: "I may come into town tomorrow."

3. Radha: "I might go shopping for tennis shoes tomorrow."

4. Arletta: "We must get the pool cleaned up."

5. Danielle: "They ought to be home by now."

6. Darren: "You should take some aspirin for your headache."

7. Tomas: "I have to call my mother before we leave."

8. Claudette: "I may drive instead of fly."

REVIEW EXERCISE 4: Questions in Statement Form

Rewrite each of the following questions in statement form.

1. Did you use to play professional football?

2. Did the Gremlins win the state championship?

3. Will you be coming to the playoffs this year?
4. Have they replaced the head coach?
5. Did you get on the basketball team?
6. Does he play golf with Mr. Stanton?
7. Has the bus already left?
8. Is Sarah trying out for the wrestling team?

REVIEW EXERCISE 5: Phrasal Verbs

Place the correct vocabulary word in each space. Use each of the following words once: *keep your eye on, keep away from, keep time, keep in mind, keep in touch, keep off, keep on, keep out, keep track of, keep up with.*

1. Can you help me _____ all the tickets we sell to the game?
2. No one can _____ Ted. He runs faster than anyone.
3. This watch needs a new battery. It doesn't _____ anymore.
4. _____ the carpet. I just had it cleaned and it's not dry yet.
5. Just _____ the ball and swing!
6. _____ practicing your pitching and you'll get it right.
7. _____ the color of your room when you pick out curtains.
8. Do you _____ with Terry, your old friend from college?
9. Kids, _____ the swimming pool when there's not an adult around.
10. Could you _____ the kids _____ of the house until they take their dirty shoes off?

10H LISTEN UP!

🎧 Now turn on your recording to listen in again as Kevin and Ted report on that game between the Bisons and the Mud Hens. Then answer these questions.

1. Is the ninth inning near the beginning or near the end of the game?
2. What's the score?
3. Is Marty Bevins pitching or hitting the ball?
4. Who won the game?
5. What was the final score?

10I WHY DO THEY DO THAT?

The Super Bowl

📖 You may have noticed that many Americans are sports fanatics. They love just about all sports. But what's America's favorite sport? While most of the rest of the world is crazy about soccer, Americans are lukewarm about it. Soccer is just beginning to become popular among young Americans, but it's not yet a national pastime in any way. Some say that baseball is number one, others argue that football is. Still others are basketball fans. Whichever sport is number one, one thing's for sure: the Super Bowl is the most-watched sporting event of the year. In fact, it's the number one, most-watched television show of the year, with 90 million viewers. What's so important about this one game? The Super Bowl is where the two best football teams from two different leagues, the National Football Conference and the American Football Conference, compete for the championship title, so it's the most important game of the year.

But that's only part of the explanation. The other part is the halftime advertisements, which are as entertaining as the game itself for many viewers. Advertisers seem to compete to present a show with their ads, and many people watch the game only for the ads. The ads are so important to advertisers that they pay $2.1 million for ads that are only shown during one Super Bowl. The halftime entertainment is also spectacular, with many big-name entertainers and a huge fireworks display.

There are also many fascinating legends about the Super Bowl. One popular legend is that the water systems in major cities are in danger of collapsing during Super Bowl halftime because there are so many simultaneous toilet flushings! There may be some truth to this, because at least one major city has had a problem with its water system during the Super Bowl. It is also claimed that sales of antacids increase 20 percent the day after the Super Bowl, and that a larger-than-usual number of people call in sick the next day instead of going to work. This may be true as well, because of the large quantities of beer consumed during the game and afterwards. California avocado growers say that they sell more avocados than usual for Super-Bowl-Sunday guacamole dip. Grocers say sales for snacks such as pretzels and potato chips double that weekend. And there is even an interesting Super Bowl legend that has to do with the stock market. If the NFC team wins, the market goes up that year. If the AFC team wins, the stock market goes down. Evidently, this is accurate about 80 percent of the time! So what do you think? Are you ready to participate in this great American tradition? If so, just be careful not to drink or eat too much! And of course, keep track of your stocks!

Lesson 10: Answer Key

Practice Exercise 1

1. John said that he was going to play hockey this weekend. 2. Sarah said that she would practice every day after school. 3. The players said that they were tired of losing. 4. Coach Silver said that they were not trying hard enough. 5. The reporter said that it was one of the most exciting games ever. 6. Gary said that they had lost the game. 7. Betty said that she had played soccer when she was a girl. 8. The woman asked where the stadium was. 9. Keith told me to give him the ball. 10. Mary asked if I preferred hockey or basketball.

Practice Exercise 2

1. Enrique said he had to get some sleep for the big game tomorrow. 2. Adrian said that each player had to play as well as possible. 3. Harry said that that player might need the team doctor. 4. Jane said that Bill ought to be at soccer practice right now. 5. The coach asked if all of us could come an hour early tomorrow. 6. Daniel said that we might be tired after the workout. 7. Derrick asked if we should go to the game tonight. 8. Lucy said that I had to work out four or five times a week. 9. Lawrence said that we could see the whole ball park from our seats. 10. The reporter said that it had to be a hard decision for Coach Matthews.

Practice Exercise 3

1. You're a fan of the Tigers? 2. Mark Sommer's pitching tonight? 3. You joined the wrestling team? 4. You're going to buy season tickets? 5. You agree with the umpire? 6. Sarah's planning on quitting the team? 7. The game's tied? 8. The game's gone into extra innings?

Review Exercise 1

Review Exercise 2

1. Jaime asked if I was hungry. 2. Meredith asked if Kevin was going to the zoo or the swimming pool. 3. Stuart asked Joe to give him a hand with the net. 4. Raul asked if I would be here tomorrow. 5. Randy said that the washing machine had been repaired this morning. 6. Tammy said that it was going to be a great game. 7. The reporter said that the fans had been having a great time all day. 8. Mack asked if I had ever seen a hockey game before. 9. The umpire told the team to play ball. 10. Coach Jordan asked Kelly if she would be able to play with her injured leg.

Review Exercise 3

1. Robin asked if I could pick her up at 10:00. 2. Jennifer said she might come into town tomorrow. 3. Radha said she might go shopping for tennis shoes tomorrow. 4. Arletta said we had to get the pool cleaned up. 5. Danielle said they ought to be home by now. 6. Darren said I should take some aspirin for my headache. 7. Tomas said he had to call his mother before we left. 8. Claudette said she might drive instead of fly.

Review Exercise 4

1. You used to play professional football? 2. The Gremlins won the state championship? 3. You'll be coming to the playoffs this year? 4. They've replaced the head coach? 5. You got on the basketball team? 6. He plays golf with Mr. Stanton? 7. The bus has already left? 8. Sarah's trying out for the wrestling team?

Review Exercise 5

1. keep track of, 2. keep up with, 3. keep time, 4. Keep off, 5. keep your eye on, 6. Keep on, 7. Keep in mind, 8. keep in touch, 9. keep away from, 10. keep . . . out

Listen Up!

1. the end, 2. a tie game, five to five, 3. hitting, 4. the Mud Hens, 5. six to five

Snail Mail Just Won't Cut It!

ARE YOU READY FOR THE LESSON?

Whether you're computer savvy or not, Lesson 11: *Snail Mail Just Won't Cut It!* may give you some helpful information about using computers and the Internet. You'll read a brief history of the Internet in *English at Work* and learn some important computer vocabulary. You'll also learn:

- The Present Perfect Tense vs. the Present Perfect Progressive Tense
- The Present Perfect Progressive Tense vs. the Past Perfect Progressive Tense
- The Future Progressive Tense
- Phrasal Verbs for the Computer

But that's not all. You'll also read about the Internet generation in *Why Do They Do That?* and learn some useful Internet and computer idioms. But let's get started with some pronunciation in *Say It Clearly!*

11A SAY IT CLEARLY!

🎧 Turn on your recording to practice two vowel sounds whose difference might be a bit tricky for you.

11B ENGLISH AT WORK

Reading: A Brief History of the Internet

🎧 The idea for the Internet began back in the early days of the Cold War. Feeling nervous about the possibility of a nuclear war, the American government began to wonder how communications within the military could be maintained. Having communication in one central location would make it vulnerable to attack. So, in deep secrecy, Rand Corporation began to work on a solution to this chilling possibility in the 1960's. Paul Baran of Rand Corporation came up with the idea for the beginnings of the Internet, a new communications system that would have neither central location nor authority and would be designed to operate in chaos. It was a brilliant solution to the possibility of a nuclear holocaust because it was intended to be decentralized from the beginning. Information would be delivered through individual nodes, each with its own authority to send and receive messages. Information would wind its way around this system until ultimately reaching its intended destination. It wouldn't matter if one or another node were destroyed, because the information would remain "in the air," received and sent among whichever nodes remained.

To realize this vision of a decentralized communications system, an ambitious project called ARPANET was assembled in the U.S., and its nodes were the high-speed supercomputers of the time. The first node was installed at U C L A in 1969, and three others were set up later that year. By the second year, this project unintentionally turned into a high-speed mail service as those working on the project began to transmit news and personal messages via this network. By the time the military segment broke off and began its own system, ARPANET had begun to warp into something different—a very large and rapidly growing network of communication comprising several different systems.

This network became a galaxy of nodes as groups and individuals began to have greater access to more powerful computers. This network evolved into the Internet as we know it today, as this cheap and wondrous information and communications tool was bound to become incredibly popular with the general public. Today it is a system that, put simply, connects everyone to everyone else. Mail is transferred among individuals from country to country, and discussions take place between people who might never have had a chance to meet in person. But of course this kind of communication is not all that happens over the Internet. It is perhaps more than anything a vast warehouse of information, making it a tool for reference and research. It is also an invaluable business tool, used by both businesses and consumers. Although governments have some control over messages and information on the Internet, there is no central control, no government that operates this network of communication. It essentially belongs to the people. This can be both a good thing and a bad thing, as such freedom necessarily allows for the exchange of any kind of information or opinion.

Ironically, what grew from a fear of the potential annihilation of the human race has given us peaceful possibilities we'd never imagined. The anarchy of the Internet is ripe with the potential for truly connecting human beings, for allowing us to understand one another in ways that would have been impossible. It is perhaps an oversimplification to assume that all problems can be worked out through communication, but communication is at least a start, and it can help avoid many conflicts. Surely the Internet is a tool unlike any other for communication, and surely the human race can greatly benefit from the ability of two people from across the world to share, even in cyberspace.

Information taken from the *Magazine of Fantasy and Science Fiction,* February 1993, Science Column #5, "Internet."

11C BUILD YOUR VOCABULARY

 To bookmark. To save a U. R. L. page in the directory of one's Internet software. *Since you go to that website so often, why don't you bookmark it?*

Browser. A computer program that enables use of the Internet. *If your computer keeps crashing when you're online, you may need to upgrade your browser.*

C. P. U. Central processing unit. The key part of a computer, the "brains" and all of the circuitry necessary for functioning. *New computers keep coming out with faster and more powerful C. P. U.'s.*

Cursor. A moveable symbol such as an arrow, a hand, or a triangle that indicates position on a screen. *Move the cursor over the "send" button and click if you're done with the message.*

Diskette. A floppy disk, a small plastic disk coated with magnetic material that is used to store data or information. *Insert a diskette into the computer so we can copy this report onto it.*

File. A complete collection of data stored on a computer. *I have several computer files where I store everything I've written.*

Hardware. The equipment components of a computer, the electronic parts such as CPU, keyboard, screen, etc. *You need to know what kind of hardware your computer has before you can add anything to it.*

Insert. To put something into a machine, such as a diskette into a computer. *If you don't insert this cable into the computer, your printer won't work.*

Interface. The connection and/or communication between different machines, such as a computer and a printer. This can also mean two people working together and communicating. *The computer and printer interface via this cable.*

Keyboard. The typewriter-like board with letters and numbers that is used to give commands to the computer. *Bill spilled coffee on his keyboard, and now he can't type anything.*

Modem. The device that connects a computer to a cable or telephone line. *You need to upgrade your modem before you can get high-speed Internet.*

Monitor. The computer screen. *Next time, I want to get a monitor capable of showing videos.*

Mouse. A small device that can be rolled to move the cursor and control various functions on the computer. *Move the cursor over the icon by rolling the mouse.*

Scanner. A device that reads pictures and printed copies and stores them as files in the computer. *If you want to put your picture on your website you can use the scanner.*

Shareware. Limited-use software that can be used on a trial basis. *Here, try this shareware on English grammar and let me know what you think.*

Software. Programs, tools or applications that are run on computer hardware. *If you use accounting software it's much easier to make budgets and file your income tax.*

Spam. Unsolicited email sent to many addresses at once, usually commercial. *Advertisers try to disguise their spam by coming up with clever subject lines.*

Upgrade. To improve something. *I'd like to upgrade to a newer, faster computer.*

Window. A box or opening on a computer screen where a program or application is displayed. *Your computer is running so slowly because you've got too many windows open.*

W. W. W. World Wide Web. A part of the Internet that is navigated by using different addresses to access different sites. *A lot of website addresses start with www.*

11D ENGLISH UNDER THE HOOD

TOPIC 1: The Present Perfect Tense vs. the Present Perfect Progressive Tense

You learned about the present perfect tense in the first lesson. Remember that it's formed with *have/has* + past participle.

We have seen that movie.

The present perfect describes an action that is finished, but it refers to a time frame that is not finished.

We have visited San Francisco twice. (In our lives.)

I worked five days last week, but I've only worked twice this week.

There is also a progressive or continuous form of this tense, the present perfect progressive. It's formed with *have/has been* + verb + *ing*.

We have been watching that movie for two hours.

The present perfect progressive describes an action that began in the past and continues into the present.

We have been visiting San Francisco for two weeks. (We are still in San Francisco.)

I have been thinking about calling you. (I started thinking about it at some point in the past, and I am still thinking about it.)

Some verbs can be used interchangeably and mean the same things in both tenses, such as *live, work* and *teach*. Notice that these verbs suggest actions that take place over a long period of time or as a process, or something that is practiced habitually, such as a hobby or a tradition.

I have worked in schools all my life.

I have been working in schools all my life.

We have come/been coming to this restaurant on our anniversary for years.

It's not common to use the verb *be* in the present perfect progressive tense.

I have been here for two hours.

We have been on the nominating committee for four months.

However, in informal conversational English, it is possible to hear the present perfect progressive form of *be*, often to talk about someone's behavior. Keep in mind that this is a very relaxed, conversational form.

You've been (being) a real jerk ever since we got here!

She's been (being) extra helpful since the baby was born.

PRACTICE EXERCISE 1: Complete each sentence with either the present perfect or the present perfect progressive form of the verb in parentheses. Keep in mind that if an action continues you need to use the present perfect progressive, but if it has ended use the present perfect.

1. We (have) _____ three thunderstorms this week, but it's sunny now.
2. The neighbors' dog (bark) _____ since 10:00 P.M.
3. My computer (make) _____ an odd sound since I turned it on.
4. The moon light (shimmer) _____ on the lake all night.
5. That phone (ring) _____ about fifty times today!

6. The baby (cry) _____ since we put her in bed.
7. Ms. Braylton (teach) _____ English for about twenty years now.
8. How long (collect) _____ you _____ glass bottles?
9. She (send) _____ me three e-mails this morning.
10. This (be) _____ such a wonderful evening.

TOPIC 2: The Present Perfect Progressive Tense vs. the Past Perfect Progressive Tense

The past perfect progressive tense is formed with *had been* + verb + *ing*.

The doctor had been seeing patients all afternoon when I walked in.

As you have seen, the present perfect progressive is used to describe actions begun in the past and continuing into the present.

The Drakes have been living in Toronto for a long time.

The past perfect progressive is used to describe actions that began and continued to happen in the past *before* another action happened.

The Gonzalez family had been living in Seattle until Mr. Gonzalez got a promotion and the family relocated to Miami.

Linda was exhausted last week because she hadn't been sleeping very well.

Notice that this tense is used to emphasize the relationship between two past actions, one of which began and continued in the past before another one.

PRACTICE EXERCISE 2: Complete the sentences with either the present perfect progressive or past perfect progressive of the verb given in parentheses.

1. Janet (not feel) _____ well for days before she finally went to the doctor.
2. Joe (study) _____ for two hours, so he'll take a break now.
3. The paper in my printer (get) _____ stuck for the last few days.
4. We (have) _____ meetings every day to discuss this problem until Bill finally came up with a good way to make it work.
5. Barry (work) _____ hard on the project for months before the new director arrived.
6. We (come) _____ to this restaurant for years, so they know us here.
7. My car (work) _____ poorly until I took it in to the mechanic.
8. The tree (not get) _____ enough water lately.
9. The printer (buzz) _____ until I turned it off and then on again.
10. Tom and Luann (see) _____ each other, but they broke up last week.

TOPIC 3: The Future Progressive Tense

The future progressive is formed with *will be* + verb + *ing*:

Jane will be working on her paper all weekend long.

There is also a future progressive formed with *go*: *be going to* + *be* + verb + *ing*. This form is based on the immediate future, which was covered in Lesson 4, and usually expresses actions that are in the near future.

Jane is going to be working on her paper all night.

Both express the same thing: an action that begins in the future and continues for a period of time further into the future. This tense can emphasize that an action will occur over a period of time, rather than happen as a one-time action.

I'll be cooking all afternoon for the dinner party.

We'll be staying at the beach house for two weeks.

It can also describe a future action that is interrupted by another action.

We'll be sleeping when you get in tonight, so please be quiet.

The movie will be starting when we get to the theater.

Often in conversational English the future progressive can be used simply to express a plan or intention. In these cases it means the same as the simple future.

Lisa will be starting graduate school in September.

We'll be leaving in five minutes.

PRACTICE EXERCISE 3: Complete the sentences with either form of the future progressive tense.

1. We (visit) _____ my cousin over the holiday weekend.
2. Dan (get) _____ home when his favorite show starts.
3. The Dreyers (move) _____ to Denmark next October.
4. Jerry (study) _____ all evening long.
5. We (clean) _____ the house during the whole weekend.
6. The election (take) _____ place next Tuesday.
7. When (go) _____ you _____ to Los Angeles?
8. What time (call) _____ you_____ me tonight?
9. The teachers (meet) _____ with parents all week long.
10. If you get home before 6:00, I (work) _____ still _____.

11E PHRASAL VERBS FOR THE COMPUTER

Back up.
To make a copy in case something happens to the files on the computer. *When you have important work that you want to save, it's always a good idea to back up the files on a computer disk.*

Click on.
To move the mouse over an icon, word, or other object and click. *If you click on this icon you can change the screen color.*

Hook up.
To connect to something. *You may need a different cable to hook the printer up to the computer.*

Key in.
To type in. *Key in this web address and it'll take you right to the information you want.*

Log in/on.
To go onto a computer network by typing in a personal code. *To check your mail, you must first log on with your ID and password.*

Log off.
To go off a computer network by signing out. *Please remember to log off after you've finished with the computer.*

Power up.
To start the power, to turn on a machine. *I need to power up the computer so I can get started on my project.*

Print out.
To make a copy of something from a computer or word processor. *I'll print out that article for you and leave it in your mailbox at work.*

Pull down.
To click on a word or item that opens up a list of options or functions. *If you click on the word "tools" it will pull down a list of options.*

Scroll down.
To move gradually to the bottom of text or graphics. *Scroll down the page bottom and you'll find the name of the web designer.*

Scroll up.
To move gradually to the top of text or graphics. *Scroll up until you find the search box, then type in your question.*

Set up.
To assemble or prepare a piece of hardware. *You have to set up the modem before you can connect to the Internet.*

Shut down.
To turn off a computer. *If you're leaving for the day, shut down your computer.*

Switch on.
To turn something on. *Can you switch on the photocopier for me, please?*

Turn off.
To shut down an operation, to stop the flow of energy by the use of a button or switch. *She turned off the spell checker before beginning to type in the document.*

Turn on.
To activate or cause to energize by the use of a button or switch. *Could you turn on the TV? I want to watch the news.*

11F REAL ENGLISH

Life Online

Man! My computer *crashed* again! And I really needed to get some messages out. I couldn't send them through the U.S. Postal Service because *snail mail* just won't *cut it*.

My whole day's been like this. When I *booted up* my computer again I had to wade through all the *spam* before I could read my e-mail. Then just as I was about to *open up* a message, the network *went down*. I guess some *hacker* had gotten into the company server and *messed* things *up*. Later, when I finally we*nt online* again, I took care of my e-mail, but then I decided to visit a *chat room*. I guess not everyone agreed with my opinions, because I really got *flamed*! I know I'm no computer *geek*, but, hey, I do enjoy a little *chatting, e-mailing* and *blogging* from time to time.

11G BRING IT ALL TOGETHER

REVIEW EXERCISE 1: Vocabulary

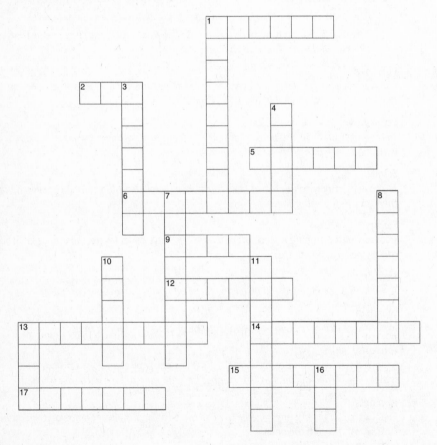

Across

1. To put something in a machine.

2. The "brain" of a computer.

5. A moveable symbol on the screen.

6. Where you can store a file.

9. A document that you've written is one.

12. An area on a computer screen where you work.

13. Limited-use software.

14. Where the keys are.
15. The physical equipment of a computer.
17. The screen.

Down
1. How machines connect.
3. To improve.
4. A device that moves things around on the screen.

7. Things that you run on a computer.
8. Something that can put photos and pictures on the computer.
10. A device that connects to the phone line.
11. A quick way to go to a Web site.
13. Unwelcome e-mail.
16. World Wide Web

REVIEW EXERCISE 2: The Present Perfect vs. the Present Perfect Progressive

Complete the following sentences with either the present perfect or the present perfect progressive.

1. It (take) _____ six months, but I finally got a job.
2. It (rain) _____ just about all day long.
3. No, Tom (not call) _____ back on the McClintock case yet.
4. You (not finish) _____ your homework yet, but you're watching TV?
5. Our team (lose) _____ a lot lately.
6. How long (listen) _____ you_____ to the radio?
7. The sky (get) _____ darker by the minute.
8. I (not buy) _____ a new computer yet.

REVIEW EXERCISE 3: The Present Perfect Progressive vs. the Past Perfect Progressive

Complete the following sentences with either the present perfect progressive or the past perfect progressive.

1. Dina (spend) _____ a few days in New York for a computer exposition.
2. The radio (play) _____ old Beatles songs all week.
3. They (eat) _____ dinner for thirty minutes when Paul finally arrived.
4. The newspaper delivery person (deliver) _____ the newspaper regularly until he got sick last week.
5. Rick (look) _____ for a new laptop for months before making a decision.
6. (take) _____ you _____ your medicine regularly?
7. I (not get) _____ much spam since we bought that new spam filter.
8. We (get) _____ coffee at the corner coffee shop until they closed.

REVIEW EXERCISE 4: The Future Progressive

Complete the sentences with the future progressive tense.

1. The doctor (make) _____ his rounds all morning.
2. Where (wait) _____ David _____ for you after work?
3. The President (speak) _____ to the press in the Rose Garden this afternoon.

4. The team (practice) _____ on Friday from 1:00 until 4:30.

5. Our children (finish) _____ their lesson soon.

6. The patient in room 43 (have) _____ surgery at 7:00 A.M.

7. How long do you think you (use) _____ the computer today?

8. (eat) _____ you _____ if I call you at 6:30 tonight?

REVIEW EXERCISE 5: Phrasal Verbs

Fill in each of the following sentences with the best phrasal verb.

logged on, power up, scroll down, logged off, back up, print out, click on, key in, set up, shut down, hook up, pull down

1. Do you know how to _____ the new printer to the CPU?

2. Do I need the "www" when I _____ a web address?

3. I've already _____ because I didn't need the network anymore.

4. I'd also like to _____ a copy of that article to read on the train.

5. Let's _____ the report on disk just as a precaution.

6. You have to _____ the "send" button if you're done writing the e-mail.

7. Once you've _____ to the network you can check if you have any e-mail.

8. Do you have the software to _____ the CD-ROM drive?

9. The electricity went off and everything _____.

10. _____ the computer and let's get to work on the project.

11. _____ the "Tools menu" and select "Language."

12. You have to _____ a little more if you want to see the rest of the pictures.

11H LISTEN UP!

Now turn on your recording and listen in as Mrs. Albany tries to work through her computer troubles with a technical support hotline. Then come back and answer the following questions.

1. What is Mrs. Albany having problems with?

2. What's the first thing Duane recommends that she do?

3. Did Mrs. Albany install the printer herself?

4. Is the printer plugged in?

5. What is the problem with the outlet where the printer is plugged in?

6. Has Duane seen that kind of problem before?

11I WHY DO THEY DO THAT?

THE INTERNET GENERATION

When Americans have trouble with their computers, they are not likely to take them to a shop to have them repaired if they have a teenager in the house. American teenagers, like many teenagers across the world, are very tech savvy. Born during the age of P. C.'s and the Internet, nearly all *Internet generation* teens have had access to a computer during their growing years. In fact, many teenagers know more about computers than your average middle-age computer specialist. Although most American schools have computers and computer classes, teenagers have learned about computers not by poring over computer textbooks or by taking courses, but through trial and error. Some teens have been given high-paying tech jobs because of their computer skills. Fourteen-year-olds getting jobs as web designers, programmers, and computer teachers making $5,000 a month is not a pipe dream; it is a reality. So next time your computer crashes, don't go to the computer technician. Just ask the fourteen-year-old next door for help.

Lesson 11: Answer Key

Practice Exercise 1
1. have had, 2. has been barking, 3. has been making, 4. has been shimmering, 5. has rung, 6. has been crying, 7. has taught/has been teaching, 8. have ... collected/been collecting, 9. has sent, 10. has been

Practice Exercise 2
1. hadn't been feeling well, 2. has been studying, 3. has been getting, 4. had been having, 5. had been working, 6. have been coming, 7. had been working, 8. hasn't been getting, 9. had been buzzing, 10. had been seeing

Practice Exercise 3
1. will be visiting/are going to be visiting, 2. will be getting/is going to be getting, 3. will be moving/are going to be moving, 4. will be studying/is going to be studying, 5. will be cleaning/are going to be cleaning, 6. will be taking/is going to be taking, 7. will ... be going/are ... going to be going, 8. will ... be calling/are ... going to be calling, 9. will be meeting/are going to be meeting, 10. will ... be working/am ... going to be working.

Review Exercise 1

Review Exercise 2
1. has taken, 2. has been raining, 3. hasn't called, 4. haven't finished, 5. has been losing, 6. have ... been listening, 7. has been getting, 8. haven't bought

Review Exercise 3
1. has been spending, 2. has been playing, 3. had been eating, 4. had been delivering, 5. had been looking 6. Have ... been taking, 7. haven't been getting, 8. had been getting

Review Exercise 4
1. will be making/is going to be making, 2. will ... be waiting/is ... going to be waiting, 3. will be speaking/is going to be speaking, 4. will be practicing/is going to be practicing, 5. will be finishing/are going to be finishing, 6. will be having/is going to be having, 7. will be using/are going to be using, 8. Will ... be eating/Are ... going to be eating

Review Exercise 5
1. hook up, 2. key in, 3. logged off, 4. print out, 5. back up, 6. click on, 7. logged on 8. set up, 9. shut down, 10. Power up, 11. Pull down, 12. scroll down

Listen Up!
1. Her printer isn't working. 2. He asks her to check the cable connections. 3. Yes. 4. Yes. 5. The outlet is controlled by a light switch, and the light switch is off. 6. Yes, very often.

She'll Win by a Landslide!

ARE YOU READY FOR THE LESSON?

Are you interested in American politics? If so, then Lesson 12: *She'll Win by a Landslide!* should be interesting to you. In this lesson, you'll learn some vocabulary about the American system of government and some phrasal verbs about winning and losing elections. You'll learn about the two sides of American politics in the reading *America Divided, But Always United*. You'll also understand the role of religion in American society a little better after reading *Why Do They Do That?* You'll also learn:

- The Progressive Form of Modals
- The Use of *would rather*
- Past Ability
- Idioms for Talking about Politics

You'll also hear about the beginnings of the international aid organization Habitat for Humanity. But let's begin the lesson with some important pronunciation in *Say It Clearly!*

12A SAY IT CLEARLY!

🎧 Turn on your recording to practice consonant clusters in English and to learn how to make them a bit easier to pronounce in natural speech.

12B ENGLISH AT WORK

READING: America Divided, But Always United

🎧 Since the early colonial days, Americans have at times been bitterly divided on important political and social issues. Even the American Revolution of 1776 did not enjoy overwhelming support among colonists, for example. Many colonial Americans wanted their independence from England, but there was a group that was deeply loyal to King George. The fight for freedom within the Thirteen Colonies was not won any more easily than the war for independence from the British.

The most tragic and dramatic example of division in American society came almost one hundred years later. The Civil War began in 1861 and ended in 1865, but there remains a legacy of injustice and division to this day. The reason for such a rift in the country—the northern and western states on one side and the southern states on the other—was the issue of states' rights, especially as applied to the ability of the federal government to prohibit slavery. When the South, whose economy was based on slavery, seceded, a bloody war was fought for four years, and in many cases brother fought brother or father fought son. Although in the end the Union was preserved, it came at a great cost, and many economic, political, and social issues were left far from resolved.

In the late 1950s and 1960s, another civil war of sorts flared up within the United

States. This was the Civil Rights Movement, a struggle to secure basic civil rights for all Americans regardless of race. The beginning of the movement is usually identified as the Montgomery (Alabama) Bus Boycott, followed by years of protests, marches, sit-ins, and the well-known August 28, 1963 March on Washington, where Martin Luther King, Jr.'s "I Have a Dream" speech was first heard.

The late 1960s produced another turbulent divide in American society, this time over the Vietnam War. This division was primarily a division between supporters of the war and the traditional views of government and power structure on one side, and opponents to the war who held newer, more progressive ideas about solving world problems on the other. As a result, the late 1960s was a time of great cultural clashes—between young and old, between new and traditional, between liberal and conservative.

This clash has of course not disappeared. On the social and political landscape of today, many issues such as abortion, gun control, the environment, gay rights, religion, and foreign policy, to name just a few, continue to divide the American people. While many Americans hold moderate views, there is also a very deep gulf between liberals and conservatives, right-wing Republicans and left-wing Democrats, the wealthy and the working class. But as American history suggests, clashes are nothing new, and divides are never impossible to close. In a sense it's possible to say that the American government, with its system of checks and balances, was set up to deal with these divisions, which are probably inevitable in free and democratic societies where people can express views and attempt to influence their country as they see fit. To deal with this, Americans have time after time opted to elect a President and a Congress with opposing views, almost by instinct, to allow the checks and balances written into the Constitution to operate and to protect the Union. There may always be intense division within this country, but there is also a stronger drive to protect, above all, the union that is the United States.

12C BUILD YOUR VOCABULARY

Administration. The executive branch of the United States government, the president and his team. *The American administration is in place for either four or eight years before a new administration replaces it.*

Congress. The Senate and the House of Representatives, elected to make laws in the U.S. *Congress passed some very controversial laws, and the president is threatening to veto.*

Conservatism. A political and social philosophy that prefers the stability and structure of very gradual change, if any. *Many states in the South are known for conservatism, although of course not everyone there is conservative.*

Democracy. A government by the people, ruled by the majority through representation. *For a country to truly be a democracy, a majority of the people must vote to demonstrate what they want to happen in their government.*

Electorate. The group of people who are entitled to vote. *The electorate makes its views known when the majority vote for one or another candidate or proposition.*

Ideology. A way of thinking or a set of beliefs, often political, social, or religious, that determines the actions or policies of a particular group. *Ideology can have such a powerful hold that it can interfere with objective judgment.*

Initiative. A way that citizens can petition to propose a law and submit it to legislators for approval. *Many people were so fed up with smoking in public that they began an initiative to ban smoking in public places.*

Liberalism. A political and social philosophy that does not adhere strictly to tradition, encourages movement and innovation, and believes that change can often be progress. *Bob Ballard was raised in a very traditional family, but once he went away to college and was exposed to other ideas he began to embrace liberalism.*

Political parties. Groups of people who align themselves around certain political goals or ideologies to form voting blocks. *The United States has two primary political parties, Republicans and Democrats, but there are several other smaller parties as well.*

Politics. Governmental policy, the guiding and influencing of governmental policy, the art of winning and holding control over government. *Many Americans believe that it is not polite to discuss religion, sex, or politics with people who are not close friends.*

Polls. The place to cast one's vote during an election; a way to gauge public opinion through questioning a certain percentage of the voting population. *Countless polls are taken before an election to help candidates determine whether their policies are popular with voters or not.*

Primary. An election where political parties choose candidates or select delegates to represent them. *Every four years, Americans vote for presidential candidates in their states' primaries.*

Public opinion. Views held by a majority of the public. *Polls are often taken to gauge public opinion so that politicians know whether their policies are popular or not.*

Republic. A government whose leader is not a monarch but is an elected official, usually a president. *The power of a republic rests with its voting citizens, but is exercised by officials elected by those citizens.*

12D ENGLISH UNDER THE HOOD

TOPIC 1: The Progressive Form of Modals

Just like other verbs, modals have progressive forms. In the present tense, the progressive form of a modal is modal + *be* + verb + *ing*.

Juana must be working late tonight.

Robert may be studying for his exams.

Progressive modals indicate an action happening right now. If you would like to review the modals and their specific meanings, turn back to Lesson 7, degrees of certainty.

PRACTICE EXERCISE 1: Fill in the blanks with the correct modal: *could, may, might, must,* or *should,* and *be* + verb + *ing.*

1. Something (burn) _____ because I smell smoke.

2. The candidate (give) _____ a press conference tonight, but I'm not sure.
3. The polls haven't changed, so the ad campaign (not work) _____.
4. Don't you have a test tomorrow? You (study) _____.
5. If people are paying attention to the scandals, the race (get) _____ close.
6. Diane is very liberal, so she (vote) _____ for McAllen.
7. I (clean) _____ instead of reading, since my house is such a mess.
8. I don't believe you! You (kid) _____ me!
9. If you don't know the candidates' positions, you (read) _____ the papers more!
10. I thought I saw Maggie's car at her mother's house, so she (visit) _____ her.

TOPIC 2: The Use of *would rather*

Would rather is a way to show a preference. Use *would rather* + base verb for the present tense form. Notice that *would* is usually contracted to *'d*.

We'd rather stay home and watch television.

Use *would rather* + *have* + past participle for the past form.

I'd rather have seen the candidate talk about his position on gun control.

Use *would rather* + *be* + verb + *ing* for the progressive form.

He'd rather be sitting in the back of the class.

When making comparisons, use *than* between the two choices, and use the same form of the verb.

Max would rather go to the movies than stay home.

I would rather have gone to the movies than rented a video.

If the second verb is the same verb as the first, you do not need to repeat the verb the second time.

Dan and Joyce would rather be sitting on the beach than at home.

PRACTICE EXERCISE 2: Fill in the sentences with the correct form of *would rather*. First use the present form, and don't forget how to make comparisons.

1. (go) _____ you _____ to the movies or the beach?
2. I (vote) _____ for a candidate I agree with _____ one I like.
3. We (take) _____ the bus _____ a taxi.
4. Jo (not go) _____ out in the rain to vote.

Now use the past form.

5. Barry (become) _____ a teacher _____ a lawyer.
6. Congressman Phelps (not be) _____ involved in such a scandal.
7. Mindy (get) _____ a newspaper _____ a magazine.

Finally, use the continuous form.

8. We (sleep) _____ right now.

9. The candidates (give) _____ prepared statements than (answer) _____ questions.

10. Everyone (feel) _____ more trusting of politicians.

TOPIC 3: Past Ability

As you know, *can* expresses ability in the present. In the past, *can* becomes *could.*

Tom could beat anybody in a race when he was in the third grade.

They couldn't make it to the meeting on time this morning.

It is also possible to use *be able to* to express ability. In the past this becomes *was/were able to.*

Tom was able to beat anybody in a race when he was in the third grade.

They weren't able to make it to the meeting on time this morning.

PRACTICE EXERCISE 3: Use either *could, be able to, couldn't,* or *wasn't/weren't able to* correctly in the following sentences.

1. Before he was in politics, Bill (say) _____ things much more freely.

2. Who (speak) _____ another language before the age of ten?

3. It rained all day yesterday, so Sandy (not go) _____ for her usual walk.

4. Nobody (get) _____ to the polls during the morning because of the weather.

5. Since I didn't have to go to work yesterday, I (watch) _____ my favorite afternoon TV talk show.

6. Because Danny studied so hard for the test, he (pass) _____ it easily.

7. Because she was so popular, Silvia (climb) _____ in the polls very easily.

8. Trent (not take) _____ the mayor seriously because he seemed so slick.

9. Randy (not beat) _____ anybody at chess until he got some training.

10. Drake was such a popular governor that he (win) _____ easily against his challenger.

12E   PHRASAL VERBS FOR WINNING AND LOSING:

Bring down.
To make the opposition look less attractive to voters and to decrease his/her popularity. To defeat. *Max Brown used every trick he knew to bring down his opponent before the election took place.*

Catch up.
To reach the same level or stage as someone else. *Although Phyllis Janz was behind for a long time, she caught up with her opponent and actually won the election.*

Clean up.
To win by a wide margin. *Joe Schmitz really cleaned up! He won in almost every county in the state.*

Hold out.
To wait until the end, to continue to make an effort to win. *Even though Ruth*

Ballard was not doing well in the polls, she decided to hold out until the end of the primaries.

Luck out.
To accomplish something seemingly through luck, to win unexpectedly. *Even though nobody expected him to win or even come in second or third, he lucked out and won the election.*

Stick with.
To remain with; to stay on a certain course. *Many people were upset with the president for lying, but they stuck with him anyway and gave him a second term.*

Stand up for.
To be strong in one's opinions. *You have to respect Elvira Anninger even if you don't agree with her, because she really stands up for her views on immigration.*

Run away with.
To win with a lot more votes than one's opponents. *Deek Janes ran away with the election with a two-thirds majority vote.*

Take off.
To have one's political popularity increase very rapidly. *When Lind came out against the proposition his candidacy really took off, and now he's the leading candidate.*

Trail behind.
To have a small percentage of the vote. *Lukas came in with 51 percent of the vote, Bender with 46.5 percent, and Krantz trailed behind with only 2.5 percent.*

Turn around.
To change the course of an election in one's favor. *Mayor Riggs was able to turn the election around when he found an issue people really cared about.*

 REAL ENGLISH

Does She Have What It Takes?

Everyone knows that Betty Camprey will not *rule out* a run for the presidency. But is she *cut out* for the most important job in the land? Does she *have what it takes*? No matter what people think, all this speculation about her run *serves a purpose*. She gets a lot of attention, and she *stays on people's minds*. It *stands to reason*, though, that she wants the job, since she has hinted at it before. Right now, she *stands* as much of *a chance* as any of the other candidates for the presidency. She really *has what it takes*. But she needs to be careful. If she doesn't make a firm decision soon she may *miss the boat*. She has to *take the bull by the horns* and *throw her hat in the ring*. If she does that, she may well quickly *rise to the top* and *win by a landslide*.

 BRING IT ALL TOGETHER

REVIEW EXERCISE 1: Vocabulary

Match each of the following words to the correct definition.

a. administration, b. congress, c. conservatism, d. democracy, e. electorate, f. ideology,

g. initiative, h. liberalism, i. political parties, j. politics, k. polls, l. primary, m. public opinion, n. republic

1. _____ Views that are considered traditional and unchanging.
2. _____ Views that emphasize tradition less and are and open to change.
3. _____ The people who vote.
4. _____ The field of governing, of influencing people and governments.
5. _____ A measure placed on the ballot by voters because they have petitioned for it.
6. _____ The first election, in which a party chooses its candidate.
7. _____ The president and his cabinet.
8. _____ Groups that represent certain political views that people choose to align with.
9. _____ A government of and by the people.
10. _____ The elected body of people who each represent their district or state and who make laws.
11. _____ A government whose leader is not a monarch, but is elected by the people.
12. _____ A place to go and vote.
13. _____ A political view or way of thinking held by one segment of the population.
14. _____ Current views held by most people at any given time.

REVIEW EXERCISE 2: The Progressive Form of Modals

Fill in the blanks with the correct modal: *could, may, might, must,* or *should,* and *be + verb + ing.*

1. I can hear the loudspeakers! The demonstration (start) _____ already.
2. After so many ad campaigns, Conway (pulling) _____ ahead in the polls.
3. It's supposed to be a relaxed family dinner, so we (not talk) _____ about politics!
4. Ron, if you feel so strongly about politics, you (get) _____ more involved.
5. Lopez (announce) _____ her candidacy this afternoon, but we'll have to see.
6. We (campaign) _____ for Abrams if we support him so much.
7. You (not discuss) _____ this issue with people unless you know their opinions.
8. Morel has hired a campaign manager, so he (run) _____ for governor.

REVIEW EXERCISE 3: The Use of *would rather*

Fill in the sentences with the correct form of *would rather.* First use the present form.

1. We (have) _____ a real choice among candidates.
2. (read) _____ you _____ the newspaper first?
3. Nat (live) _____ in Washington _____ California.

Use the past form.

4. Lynn (listen) _____ to the debate on the radio than (see) _____ it on TV.

5. I think he (not have) _____ to answer that question.

Use the continuous form.

6. Letty (go) _____ to work _____ (stay) _____ home.

7. (take) _____ you _____ a trip up the coast?

8. Everybody (work) _____ right now than sitting in this meeting.

REVIEW EXERCISE 4: Past Ability

Use either *could, be able to, couldn't,* or *wasn't/weren't able to* correctly in the following sentences.

1. Daniels (gain) _____ a lot of support from older voters because of the stand he took on prescription medicine.

2. Voters (read) _____ about important issues in the brochures that were sent out.

3. We (decide) _____ on the ballot initiative only after talking to many people.

4. People (not believe) _____ anything the candidate said after he was caught in a lie.

5. Which candidates (get) _____ their names on the ballots this year?

6. The campaign volunteers (sleep) _____ the night before election day.

7. Sally (not list) _____ any reasons for why I should support her favorite candidate.

8. Nobody (feel) _____ confident about the election because it was so close.

REVIEW EXERCISE 5: Phrasal Verbs

Fill in the blanks with one of the following phrasal verbs.

bring down, catch up, clean up, luck out, stick with, stand up for, run away with, take off, trail behind, turn around

1. Since this is the first election you've ever run in and you won, do you feel that you _____, or was it hard work?

2. The former governor did so well in his run for Senate, beating everyone by a wide margin, that he really _____ the election.

3. The only way to win is to work hard and _____ it or people will think you aren't serious.

4. A little-known governor from a small state made history by _____ the powerful president.

5. It's not impossible to change the course of this election, but it will take a lot of campaigning to _____ this election _____.

6. People like a candidate who _____ his views even if they don't agree with those positions.

7. Those candidates who _____ in the early primary vote usually drop out of the race.

8. What does it take to _____ with the front-runner? Hard work, dedication and luck!

9. The senator's reelection campaign has begun to _____ ever since the disclosure of his opponent's financial dealings.

10. Wow! What an election! Nobody expected this to happen, but the underdog candidate really _____ and won by a very large margin.

12H LISTEN UP!

Turn on your recording and listen to a short article about Habitat for Humanity and a famous ex-presidential couple. Then answer the following questions.

1. Are Jimmy and Rosalynn Carter the founders of Habitat for Humanity?
2. Were the Fullers a poor couple in need of housing?
3. Have the Carters themselves helped build homes for the needy?
4. Does Habitat for Humanity simply hand out money for homes?
5. Does Habitat for Humanity work only in the United States?

12I WHY DO THEY DO THAT?

Religion in the U.S.

While people of most wealthy countries place less importance on religion, many Americans view religion as an important—or central—part of their lives. In fact, the United States is the only wealthy, developed country whose people say that religion is significant to them. Six out of ten Americans say that religion is very important in their lives. This is four times greater than the people of Europe and twice that of the people of Canada. The U.S. is more similar to a poorer nation in religious devotion than to other wealthy, developed nations, and despite an ostensible separation of church and state, religion is often very closely tied to politics in the United States.

Why is religion so important in the U.S.? It could stem from the reason some of the first colonists came to this country. The pilgrims, for example, came to the New World to escape religious persecution. They wanted the freedom to worship as they chose and not as the monarchies of Europe told them to. The freedoms they enjoyed in the New World drew other religious groups, first in the form of Christian sects from Europe and then later as people of every faith from every corner of the world. Freedom of religion was written into the American Constitution, and a thirst for this religious freedom was just one of the engines that drove immigration into the United States, making it a very powerful aspect of the culture of this country. Religion has, predictably, continued to occupy an important position in American life.

But religion, like so much else in the United States, is a very diverse issue. Even though certain religious groups are outspoken and very actively involved in public and political life, no one religious group can claim to speak for a majority of Americans. According to the American Religious Identity Survey*, conducted in 2001 by sociologists from the Graduate School of the City University of New York, over 75 percent of Americans identify themselves as Christian, but this identity ranges from Episcopalians to Methodists to Roman Catholics to Mormons to Evangelicals. Nearly

*The data from this survey can be found online at *http://www.gc.cuny.edu/studies/aris_index.htm* 1

1.5 percent of the population is Jewish, and Muslims, Hindus, Buddhists, Unitarian-Universalists, and other groups each account for less than 1 percent of Americans. Over 13 percent of the population identifies itself as non-religious or sectarian, and the numbers of followers of Sikhism, Baha'i, Taoism, and Native American beliefs continue to rise. Naturally, how Americans practice their many religions—if they have one at all—varies greatly as well, both from region to region and from person to person. It is perhaps safest to treat religion, then, as a personal matter when dealing with an individual American, because even though statistics show that it is probably important in that person's life, it's very hard to predict exactly what religion means to him or her.

Lesson 12: Answer Key

Practice Exercise 1	1. must be burning, 2. may/might/could be giving, 3. must not be working, 4. should be studying, 5. could/may/might be getting, 6. must be voting, 7. should be cleaning, 8. must be kidding, 9. should be reading, 10. must be visiting
Practice Exercise 2	1. Would … rather go, 2. would rather vote … than, 3. would rather take … than, 4. would rather not go, 5. would rather have become … than, 6. would rather not have been, 7. would rather have gotten … than, 8. would rather be sleeping, 9. would rather be giving … answering, 10. would rather be feeling
Practice Exercise 3	1. could/was able to say, 2. could/was able to speak, 3. couldn't/wasn't able to go, 4. could/was able to get, 5. could/was able to watch, 6. could/was able to pass, 7. could/was able to climb, 8. couldn't/wasn't able to take, 9. couldn't/wasn't able to beat, 10. could/was able to win
Review Exercise 1	1. c, 2. h, 3. e, 4. j, 5. g, 6. l, 7. a, 8. i, 9. d, 10. b, 11. n, 12. k, 13. f, 14. m
Review Exercise 2	1. must be starting, 2. could/may/might be pulling, 3. should not be talking, 4. should be getting, 5. might/may/could be announcing, 6. should be campaigning, 7. should not be discussing, 8. must be running
Review Exercise 3	1. would rather have, 2. Would … rather read, 3. would rather live … than, 4. would rather have listened … seen, 5. would rather not have had, 6. would rather be going … than … staying, 7. Would … rather be taking, 8. would rather be working
Review Exercise 4	1. could/was able to gain, 2. could/were able to read, 3. could/were able to decide, 4. couldn't/weren't able to believe, 5. could/were able to get, 6. couldn't/weren't able to sleep, 7. couldn't/wasn't able to list, 8. could/was able to feel
Review Exercise 5	1. lucked out, 2. ran away with, 3. stick with, 4. bringing down, 5. turn … around, 6. stands up for, 7. trail behind, 8. catch up, 9. take off, 10. cleaned up
Listen Up!	1. No. Millard and Linda Fuller founded the organization. 2. No, they were wealthy. 3. Yes. 4. No, it is a partnership between new homeowners and volunteers. 5. No.

Pride of Ownership

ARE YOU READY FOR THE LESSON?

Are you interested in buying a house? Lesson 13: *Pride of Ownership* is packed with information about buying a home, along with important vocabulary words related to real estate. You will also learn:

- Past Forms of *should* and *shouldn't*
- *Be supposed to* and *be to*
- Making Suggestions with *could*
- Phrasal Verbs for Buying and Selling a House

You'll learn a few real estate idioms in *Real English,* and then you'll read about the American dream of home ownership and why it's so important to own a home in the U.S. But right now let's take a look at some reductions for *could* and *should*.

13A SAY IT CLEARLY!

🎧 Turn on your recording to practice more reductions in natural, conversational English.

13B ENGLISH AT WORK

Dialogue: Who Needs Buyer's Remorse?

📖 Kareen has been looking at houses for several months. She's found a house she wants to buy, but she's feeling pretty nervous about making such a big financial commitment. Listen in as she speaks to Nancy, her real estate agent, on the phone.

🎧

Kareen Hello?

Nancy Hi, Kareen! Nancy Plumber.

Kareen Hi, Nancy. What's the good word?

Nancy Well, I talked to the agent for Carlton Street, and I think we can get them to come down on their price. Their appraisal didn't come in as high as they thought it would.

Kareen Nancy, I don't know. I mean, it's so much money . . . How much do you think we could get it for?

Nancy I think we can get them to come down by about $25,000, maybe.

Kareen Really? But that's still so much money. I just don't know if I'm really ready for this. It needs some work, and I can't afford to pay for a big mortgage and then pay to have some work done on it, too.

Nancy Why don't we see what kind of a loan we can get? We could either put zero down or make a down payment of 5 percent, and then you could use your cash to fix it up. There are all kinds of ways you can get money to fix up a place without paying a whole lot out.

Kareen But then I'd have to pay P. M. I., wouldn't I?

Nancy   That's true, but in today's market your equity will grow really fast. In a year or two when it's worth more you can refinance and get rid of the P. M. I. payments.

Kareen   But it's so much money. What if I can't make the payments? Then I'd have to go into foreclosure and be back at zero again.

Nancy   You're not going to go into foreclosure! I wouldn't be selling you this house if I thought that you couldn't afford it. Look, I can go back into my computer and check to see what other listings there are. Maybe there's something in a price range you'll feel more comfortable with.

Kareen   No, we've already looked at everything out there .... What if there are problems? What if the plumbing's about to go or something?

Nancy   The owners are required by law to provide a full disclosure before escrow closes and you take possession. If there's something wrong, they have to fix it. There are laws to protect you.

Kareen   Well ... It is a really nice house ... How much did you say you thought we could get it for again?

13C BUILD YOUR VOCABULARY

Amortization. Payments with interest that gradually decrease the interest and balance of a loan while the payment stays the same. *Would you like a loan that amortizes over 15 years or 30 years?*

Appraisal. Property value determined by a lending institution such as a bank; largely determined through comparison of similar properties in the same neighborhood. *The bank appraised the value of your house at $350,000.*

Closing costs. Loan costs that are not included in the loan but must be paid in cash at the time escrow closes. *Your closing costs will be approximately $3500. You need to pay these before taking possession of the property.*

Disclosure. Information given by a seller revealing potential problems with a product that is being sold. *Every seller must provide complete disclosure to the buyer of property.*

Down payment. A percentage of the full price paid in advance for the purchase of a product. *If you have a good stable income you can buy a new house with a small down payment.*

Escrow. A place for property to be held in trust, such as when it is being transferred to a new owner. *A renter's security deposit will be held in escrow until the termination of the lease agreement.*

Equity. The dollar value above the amount owed for property; the difference between what something is worth and the amount a person still owes for it. *Paying a mortgage is called "building equity" because the payments bring down the total amount owed.*

Equity Line. A loan based upon a percentage of the value of one's home. The money can be used at will by the borrower but must be paid back to the lender with interest. *Many homeowners take out an equity line so that they can repair problems or do remodeling in their homes.*

Foreclosure. The right of a bank or lien holder of a mortgage to take possession of a property when the property owner is several months behind on his or her payments on the loan. *Be careful! If you don't pay your mortgage for several months, your home may go into foreclosure.*

HUD. Housing and Urban Development, a department within the U.S. government that has the purchasing of property under its jurisdiction. *HUD has just changed the down-payment policy for first-time buyers.*

Lien. A legal financial claim against a property that must be paid when property is sold. *Be sure you tell your realtor and your lender if you have a lien on your property. They will know what to do about it.*

Listing. A property that is put on sale and included in a list of other properties that are for sale. *I took a listing from the Jones family at 3234 Bridge Street yesterday. Can you add it to the other listings?*

Mortgage. A legal document where property is given as security for repayment of a loan. *When you figure your monthly expenses, your mortgage is probably your biggest expense.*

P. M. I. Private mortgage insurance. Additional insurance usually paid on the purchase of a house when the down payment is below 20 percent. *If you put at least 20 percent down on the property, your mortgage payments will be lower because you won't have to pay P. M. I.*

Points. Extra money that can be paid to keep the interest rate lower when the loan is made. A point is one percent of the amount of mortgage. *I can give you a 5.2 percent loan, but you'll have to pay points. If you don't want to pay any points, your rate will be higher.*

Principal. The amount owed on a property excluding taxes, interest, and insurance. *Wow! You've brought your principal down quickly by paying an extra $100 a month.*

Refinance. To pay off an existing loan and take out another loan on the same property. This is usually done to lower the payment or to take out additional money from the loan. *If you purchased your house at a rate of 7.25 percent, now's a good time to refinance since rates are below 6 percent.*

Title. A legal document that proves a person's ownership of a property. *Once escrow closes, you'll take title to the property.*

13D ENGLISH UNDER THE HOOD

TOPIC 1: Past Forms of *should* and *shouldn't*

The past form of *should* is *should have* + past participle. This is generally used to express regret about something in the past, or the wish that something had been done differently. To form the negative, use *not* after *should*.

You should have bought a house last year. The market was better for buyers.

We shouldn't have chosen that real estate agency!

PRACTICE EXERCISE 1: Fill in the blanks with either the positive or negative form of *should have* + past participle.

1. You (turn) _____ a few miles back; I think we've come too far.
2. You (not keep) _____ news of your marriage a secret for so long!
3. (not tell) _____ you_____ your doctor that you're planning on getting pregnant?
4. You (go) _____ to the beach with us yesterday.
5. (stay) _____ you_____ out so late on a Tuesday night?
6. I (buy) _____ an apartment rather than rented so I could build equity.
7. The realtor (be) _____ here by now.
8. Kenny (get) _____ paid last Friday, but he never got his check.
9. I lost the entire file! I (save) _____ it!
10. You were in Los Angeles last weekend? You (call) _____ me!

TOPIC 2: *Be supposed to* and *be to*

Be supposed to + base form of the verb expresses an obligation or an expectation, but this construction leaves doubt whether this will happen or not.

The students are supposed to arrive on time, but they often come late.

We're supposed to have a meeting at 3:00 today, but Jack's not here yet.

The construction *be to* also expresses expectation and obligation, but it is stronger than *supposed to* and implies rules or regulations. It is mostly used in written documents. It can be used in speech, but it implies a certain degree of authority.

Employees are to report to the security office for new ID cards.

All food and beverages are to be left outside the library.

PRACTICE EXERCISE 2: Fill in the blanks with either *be supposed to* or *be to*.

1. Who (walk) _____ the dog tonight?
2. What time (be) _____ you_____ at the meeting in the morning?
3. All employees (meet) _____ with the manager before the end of the month.
4. What time (return) _____ your parents _____ from the party?
5. The doctor said I (stay) _____ home in bed for a few days.
6. We (not dress) _____ casually for the big event tonight.
7. Someone (come) _____ from the bank today to appraise the house.
8. It (rain) _____ all day tomorrow.
9. You (not walk) _____ home alone so late at night, young lady!
10. The boss said we (expect) _____ more layoffs by the end of the month.

TOPIC 3: Making Suggestions with *could*

Use *could* + base form of the verb to make a future suggestion.

We could go to a movie tonight.

Use *could have* + past participle to make a suggestion about the past.

We could have met you at the theater if you had to work late.

PRACTICE EXERCISE 3: Fill in the blanks with the correct form of *could* to make suggestions.

1. We (go) _____ to that new Mexican restaurant tonight.
2. We (watch) _____ the game together on my big-screen TV.
3. There are a lot of things we (do) _____ when we visited Chicago.
4. You (study) _____ photography at an arts school after you graduate.
5. You (take) _____ your house off the market and later sell it for more.
6. We (go) _____ to the opera last night.
7. We (take) _____ the train instead of a bus yesterday.
8. You (call) _____ my realtor if you're not happy with yours.
9. We (drive) _____ on the back roads to avoid the traffic.
10. You (stay) _____ here last night instead of in a hotel.

13E PHRASAL VERBS FOR BUYING AND SELLING A HOUSE

Back out.
To retreat from something you are involved in; to exit. *When Jack heard how much money was involved, he backed out of the investment.*

Clean up.
To clean, to organize an area. *If you're going to bake cookies, please clean up after you're finished.*

Clean out.
To completely clean a space, to clear a space of clutter or garbage. *I found your old yearbook when I was cleaning out the basement this morning!*

Come across.
a) To find something by accident. *When I was looking for my insurance statement I came across some old love letters from you.*
b) To make an impression on others. *If you want to come across as a good candidate for this job, you need to dress and act the part.*

Do without.
To manage or perform adequately without something. *I'll have to do without a car for a few months until I can save enough money to buy one.*

Fix up.
To repair, to make nicer or more attractive. *We fixed up our new condo when we bought it, and now it looks great.*

Get stuck with.
To be left with something or someone unwanted. To acquire something that is too expensive. *Since I got my divorce, my house has been too expensive for me, and I got stuck with the payments.*

Make room for.
To add or create additional space for something. *We're going to remodel the house to make room for the new baby.*

Move in.
To start to live in a new house. *A nice young couple moved in next door.*

Put down.
To pay money as a down payment. *They put $15,000 down on their new house.*

Take advantage of.

a) To accept or profit from something that would not ordinarily be available. *I took advantage of the city's special anti-pollution offer for a discounted electric lawn mower.*

b) To manipulate or use someone in an unfair way. *Todd took advantage of Betsy's innocent nature when he asked her for that money.*

Want out of.
Desire an end to some obligation. *I've decided I can't afford to buy a new house right now, so I want out of the deal.*

Work out.
To resolve a complicated problem. *I think we can work out a way for you to buy this property without putting a lot of money into a down payment.*

13F REAL ENGLISH

Real Estate
Come to Casa Especial Realty, your *neighborhood specialists*. No matter what your tastes and budget may be, for *pride of ownership* we've got the place for you. Here's a great little *fixer-upper* with *curb appeal*. It's a *2 on 1*, so live in one and rent the other. Let the *helper unit* pay your mortgage. If you've got the time and energy *to fix* something *up*, this one's *a steal*. It just needs a little *upgrading* to make it *home sweet home*. So give us a call for more details. Or *stop by* our *open house* on Tuesday, the 11th.

13G BRING IT ALL TOGETHER

REVIEW EXERCISE 1: Vocabulary
Match each of the following words to the definition or descriptions given below.

a. amortization; b. appraisal; c. closing costs; d. disclosure; e. down payment; f. escrow; g. equity; h. equity line; i. foreclosure; j. HUD; k. lien; l. listing; m. points; n. principal; o. mortgage; p. P. M. I.; q. refinance; r. title

Put the letter of the word that is defined on the line next to its definition.

1. _____ The expenses paid for at the end of an escrow.

2. _____ Legal action taken by the bank if you do not pay your mortgage for several months.

3. _____ Your loan gets paid down little by little.

4. _____ The amount of cash brought in at the beginning of a property purchase.

5. _____ Payment to the lender that keeps the interest rate down.

6. _____ A legal document that proves property ownership.

7. _____ To take out a loan after the property has been purchased.

8. _____ Property is held in trust during its sale.

9. _____ The bank determines the value of a property.

10. _____ A property that is for sale grouped together with others.

11. _____ Problems described in a legal document by the seller to the buyer.

12. _____ A government agency that is responsible for home ownership.

13. _____ The value of the property above the amount of money owed on it.

14. _____ The balance of the loan not including interest.

15. _____ A legal document showing that money is owed on a property.

16. _____ A bank loans money on a percentage of the property's equity.

17. _____ Insurance on property when the buyer pays less than 20 percent as a down payment.

18. _____ A financial legal claim on a property that the property owner owes.

REVIEW EXERCISE 2: Past Forms of *should* and *shouldn't*

Complete each sentence with the correct past form of *should* plus the verb given in parentheses.

1. We (get) _____ together when you were in town last month.

2. You (be) _____ with me when I was looking for your new dress.

3. You (not leave) _____ before speaking with the realtor.

4. What do you think I (do) _____ when they offered me so little for the condo?

5. You and your wife (visit) _____ Uncle Will while you were in town.

6. We (not accept) _____ their offer without talking with our lawyer.

7. We (not move) _____ to this city without getting to know the school district.

8. I (ask) _____ the inspector about the water damage on the first floor.

REVIEW EXERCISE 3: *Be supposed to* and *be to*

Complete the following sentences with the correct form of *be supposed to* or *be to* with the verb given in parentheses. Be careful of the tense.

1. I (finish) _____ reading this book tonight.

2. All visitors (sign) _____ in at the security desk.

3. The appraiser (see) _____ the house yesterday.

4. The doctor said that I (not eat) _____ anything at all before the tests.

5. When (go) _____ you _____ to Mexico?

6. John (return) _____ by nine tonight.

7. Children, you (not play) _____ ball in the house!

8. The defendant (be taken) _____ into custody immediately.

REVIEW EXERCISE 4: Making Suggestions with *could*

1. If you don't want to move, we (take) _____ the house off the market.
2. We (walk) _____ to the church. It was only a few blocks.
3. You (clean) _____ the kitchen before the guests arrived.
4. We (take) _____ my car to the mountains. It has a full gas tank.
5. We (deliver) _____ the flowers before we go out of town.
6. I (pick up) _____ you _____ at your house and take you to work if necessary.
7. I've already seen that movie, but I (see) _____ it again.
8. We (take) _____ a picture of the property and post it online.

REVIEW EXERCISE 5: Phrasal Verbs for Buying and Selling a House

Fill in each sentence with one of the following:

back out, clean up, clean out, came across, do without, fix up, get stuck with, make room for, move in, take advantage of, want out, work out

1. Look what I _____ when I was going through some old family photos.
2. This would be such a cute place to _____ if we could afford it.
3. Jack says he _____ of the big real estate deal he's involved with.
4. I don't want to _____ the bill, so if you want it you'll have to pay for it.
5. Our backyard looks great now that we've _____ it _____.
6. The marriage counselor said that they could _____ their problems and have a better marriage.
7. You'll just have to _____ a nicer kitchen until we can afford to remodel it.
8. Once you have signed the contract you have three business days to _____ if you change your mind.
9. You'll have to hurry if you want to _____ this great opportunity!
10. The Clarksons moved a lot out of their attic to _____ a new home office up there.
11. We need to _____ the garage and get rid of all the junk.
12. It looks like a new family is _____ to that old house down the street.

13H LISTEN UP!

🎧 Turn on your recording and listen to the article on a homeowner's nightmare: termites. Then come back and answer the following questions.

📖

1. What insects are termites similar to?
2. Is a termite inspection usually required when selling a home?
3. What is swarming?
4. When do swarms usually happen?

5. What other clues are there that a house is infested with termites?

6. What are the two ways termites can be controlled?

7. Do these solutions last forever?

 131 WHY DO THEY DO THAT?

The American Dream of Home Ownership

Everyone knows that a big part of the *American dream* is to own one's own home. What a lot of people don't realize is the role home ownership has played in the nation's sovereignty, and how important this concept is to American history. In the England of 200 years ago, property ownership was passed from the father to the eldest son. Even if a landholder wanted to share his property with all of his sons, by law he was not permitted to split his property among more than one heir. This drove many of the early colonists to the New World because they could not inherit property. Property ownership therefore was a very important issue to many early European-Americans, and it became a critical factor in the decision to seek independence from England. Landowners wanted to protect their right to own land, because land ownership meant power. It was these same landowners who decided how the American government should be formed. So naturally the issue of land ownership was written into the laws of this country, and at first, only landowners were allowed to vote. But the concept of land ownership began to evolve, and such important historical figures as Thomas Jefferson believed land ownership to be the right of every American. Over time the government began to encourage all Americans to own their own homes.

Even the definition of home ownership has changed over time. Today in the U.S., home ownership means not just owning a house, but also owning the land the house is built on as well as, in most cases, a piece of surrounding land. This gives homeowners the right to make most of the decisions about the use of that land. So home ownership in the U.S. is such a big part of the *American dream* because with it comes the freedom to own a small piece of one's country.

Lesson 13: Answer Key

Practice Exercise 1	1. should have turned, 2. shouldn't have kept, 3. Shouldn't . . . have told, 4. should have gone, 5. Should . . . have stayed, 6. should have bought, 7. should have been, 8. should have gotten, 9. should have saved, 10. should have called
Practice Exercise 2	1. is supposed to walk, 2. are . . . supposed to be, 3. are to meet, 4. are . . . supposed to return, 5. am/was supposed to stay/am/was to stay, 6. are not supposed to dress, 7. is supposed to come, 8. is supposed to rain, 9. are not to walk, 10. are to expect
Practice Exercise 3	1. could go, 2. could watch, 3. could have done, 4. could study, 5. could take, 6. could have gone, 7. could have taken, 8. could call, 9. could drive, 10. could have stayed
Review Exercise 1	1. c, 2. i, 3. a, 4. e, 5. m, 6. r, 7. q, 8. f, 9. b, 10. l, 11. d, 12. j, 13. g, 14. n, 15. o, 16. h, 17. p, 18. k
Review Exercise 2	1. should have gotten, 2. should have been, 3. shouldn't have left, 4. should have done, 5. should have visited, 6. shouldn't have accepted, 7. shouldn't have moved, 8. should have asked
Review Exercise 3	1. am supposed to finish, 2. are to sign, 3. was supposed to see, 4. was not to eat, 5. are . . . supposed to go, 6. is supposed to return, 7. are not to play, 8. is to be taken
Review Exercise 4	1. could take, 2. could have walked, 3. could have cleaned, 4. could take, 5. could deliver, 6. could pick . . . up, 7. could see, 8. could take

Review Exercise 5　　　1. came across, 2. fix up, 3. wants out, 4. get stuck with, 5. cleaned . . . up, 6. work out, 7. do without, 8. back out, 9. take advantage of, 10. make room for 11. clean out, 12. moving in

Listen Up!　　　　　　1. Ants. 2. Yes. 3. When termites come out into a house and fly around. 4. In the spring. 5. Small tunnels in wood that termites have eaten, mud tubes leading from a home into the ground. 6. Insecticides (termiticides) or baits. 7. No, only a few years.

Lesson 14

Hit the Books!

ARE YOU READY FOR THE LESSON?

If you are interested in learning about American schools, then Lesson 14: *Hit the Books!* will give you a lot of important information. You'll listen in on a conversation between a parent and a teacher, and you'll learn more about American teachers in *Why Do They Do That?* You will learn some vocabulary useful for understanding the American educational system as well. In addition, you will learn:

• Verbs Followed by Infinitives
• Adjectives Followed by Infinitives and *It* Plus Infinitive
• Verbs Followed by Nouns or Pronouns Plus Infinitives
• Phrasal Verbs for School

But there's more. You'll also learn some good idioms about studying and test taking. So let's get started with some reductions in *Say It Clearly!*

14A SAY IT CLEARLY!

Turn on your recording to practice some common reductions that will make your English sound more natural.

14B ENGLISH AT WORK

DIALOGUE: He's Always Been a Good Student!

Mrs. Beck is meeting with her son's teacher, Ms. Rendon. Her son is usually a good student, but his grades have been slipping in English class and she's a little worried about him.

Mrs. Beck   Hello, Ms. Rendon, I'm Laura Beck, James' mother. How are you?

Ms. Rendon   Mrs. Beck, so nice to meet you. Yes, have a seat. I've just been reviewing James' work. Let's see.

Mrs. Beck   Yes, James has always been such a good student. I don't know what's happened to him.

Ms. Rendon   Honestly, a lot of kids' grades go down around their sophomore or junior year, especially boys.

Mrs. Beck   I don't know whether to be comforted by that or not, but high school is when his G. P. A. is the most important. He wants to go to a university, but if he keeps getting grades like this he'll have to go to a junior college first.

Ms. Rendon   Well, sometimes kids need a little time to mature before going to a university. Maybe a J. C. isn't such a bad thing for some kids.

Mrs. Beck   His father and I both went straight to universities; we expect James to do the same.

Ms. Rendon	OK, well, he hasn't been doing his homework. That's one problem. I don't have many entries for homework assignments, and the homework prepares the kids for the exams. His exam scores are a little lower than they used to be. His lower grade this semester is a consequence of not turning in his homework and not scoring well on tests. He hasn't done much participating in classroom discussions either. He probably isn't reading his assignments or maybe he just doesn't understand what he's reading. I've asked him about it, but he just shrugs his shoulders, so I'm not sure what the problem is. Sometimes it's not the class or the material. Sometimes it's not the subject that causes a student to lose interest or not do well in class.
Mrs. Beck	Everything's fine at home. We have a very close family, so I don't think it has anything to do with his home life.
Ms. Rendon	Have you spoken to his counselor?
Mrs. Beck	No.
Ms. Rendon	Well, have you asked James why he's not doing well in class?
Mrs. Beck	I've tried, but he just gives me a vague response. I can't get anything out of him.
Ms. Rendon	If he won't tell me and he won't tell you, then you might want to talk to his counselor.
Mrs. Beck	OK, I think I'll do that. I'm also going to talk to him about his assignments. Do you have a syllabus with the assignments?
Ms. Rendon	Yes, I'll get you one. Remember that he may have some issues going on in his life that you may not know about. Kids at this age really start keeping their problems to themselves. Other than his grades going down, he's a good kid. I'm sure this is just a passing concern.
Mrs. Beck	OK, Ms. Rendon, I appreciate all your help.
Ms. Rendon	No problem. Take care.

14C BUILD YOUR VOCABULARY

BA. Bachelor of Arts. A four-year degree in the arts or humanities. *It took Rob five and a half years to complete his BA because he was working full time while in school.*

(Course) Catalog. A book listing courses available at a school during a particular semester. *Let's look in the catalog to find the art history class we want to take.*

Course. A specific class. *Sam normally takes five or six courses a semester.*

Credit. A unit of value that each course is worth. Degrees require a certain number of credits overall. *My French class is worth three credits, but my biology class is worth four because there's a lab session each week.*

Curriculum. Program of courses offered by a school. *Maisie Brown had been designing the school curriculum since she became the school's director.*

Dean. The head administrator of a section of a school or university. *The dean called a staff meeting to see if there was a better way to organize the program schedule.*

Degree. A title conferred by a university that denotes that a course of study has been completed, such as BA, MA, or PhD. *Once I got my BA, I decided to get a job and work for a while before going back to school for any other degrees.*

Dissertation. A long and exhaustive written study of a particular subject that is part of a doctoral program. *Rimouna is writing her dissertation on Arab women writers in translation.*

Doctorate. PhD, the highest degree conferred by a university. *It took Jason six years to complete his doctorate in linguistics.*

Enroll. To enter a school with the intent of studying there; to sign up for a school program or course. *There are thirty students enrolled in one class and twelve enrolled in another.*

Exam. Short for "examination." A formal method for determining progress, knowledge, or ability in a subject or course. *Your grade in this course will be determined by a combination of your midterm exam, final exam, and term paper scores.*

Freshman. A first-year student at a high school or college. *There are many organizations to help freshmen make the transition to living away from home.*

Immunization record. A record of shots or immunizations needed before a student can be registered for school. *Nara had to take her children to the public health center, because they needed to get a few more shots for their immunization records.*

Junior. A third-year student at a high school or college. *By the time Paul was a junior in high school he'd already decided exactly where he wanted to go to college.*

MA. Master of Arts, Masters. A postgraduate degree that involves a specific series of courses in the arts and usually a thesis involving research or a creative project. *A lot of people wait until they've worked for a while before they go back to school to get an MA.*

Major. The primary study emphasis of a college student. *Don't worry too much if you're not sure of your major during your first year at school; just take classes that interest you.*

PhD. The highest degree that can be attained through a university education. *Polly knew she would have to dedicate the next eight years of her life to work on a PhD.*

Principal. The head of an elementary or secondary school. *The teacher sent Robert to the principal because he was disruptive in class.*

P. T. A. Parent Teacher Association; an organization that enables parents and teachers of elementary and high-school students to work together to make their schools better. *As P. T. A. president, Millie Brown organized parents to help paint the school for the new school year.*

Recess. A break from school; a break from studying. *What will you be doing during the spring recess?*

Register. To fill out forms to attend a class; to formally enroll. *Kam needed some help in filling out all the forms when she registered for class.*

Semester. One half of a school year, usually about eighteen weeks. *Luba decided to go back to school just before spring semester began.*

Seminar. An advanced or graduate group studying under an instructor where students share their independent research through reports and discussion. *Professor Haggart leads interesting philosophy seminars.*

Senior. A fourth-year student at a high school or college. *Many high schools have a tradition that most seniors skip school on a particular day and go to the beach or a lake.*

Sophomore. A second-year high-school or college student. *Just because he's a sophomore, Rick thinks he's got everything figured out.*

Standards. The model established by an authority of what should be covered in a course of study. *Look to the state education department to find the standards you need to fulfill when you plan your lessons.*

Standardized testing. A program of testing set up by the state or national government that tests students' knowledge of subjects. This type of testing compares students and is often used in admissions to colleges and graduate schools. *In order to get into a university, you must take some sort of standardized test like the A. C. T. or S. A. T.*

Term paper. A major written paper for a course in high school or college. *Jack got an A on his term paper for his U.S. history class.*

14D ENGLISH UNDER THE HOOD

You've seen many examples of infinitives in this course already. An infinitive is the basic form of a verb preceded by the preposition *to*, as in *to dance, to sing, to see* or *to study.* The infinitive has many different uses. It can function as the subject of the sentence:

To listen to beautiful music is a pleasure.

To work hard and stay in school should be your goal.

An infinitive can also function as a direct object:

We prefer to watch a movie on Friday nights.

Jason yearns to see his girlfriend again.

An infinitive of purpose explains why something is done. It can be a simple infinitive or an entire phrase:

I am going to the library to study.

They went to the store to buy a new computer.

In this section we're going to take a closer look at three of the more important uses of infinitives.

TOPIC 1: Verbs Followed by Infinitives

Many verbs in English are followed by infinitives:

I want to go to the movies tonight.

The children forgot to do their homework assignments.

There isn't an easy rule to explain which verbs are followed by infinitives. They just have to be memorized and practiced. Here is a list of some of the more common ones:

afford, agree, appear, ask, begin, claim, consent, continue, decide, demand, deserve, expect, fail, forget, hate, hope, learn, like, love, manage, need, offer, plan, prefer, prepare, pretend, promise, refuse, seem, can't stand, start, try, volunteer, wait, want, wish.

Cindy can't afford to buy a new car today.

We managed to make it to work on time despite the traffic.

Paul volunteered to help clean up the park.

PRACTICE EXERCISE 1: Fill in the blanks with the best verb from the following list.

play   visit   buy   cry   speak   ride   see   be   start   go

1. We hope _____ a house some day.
2. Jay continues _____ his bicycle to work.
3. Mary intends _____ to college after she graduates.
4. You seem _____ a little tired.
5. Nancy likes _____ the violin.
6. I can't stand _____ you cry.
7. You will learn _____ English very well.
8. A few students continue _____ their teachers after graduating.
9. June expects _____ her own business someday.
10. The girls started _____ when they realized they were lost.

TOPIC 2: Adjectives Followed by Infinitives and *It* Plus Infinitive

There are also a lot of adjectives in English that can be followed directly by an infinitive.

I'm surprised to see you here!

Jason was lucky to find a new job so quickly.

As a general rule, adjectives that are followed by infinitives describe people's emotions or feelings about something. Here's a list of the more common ones:

afraid, amazed, anxious, ashamed, astonished, careful, certain, delighted, determined, disappointed, eager, glad, happy, hesitant, horrified, liable, likely, lucky, pleased, proud, ready, relieved, reluctant, sad, shocked, sorry, surprised, upset, willing.

Hank was surprised to see his professor at the restaurant.

We were horrified to learn of the scandal at college.

Remember that the infinitive can also be used as a subject of a sentence, and often these sentences will end with an adjective.

To jump into Niagara Falls is foolish!

To study hard is important.

These sentences can be restated so that the infinitives follow the adjectives. Just put *it is* at the beginning, and then the adjective, and then the infinitive and the rest of the sentence.

It is foolish to jump into Niagara Falls!

It is important to study hard.

PRACTICE EXERCISE 2: Fill in each blank with the best verb from the following list.

give, try, hear, learn, see, discover, know, help, be able, sleep

1. The students were thrilled _____ about animals by going to the zoo.
2. I'm reluctant _____ you a passing grade because you haven't tried.
3. Aren't you anxious _____ what he looks like now, after all these years?
4. The researchers were eager _____ the cause of the genetic mutation.
5. It is very pleasant _____ late on a Saturday morning.
6. Henry is proud _____ to retire early.
7. It is important for you _____ a little harder.
8. It is kind of you _____ me like this.
9. I was happy _____ the movie that everyone had been talking about.
10. It is upsetting _____ that you called while I was away.

TOPIC 3: Verbs Followed by Nouns or Pronouns Plus Infinitives

Another important use of infinitives is with certain verbs that are also followed by a noun or a pronoun.

Richard asked his friend to help him move.

He reminded me to mail my check.

As you can see, the formula is: subject + verb + noun/pronoun + infinitive. Here is a list of the most common verbs that can be followed by a noun or a pronoun and then an infinitive:

advise, allow, ask, beg, cause, challenge, convince, dare, encourage, expect, forbid, force, get, hire, implore, invite, need, order, permit, persuade, remind, require, teach, tell, urge, want, warn, would like.

They hired a new assistant to help them organize the records.

How can I convince you to reconsider your decision?

The boys persuaded their parents to let them go to the party.

PRACTICE EXERCISE 3: Make logical sentences out of the following words. Always start with the first word.

1. I / you / advise / to transfer to a different class.
2. Dan / to arm wrestle him / Ralph / challenged.
3. Linda / to read her his short story / begged / Jorge.
4. Doris / me / with her / invited / to go shopping.
5. Will you / me / to accompany you / permit?
6. I / the job / to do / you / hired.
7. Gabby / the leader / to be / you / needs.
8. Would you / to drive your car / like / me?
9. Jerry / him / some free time / his mother / to give / convinced.
10. The students / mercy / to have / the professor / begged.

PHRASAL VERBS FOR SCHOOL

Drop out.
To leave something before completion. *Derrick dropped out of school when he turned sixteen.*

Fall behind.
To have a lot of work that is unfinished and late. *Robert's schedule was so hectic that he fell behind on his project and had to ask to have the deadline extended.*

Figure out.
To solve a problem, to find an answer or solution. *Ted and Jennifer worked together to figure out the answers to their math homework.*

Get through to.
a) To communicate to someone so that he or she understands. *If students don't enjoy a subject, it can be difficult for a teacher to get through to them.*

b) To be able to make an emotional or personal connection to another person; to bond with someone. *Often the best people to get through to alcoholics are those who have been alcoholics themselves.*

c) To connect with someone by telephone after difficulty. *I finally got through to the insurance company after waiting for ten minutes.*

Look into.
To check carefully. *We really need to look into the problem of so many students dropping out of school.*

Look over.
To examine quickly, to glance at. *Could you look over my application to make sure I've filled it in correctly?*

Stay in.
To finish something you started, to remain. *Derrick's girlfriend Alma decided not to drop out of school like he did.*

Stick it out.
To continue to do something that might be difficult. *I'm not sure I can really handle medical school, but I'm going to stick it out for a while anyway.*

Read over.
To review quickly. *Class, be sure you read over the material before the quiz tomorrow.*

Turn on.
a) To excite, stimulate. *Mrs. Barrett really knew how to turn the kids on to reading.*

b) To start the power of an electrical product. *You have to put batteries in this radio before you can turn it on.*

 REAL ENGLISH

Life on Campus

Being a college student is hard work. I don't have a lot of *time to kill* when I can just *kick back* and relax. I always have to *hit the books*. And finals week begins on Monday, so I really have to *stick to* my books. If I *goof off* too much *I'll miss the boat*. So I'm going to *take my time* to prepare for the tests. I'll *learn* as much as I can *by heart*. If I don't *get it* I can't just guess *off the top of my head*. I'll *go blank* during the test! But once the test is over, I'll be free for another week. That's when I'll *crash*.

14G BRING IT ALL TOGETHER

REVIEW EXERCISE 1: Vocabulary

Fill in the blanks with the following words.

(course) catalog; courses; curriculum; degree; dean; enrolled; exams; immunization record; major; principal; P. T. A.; recess; register; semester; seminar; standards; standardized tests; term paper

1. If you look at the _____ for the E. S. L. program, you will find that along with grammar, reading, writing, listening, and speaking, students need to understand daily life in the United States as well.

2. Mrs. Carroll will retire after thirty years of distinguished service as the _____ of Hamilton Middle School.

3. You need to take at least three English _____ before you graduate.

4. Did you check the _____ to see what day your class starts?

5. When you _____ for school, be sure you have your social security number, address, and phone number.

6. If you are an independent type of student but you enjoy discussing what you learn, you should sign up for a _____.

7. Are you taking your _____ now, or do you just have papers to write?

8. _____ Jameson gave a moving speech at the graduation ceremony.

9. Joe's father is wondering how useful a _____ in philosophy is.

10. An _____ is required for every new student before classes begin.

11. Teachers often don't like to give _____ because they do not measure a child's creativity.

12. This college is known for a _____ that emphasizes social sciences and fields specific to life in large cities.

13. To be involved with your children's school, join the _____.

14. You won't become a senior until your seventh _____ of high school.

15. Ms. Jones needed a class roster so she could see how many students were _____ in her class.

16. The children played volleyball during _____.

17. You are required to write a _____ if you want to pass this course.

18. Many students do not choose their _____ until their junior year of college.

REVIEW EXERCISE 2: Verbs Followed by Infinitives

Fill in the blanks with the correct form of the verb in parentheses.

1. He wants (get) _____ a new DVD player.

2. Everyone was excited (meet) _____ the new senator.

3. Don't begin (watch) _____ the movie until I get back.

4. We prefer (sit) _____ next to the exit door.

5. We stopped (wait) _____ for you.

6. The video continued (roll) _____ even though class was over.

7. You need (start) _____ your test right now.

8. Do you plan (visit) _____ your mother over recess?

REVIEW EXERCISE 3: Adjectives Followed by Infinitives and *It* Plus Infinitive

Fill in the sentences with an appropriate verb.

stay, take, speak, have, learn, win, find, hear

1. _____ general math is part of a high-school curriculum.

2. _____ the bus is the best way to get there.

3. It isn't easy _____ another language well.

4. It is helpful _____ a car in California.

5. _____ in Vermont for the weekend would be a great little vacation.

6. I was shocked _____ that your father had died.

7. We were lucky _____ seats in such a crowded lecture hall.

8. Is he certain _____ the title?

REVIEW EXERCISE 4: Verbs Followed by Nouns or Pronouns Plus Infinitives

Fill in the sentences with a verb from the list.

write, take care of, plead, walk, give, roll over, set, prepare

1. I dare you _____ across that log.

2. Pat reminded me _____ the alarm so we'd wake up early.

3. Did you expect the boss _____ you a promotion?

4. The teacher warned her students _____ for the test.

5. Did you teach your dog _____?

6. The professor required his students _____ a term paper.

7. The lawyer advised his client _____ guilty.

8. The director hired a new employee _____ the extra work.

REVIEW EXERCISE 5: Phrasal Verbs for School

Fill in the following blanks with the appropriate phrasal verb.

drop out of, fall behind, figure out, get through to, look into, look over, stay in, stick it out, read over, turn on

1. If you think you want to apply to a certain college, you'd better _____ it first.

2. It's usually very difficult for adults to _____ teenagers, because they relate better to younger people.

3. College freshmen often get homesick if they go to school in a different city, but if they _____ they'll start to feel better after a while.

4. Take a few minutes to _____ your poem and then recite it to your classmates.

5. Jeremy was out sick for a month so he _____ in his schoolwork.

6. If you get a good job offer, you may want to _____ school.

7. It takes a while to _____ what you want to study in school.

8. I've decided to _____ junior college for one more year, and then I'll transfer to the university.

9. Mr. Jones really knew how to _____ students _____ to science.

10. Jim, could you please _____ my paper before I turn it in?

14H LISTEN UP!

Listen in as Scott registers by phone for a Spanish class at Jackson Junior College. Then answer the following questions.

1. Did Scott successfully register for a Spanish class?

2. What campus did he want?

3. On which campus did the computer voice give him a Spanish class?

4. What did Scott ask for when he discovered the mistake?

5. Did the voice help him with his problem?

6. What did the computer do at the end of the conversation?

14I WHY DO THEY DO THAT?

American Teachers

Compared to teachers in many other countries, American teachers, like the rest of American society, are rather informal. They usually dress casually when they teach. Male teachers rarely wear jackets and ties, and female teachers prefer not to wear suits and heels. Some teachers even wear jeans. Teaching involves a lot of standing, bending, and moving around, so they prefer to be comfortable. And dress isn't the only casual area of teaching. While in most countries students use a formal title when addressing their teachers, it is not always necessary to do this in the U.S. American teachers in elementary and secondary schools prefer to be called by the titles "Mr.," "Mrs.," or "Ms.," with their last names. University professors sometimes like to be called by the title "Professor" or even "Doctor," but many others do not. In universities and adult education, teachers often like to be called by their first names, perhaps because many of their students may be older than they are, or perhaps because they feel that an informal atmosphere encourages learning and free discussion of ideas.

Discussion is a key factor in American education. American students rarely sit quietly in the classroom listening to the teacher lecture. They are encouraged to ask questions at any point. The teachers do not think of themselves as having all the answers, and they will openly say so and offer to look for the answers they do not have or challenge the students to find the answers. They want their students to debate and disagree with them and their classmates openly, because this is considered important for the development of critical and independent thinking. Teachers will often bring up thought-provoking questions that the students are expected to discuss. In fact, students' grades are often at least partially determined by their interaction in the classroom. This should come as no surprise, as the U.S. is often thought of as a place of competitive individualism and independent thinking. It's to be expected that the American classroom should foster these values.

Lesson 14: Answer Key

Practice Exercise 1	1. to buy, 2. to ride, 3. to go, 4. to be, 5. to play, 6. to see, 7. to speak, 8. to visit, 9. to start, 10. to cry
Practice Exercise 2	1. to learn, 2. to give, 3. to know, 4. to discover, 5. to sleep, 6. to be able, 7. to try, 8. to help, 9. to see, 10. to hear
Practice Exercise 3	1. I advise you to transfer to a different class. 2. Dan challenged Ralph to arm wrestle him. 3. Linda begged Jorge to read her his short story. 4. Doris invited me to go shopping with her. 5. Will you permit me to accompany you? 6. I hired you to do the job. 7. Gabby needs you to be the leader. 8. Would you like me to drive your car? 9. Jerry convinced his mother to give him some free time. 10. The students begged the professor to have mercy
Review Exercise 1	1. standards, 2. principal, 3. courses, 4. (course) catalog, 5. register, 6. seminar, 7. exams, 8. Dean, 9. degree, 10. immunization record, 11. standardized tests, 12. curriculum, 13. P. T. A., 14. semester, 15. enrolled, 16. recess, 17. term paper, 18. major
Review Exercise 2	1. to get, 2. to meet, 3. to watch, 4. to sit, 5. to wait, 6. to roll, 7. to start, 8. to visit
Review Exercise 3	1. To learn, 2. To take, 3. to speak, 4. to have, 5. To stay, 6. to hear, 7. to find, 8. to win
Review Exercise 4	1. to walk, 2. to set, 3. to give, 4. to prepare, 5. to roll over, 6. to write, 7. to plead, 8. to take care of
Review Exercise 5	1. look into, 2. get through to, 3. stick it out, 4. read over, 5. fell behind, 6. drop out of, 7. figure out, 8. stay in, 9. turn . . . on, 10. look over
Listen Up!	1. No, he didn't. 2. The Jackson campus. 3. The Johnson campus. 4. To talk to a real person. 5. No, it didn't. 6. It hung up.

Lesson 15

Let's Get Together Sometime!

ARE YOU READY FOR THE LESSON?

If you enjoy meeting new people and getting together with your friends, you'll find Lesson 15: *Let's Get Together Sometime!* helpful. In this lesson, you'll read a dialogue about meeting someone new, and you'll learn some vocabulary for fun things Americans like to do. The phrasal verbs and idioms in this lesson have to do with relationships and entertainment. And if you were wondering about certain American social customs, you may find the answers to your questions in *Why Do They Do That?* You'll also learn about:

• Verbs Followed by Gerunds

• Verbs Followed by Prepositions and Gerunds

• *Go* Plus Gerunds

And in *Listen Up!* you'll hear about one way that some Americans meet new people, find romance, and make friends. Let's begin as usual with a pronunciation segment in *Say It Clearly!*

15A SAY IT CLEARLY!

🎧 Turn on your recording to warm up with a pronunciation segment.

15B ENGLISH AT WORK

Dialogue: Who's That Over There?

📖 Dale and Ted are colleagues who are enjoying a beer together after work at a local pub. They spot a woman they work with, and she's with a friend of hers who they don't know but who really gets their attention.

🎧

Dale Man, I thought this week would never end.

Ted Yeah, here's to Fridays. Bottoms up.

Dale Hey, Ted. Isn't that Tina from Accounting? In that booth over there?

Ted Where? Oh, yeah, it is. And who's that girl sitting with her?

Dale Wow.

Ted You know, it's been a while since we've spoken to good old Tina. Maybe it's time we said "hello" to her.

Dale Yeah, good idea.

(They walk over.)

Dale Tina!

Ted: Hey, Tina!

Dale We haven't seen you for so long!

Tina Um, hi guys. What's going on? You just saw me this morning.

Dale Oh, right, um ... Well, we mean outside the office.

Tina	OK. Hi ... Oh. Maggie, this is Ted and this is Dale. They work at Northern with me.
Ted	Hi.
Dale	Hello, there.
Maggie	Hello. So, what do you guys do at Tina's company? You're in Accounting, too?
Ted	No!
Dale	No way. IT.
Maggie	I.T., huh? You're into computers?
Ted	Well, not like, enough to spend weekends at conventions or anything, but, you know, enough to keep the engines of commerce well oiled.
Maggie	So, you go and fix problems when people call up with jammed printers and things?
Tina	(laughs) They're actually pretty good at it, too.
Dale	Yeah, ahem ... So, Maggie, how do you know Tina?
Maggie	Oh, we've known each other a long time. We grew up in the same town, went to high school together ...
Tina	Yeah, we're ancient friends.
Ted	So why are you visiting Tina?
Maggie	Well, I'm, um ...
Dale	Hey, there's a street fair this weekend. You gonna be around tomorrow? Do you wanna go with us?
Tina	Uh ...
Maggie	Sure.
Dale	Great. And maybe some bowling afterwards? Do you like bowling?
Maggie	Bowling? It's all right.
Ted	I think she's more the adventurous type, or the rugged outdoors type. I bet you like hiking and camping.
Maggie	Yeah, actually I do like hiking and camping, and I really like rock climbing.
Ted	Rock climbing? Cool. What else do you do for fun?
Maggie	I like skydiving, too.
Dale	Do you like skiing?
Maggie	I love skiing, and surfing.
Dale	Wow! That's great!
Maggie	Hey, listen, would you guys excuse me for a minute? I'll be right back.

(After Maggie leaves)

Dale	Wow, she's great.
Ted	Bowling? You think you're gonna grab her attention with bowling?
Dale	Oh, listen to you. "... more the adventurous type ... the rugged outdoors ..."
Tina	Okay, listen studs, I think you're both out of your league.
Ted	Oh yeah? Why?
Tina	Well, Maggie's visiting me so we can spend some time together before her big day.
Dale	Big day?
Ted	She's not ...
Tina	Yup. She's getting married in a few weeks.

Dale Oh...

Tina Yeah. I think you two just bowled a gutter ball.

15C BUILD YOUR VOCABULARY

Bird-watching. Observing and identifying birds in their natural environment. *Lola and Jim have become avid bird watchers since they first spotted a variety of blue jays in their yard.*

Book group. A group of people organized like a club to read and discuss books. *Our book group is meeting next Tuesday and I haven't even started the book we have to read!*

Bowling. A game where a heavy ball is rolled down an alley to knock down pins. A "gutter ball" means that the ball rolled into a trench on either side of the alley and all the pins were missed. *Every Friday night the Smythes and the MacWilliams get together to go bowling.*

Bungee jumping. A sport where a person, attached to a strong rubber cord, jumps from a great height. *Nathan goes bungee jumping about twice a year because he loves the feeling of flying through the air and then being snapped back up by the bungee cord.*

Camping. Temporarily living outdoors, usually in a tent without any luxuries. *Ramon's favorite type of vacation is camping in the mountains because he loves the serenity of nature.*

Canoeing. Boating in a small narrow craft that is propelled by paddling. *One of Jim's favorite hobbies is canoeing in Mission Bay.*

Chat room. A "space" on the Internet where people can post and read opinions about various topics, interests or current beliefs. *If you're a parent, you should carefully monitor the chat rooms your child might visit.*

Clubbing. Going out to discos. *When Ron was in his twenties he used to go clubbing every Saturday night.*

Dinner party. A small party organized around a dinner, where a group of people is invited to someone's house for dinner, drinks, and dessert. *Steven is a great cook with a wonderful apartment, so guests to his dinner parties are lucky!*

Get-together. A party, usually informal, sometimes for a certain purpose, but often simply social. *We're having a small get-together on Friday to watch the new documentary that Mark has just finished filming.*

Hiking. Taking a long walk, often in the mountains or forest, for pleasure or exercise. *Victor goes hiking in the mountains or the desert whenever he can.*

Horseback riding. Riding a horse for pleasure. *The Jameson twins go horseback riding in the country almost every weekend.*

Jogging. Running at a slow pace for cardiovascular exercise. *When John Kennedy was President he made jogging popular in the United States.*

Mingle. To mix and converse with various people in a social setting. *It's Jessica's party, so she is expected to mingle with all the guests.*

Rock climbing. Climbing up high, steep rocks, often by pulling oneself by the hands. *Yosemite is a great place for rock climbing, but you need experience.*

Roller-blading. Moving on a pair of boots with a single row of wheels. *The Park family enjoys roller blading in the park near their house.*

Sailing. Traveling in a boat powered by the wind pushing sails. *Now that Martha no longer gets seasick, she finds sailing to be a very calming experience.*

Skateboarding. Moving rapidly while standing on a board with rollers attached to it. *When Anthony was about fourteen, he broke his arm while skateboarding.*

Sightseeing. Visiting interesting tourist attractions. *Travis and Vicky did a lot of sightseeing on their trip to London.*

Skiing. Sliding over the snow on two long wooden planks, usually down a mountain. *It's traditional for college students to take skiing holidays in nearby mountains during spring break.*

Skydiving. Jumping out of an airplane and falling until using a parachute to land. *Bernice didn't think she'd like skydiving, but once she tried it she became addicted to the feeling of free-falling through the air.*

Surfing. Riding on ocean waves while standing on or leaning against a board. *The Beach Boys became famous for their songs about surfing and California.*

Window-shopping. Looking at new merchandise without intending to buy anything. *When Walter and Priscilla were newlyweds, they often went window-shopping because they just didn't have enough money to buy what they liked.*

Whale watching. Going out on a boat to watch the whales in the ocean. *Southern California is a great place to go whale watching.*

Working out. Going to a gym and lifting weights to build muscle. *Bob used to be overweight, but since he started running and working out he's really gotten a great body.*

15D ENGLISH UNDER THE HOOD

The gerund is the *-ing* form of a verb that is used as a noun, such as *singing, dancing, looking,* or *sleeping.* A gerund can be used as the subject of a sentence:

Smoking is prohibited.

Walking is good exercise.

A gerund can also function as the object of a verb:

We hate waiting in line.

My son loves playing video games.

A gerund can also function as the object of a preposition.

We spoke about moving to Chicago.

They're responsible for paying the bill on time.

In this section we're going to take a closer look at three other important uses of gerunds.

TOPIC 1: Verbs Followed by Gerunds

In Lesson 14 we looked at verbs that are followed by infinitives, such as *want to go*, *forget to do*, and *start to rain*. In this section we'll look at other verbs that are followed not by the infinitive, but by a gerund.

Do you enjoy studying foreign languages?

Terry denied taking the money off of Jack's desk.

Once again, there isn't any easy rule to explain which verbs are followed by gerunds instead of infinitives. They just have to be memorized, and of course practiced. Here's a list of some of the more common ones:

admit, advise, anticipate, appreciate, avoid, begin, consider, continue, delay, deny, discuss, dislike, enjoy, finish, forget, hate, can't help, can't stand, keep, like, love, mind, miss, postpone, practice, prefer, quit, recall, recollect, recommend, regret, remember, resent, resist, risk, start, stop, suggest, tolerate, try, understand.

Harry forgot leaving his keys in the car.

I can't stand waiting in line!

Did you try talking to your boss about your concerns?

PRACTICE EXERCISE 1: Choose from the following list to fill in the blank with the best gerund.

be, smoke, give, pull, call, jog, watch , travel, meet, study

1. I tried _____ for exercise, but it hurts my knees.
2. We prefer _____ our mother "Mom."
3. Terry regrets _____ out her phone number to so many guys she meets.
4. Quit _____ on my shirt! You're going to rip it!
5. Do you enjoy _____ movies?
6. Have you finished _____ for the exam?
7. You have to resolve to quit _____ this New Year.
8. To avoid _____ late, set your clock ahead ten minutes.
9. The Smythes anticipate _____ to Europe this summer.
10. We'll have to postpone _____ on the project until next week.

TOPIC 2: Verbs Followed by Prepositions Plus Gerunds

Some common verbs are followed not just by a gerund, but by a preposition and a gerund.

She complained about standing in line.

We stopped the thief from stealing the woman's purse.

Again, there's no easy rule for determining which verbs are followed by prepositions and gerunds. Here is a list of some of the most common and important ones. Notice that several of these expressions consist of *to be* plus an adjective. It's really the adjective in these cases that calls for the preposition plus gerund, but they're listed here for convenience.

to be excited about, to be concerned about, to be worried about, to complain about, to dream about/of, to talk about/of, to think about/of, to apologize for, to blame someone for, to forgive someone for, to be responsible for, to thank someone for, to keep someone from, to prevent someone from, to stop someone from, to believe in, to be interested in, to take part in, to succeed in, to insist on, to look forward to, to be opposed to, to be accustomed to, to be capable of

The children are excited about leaving on vacation next week.

I apologized to my colleague for submitting the reports late.

We're not accustomed to eating so late.

He kept his friend from learning the truth.

PRACTICE EXERCISE 2: Fill in each blank with the most appropriate verb plus preposition.

insist on, dissuade from, apologize for, concerned about, plan on, thank for, believe in, accustomed to, excited about, complain about

1. Jim's father tried to _____ him _____ buying such an expensive house.
2. Many people _____ praying even if they don't practice a religion.
3. Is it too late to _____ breaking your favorite doll when we were children?
4. Does she _____ having a two-week vacation?
5. I'm sorry. I'm not _____ eating so late at night.
6. Is anyone else _____ graduating from college?
7. If you _____ having your way, I guess I'll let you pay for dinner.
8. The boys are _____ leaving their puppy alone at night.
9. Could you please _____ Mary again _____ fixing such a lovely dinner?
10. It must be tiring for you to hear me _____ having a headache all the time.

TOPIC 3: *Go* Plus Gerunds

The verb *go* can be followed by certain gerunds in idiomatic expressions used to describe some kind of an activity, usually pleasurable or recreational.

go dancing, go swimming, go sailing, go shopping, go camping

The verb *go* can be in any tense, or with modals.

Let's go dancing.

We went swimming yesterday, but we should have gone sailing.

The Parkers have never gone camping before.

PRACTICE EXERCISE 3: Fill in the sentences with *go* plus an appropriate gerund.

ski, sightsee, grocery shop, run, sail, hike, whale watch, camp

1. If you like the snow you can _____.

2. When visiting a new city, most people like to _____ to see new things.

3. If you need food, it's time to _____.

4. A great way to lose weight and get in shape is to _____.

5. Rich and Kathy _____ in their new boat last weekend.

6. Have you ever _____ on the trails in these mountains?

7. If you think whales are interesting, you can _____ in the bay.

8. Should we _____ in the new tent we just bought?

15E PHRASAL VERBS ABOUT RELATIONSHIPS:

Ask out.
To ask someone to go on a date. *I'd really like to ask Susan out. I wonder if she'd go to dinner with me?*

Break up.
To end a relationship. *Jordan was devastated when Suzanne broke up with him.*

Call off.
To end or cancel something, such as a date, a party, a relationship, a project, etc. *Jack is calling off the party for this weekend because his wife is not feeling well.*

Call up.
To make contact with someone by telephone. *Don just called me up to tell me he was going to Boston for a few weeks.*

Dress up.
To wear formal or fancy clothes. *Since we're going to a formal reception we need to dress up.*

Drop by.
To stop and visit someone very briefly. *Can we drop by the Wilsons' before going out to dinner so that I can give them these cookies?*

Fall for.
To become seriously attracted or attached to someone. *Gordan has really fallen for Melissa, but she doesn't seem to know it.*

Fix up.
To try to arrange a romantic relationship between two people. *Hey, Jim, do you think you could fix me up with your sister, Lana?*

Get back together.
To renew a romantic relationship that had ended. *Did you hear that Deb and Gerrick got back together after four months of separation?*

Get together.
To meet with friends in a social setting. *Let's get together this weekend for dinner at The Celadon on Fifth Avenue.*

Go in for.
To enjoy or to like, as in a sport. *Trish really goes in for field hockey.*

Go out.
To go somewhere for a social outing with friends, particularly in the evening and on the weekends. *The whole group of friends went out to dinner and a movie last Friday night.*

Go out with.
To date someone repeatedly, to be in a relationship. *Emily's been going out with Dave for about two months now.*

Make up.
To resolve a conflict, to apologize. *I was really mad at my Mom this weekend, but we made up.*

Split up.
To end a relationship. *Donna and Jim fight all the time—they should just split up.*

15F   REAL ENGLISH

She's a Real Knockout!

It's Friday, *T. G. I. F. day*, and *man* am I *looking forward to* the weekend! I work so hard during the week that when Friday *rolls around* I'm ready to *kick up my heels* and *have a night on the town*. Tonight I've got a *hot date* with a woman that I'm *in love with*. She's a real *knockout*! I'm getting *dressed to kill*, taking her to the best restaurant around, and then we'll go out and *paint the town red*, you know, *the works*! We're really gonna *go all out*. I just know it's gonna *be a blast*!

15G   BRING IT ALL TOGETHER

REVIEW EXERCISE 1: Vocabulary

Match the following vocabulary words with their definitions by placing the letter of the word next to its description.

a. bird-watching; b. bowling; c. bungee jumping; d. camping; e. canoeing; f. hiking; g. horseback riding; h. jogging; i. rock climbing; j. roller-blading; k. sailing; l. skateboarding; m. sightseeing; n. skiing; o. skydiving; p. surfing; q. window-shopping; r. whale watching

1. _____ Jumping from a high place with a cord attached to the body.
2. _____ Visiting interesting places, often while on vacation.
3. _____ Riding in a long, narrow boat and moving with a paddle.
4. _____ Climbing up the sides of high rocks.
5. _____ Riding over the snow on long sticks.
6. _____ Temporarily living in nature and sleeping in a tent.
7. _____ Jumping out of an airplane with a parachute.
8. _____ Riding on boots that have a line of wheels on them.
9. _____ Riding a horse for pleasure.
10. _____ Going out on a boat to watch whales.
11. _____ Rolling a ball to knock over pins.
12. _____ Looking at window displays in stores.

13. _____ Riding on a board that has small wheels attached to it.
14. _____ Observing birds in their natural environments.
15. _____ Riding ocean waves on a board.
16. _____ Walking on long trails, often in the mountains.
17. _____ Riding on a boat powered by the wind.
18. _____ Running at a slow, rhythmic pace for exercise.

REVIEW EXERCISE 2: Verbs Followed by Gerunds

Finish the sentences by choosing an appropriate verb and using its gerund form.

borrow, take, get up, eat, tell, buy, steal, lose

1. The suspect wouldn't admit _____ the car.
2. We can't risk _____ this contract.
3. How do you suggest _____ a new house with no money?
4. Frank doesn't recall _____ money from Greg.
5. Gerry can't stand _____ dinner this late.
6. Have you ever considered _____ the bus to work?
7. Do you mind _____ me your name?
8. We hate _____ so early for work!

REVIEW EXERCISE 3: Verbs Followed by Prepositions and Gerunds

Fill in each of the following blanks with the correct preposition and gerund form of the verb given in parentheses.

1. The police are trying to keep that man (hurt) _____ himself or anyone else.
2. Melissa, will you please forgive me (be) _____ such a fool?
3. Do you want to take part (plan) _____ a party for the boss?
4. Mary's father blamed Jim (cause) _____ the car accident.
5. The judges congratulated Susan (win) _____ the contest.
6. We plan (flying) _____ to London via Reykjavik.
7. Don't worry (get) _____ to the party late.
8. The alarm will prevent thieves (break) _____ into the house.

REVIEW EXERCISE 4: Go Plus Gerunds

Fill in each sentence with *go* plus an appropriate gerund.

1. Jack's an avid fisherman who _____ just about every weekend.
2. I love discos! Let's _____ this Saturday.
3. Do you want to _____ in our new sailboat this weekend?
4. On our first day in Amsterdam we _____ all over the city.
5. There are some great rocks and small cliffs where we could _____.
6. Jerry gets up at 6:00 A.M. every day and _____ for exercise.
7. The new bowling alley is open, so do you want to _____?
8. I _____ on the bike trails along the river last weekend.

REVIEW EXERCISE 5: Phrasal Verbs

Fill in the blanks with the following phrasal verbs.

ask out, broke up, called off, call up, dress up, dropped by, fell for, get back together, get together, going out, going out with, make up, split up

1. We have to _____ for the formal wedding we're going to.
2. Did you hear that Margaret and Dave _____, and he's already dating again!
3. Deb is _____ Ben on a second date to the opera tonight.
4. The Denvers _____ this morning for just a few minutes to say "hello."
5. I'd like to see Denny and Samantha _____, because they were a great couple.
6. Due to the snowstorm, classes have been _____ for the day.
7. Why doesn't Nick _____ her _____ to the movies or dinner?
8. Are we _____ tonight, or are you too tired to do anything?
9. I'll _____ you _____ later tonight if you give me your number.
10. Alexia and Gordon _____ after two years, but they seem to still be friends.
11. If a couple fights in the evening, they should try to _____ before going to bed.
12. Let's _____ sometime and go to a movie or have dinner or something.
13. Cal's been moping around since he _____ a woman who's already married.

15H LISTEN UP!

🎧 Turn on your recording and listen to a short article on new and traditional ways for people to meet one another, make new friends, or find romance. Then answer these questions.

📖

1. Are work, school, and family and friends listed as traditional ways to meet people or less-traditional ways?
2. What type of ad can be put in the newspaper to help meet someone special?
3. Are singles groups organized around specific interests?
4. What types of activities do they organize for people to meet?
5. What is it called when people only have a few minutes to get to know one another and see if there's a spark of interest?
6. What is the name of the "space" where people can talk on the Internet?
7. Is Internet dating seen as very strange by everyone nowadays?

15I WHY DO THEY DO THAT?

Drop by Anytime!

As you've probably noticed, there are many expressions and greetings in English that may seem to mean something other than what they really mean. For example, the most common American greeting is "Hello, how are you?" This isn't actually a question about your state of mind or physical health; it's simply a way to say "hello." So, when you are greeted this way, it would be best not to start talking about your upcoming divorce, or about how broke you are, or about how much your back is hurting you. Equally, it would surprise Americans if you answered that you just got a raise, and your kids are getting high grades, and ... The best response is simply "Fine, thanks, how are you?"

When Americans run into people they haven't seen for a while, or sometimes when they meet new people, it is customary to say something like, "Let's get together sometime." The other person responds by agreeing that they should get together. If this is as far as it goes, it is just a cordial way to say, "See you around." It may not truly be an invitation to get together. It only becomes a concrete plan when something more specific is said, such as for example, "What about this weekend?" or "Give me your number, and I'll give you a call so we can make plans."

A very common American invitation is, "Why don't you drop by sometime?" But be careful! This is by no means an invitation to literally stop by someone's home at any time. Americans are generally open to receiving invited guests in their homes, but not without an invitation for a specific date and time. In fact, arriving at someone's home unannounced is considered rude. So, if you're invited to drop by anytime, make sure you call first and agree on a specific date and time with your host.

Lesson 15: Answer Key

Practice Exercise 1	1. jogging, 2. calling, 3. giving, 4. pulling, 5. watching, 6. studying, 7. smoking, 8. being, 9. traveling, 10. meeting
Practice Exercise 2	1. dissuade ... from, 2. believe in, 3. apologize for, 4. plan on, 5. accustomed to, 6. excited about, 7. insist on, 8. concerned about, 9. thank ... for, 10. complain about
Practice Exercise 3	1. go skiing, 2. go sightseeing, 3. go grocery shopping, 4. go running, 5. went sailing, 6. gone hiking, 7. go whale watching, 8. go camping
Review Exercise 1	1. c, 2. m, 3. e, 4. i, 5. n, 6. d, 7. o, 8. j, 9. g, 10. r, 11. b, 12. q, 13. l, 14. a, 15. p, 16. f, 17. k, 18. h
Review Exercise 2	1. stealing, 2. losing, 3. buying, 4. borrowing, 5. eating, 6. taking, 7. telling, 8. getting up
Review Exercise 3	1. from hurting, 2. for being, 3. in planning, 4. for causing, 5. on / for winning, 6. on flying, 7. about getting, 8. from breaking
Review Exercise 4	1. goes fishing, 2. go dancing, 3. go sailing, 4. went sightseeing, 5. go rock climbing, 6. goes jogging, 7. go bowling, 8. went biking
Review Exercise 5	1. dress up, 2. broke up, 3. going out with, 4. dropped by 5. get back together, 6. called off, 7. ask ... out, 8. going out, 9. call ... up, 10. split up, 11. make up, 12. get together, 13. fell for
Listen Up!	1. Traditional. 2. A personal ad. 3. Yes. 4. Parties, outings or other events. 5. Three-minute dating. 6. A chat room. 7. No.

Lesson 16

Watercooler Conversations

ARE YOU READY FOR THE LESSON?

If you were wondering about American work life, Lesson 16: *Watercooler Conversations* will answer some of your questions. You'll learn about American job satisfaction in *English at Work* and on-the-job romances in *Listen Up!* You will also learn some work-related phrasal verbs with *take* and on-the-job idioms. But there's more. You will also learn:

- Passive and Past Forms of Infinitives and Gerunds
- Passive Infinitives and Gerunds after *need*
- Using Possessives to Modify Gerunds

You'll also be learning what "watercooler conversations" are in *Why Do They Do That?* So let's get started with a pronunciation warm-up in *Say It Clearly!*

16A SAY IT CLEARLY!

🎧 Turn on your recording to practice a very common vowel sound.

16B ENGLISH AT WORK

DIALOGUE: What Do You Think About the New Boss?

Three colleagues at Trenton Enterprises are in the break room discussing their new boss, as well as the rumors that they've heard of layoffs in their company.

🎧

Jim I don't know about the new boss, Bagley. He reminds me too much of Conner—you know, the director they hired right before we got downsized.

Ed Oh, yeah, I remember that guy. He had the same poker face. None of us knew what was happening until it happened. I hope the company didn't hire Bagley to do the same sort of job.

Carol Well, I say we should give him a chance. He seems like a real professional to me.

Terry I don't know, Carol. I keep hearing rumors about more layoffs in other divisions. Why would they suddenly get rid of Ferguson, who was here for years, and hire someone new? I can't afford to lose my job right now.

Ed They didn't get rid of Ferguson. She got a promotion.

Terry More like she was put out to pasture, I think. I really think she's on her way out.

Carol You're such a pessimist. No one is going to lose their job.

Terry That's easy for you to say! You've got something to fall back on, since you used to teach. I'd have to live on unemployment.

Ed Well, look on the bright side. Maybe you'll get a nice severance package and be able to sit around doing nothing for a few months with a salary!

Terry   I'd rather work for that salary and not have to worry about finding a new job in a few months. I've been on unemployment before, and it's no picnic. I could barely make ends meet. I couldn't find a new job for months, and I ended up freelancing. No security, no benefits ...

Carol   Look guys, let's not blow things out of proportion. We don't know that the company's going to lay people off. It's just a rumor. We have no real reason to think that they hired Bagley to clean house. The whole company is doing pretty well, and we know for a fact that our division is up.

Jim   Well, I hope you're right.

The new director, Mr. Bagley, walks into the break room.

Bagley   Is this coffee still drinkable?

Carol   Oh, Mr. Bagley. Good morning.

Bagley   'Morning, Carol ... Jim, Terry ... uh, Ed?

Ed   Yes, that's right.

Bagley   Hey, not bad for my second week on the job, right? Oh, you can call me George. I'd prefer that. "Mr. Bagley" 's too formal. Say, Terry, I'd like to talk to you.

Terry   Sure. What's up?

George   I want to get your feedback on creating some new positions. I'd like to hire some people, but I want to make sure we put them where they'll be most effective. You've been in the division for a while, I think, so you must have insight into how things really flow around here.

Terry   Okay, sure. I'd be happy to talk to you about that.

George   Great. Are you free at around 11:00?

Terry   Sure. See you then.

George leaves.

Ed   Hmmm, new positions. I guess we're not doing so bad after all.

Carol   Yeah, no need to run out and beef up your résumè, Terry!

16C BUILD YOUR VOCABULARY

Benefits. Awards other than a salary paid to an employee, such as medical coverage or vacation leave. *Many prospective employees ask about benefits during a job interview.*

C. E. O. Chief Executive Officer. The company executive with the most decision-making power. *The C. E. O. of Hastings, Inc., James Williams, made the decision to open a new plant in Pittsburgh.*

Conference call. A telephone call that allows several people in different locations to conduct business over the phone at the same time. *After the project manager moved to another city, he started directing business with his employees via conference calls.*

Cubicle. A semi-separated office space defined by partitions that generally rise halfway to the ceiling. *Since Jim's cubicle is next to Sarah's, he can hear how much she talks on the phone.*

Deductions. Money taken out of a paycheck for taxes, insurance, retirement plans, etc.

Every year it seems like there are more and more deductions and less and less money that goes into my bank account.

Fire. To dismiss from a job. *Bob doesn't like to fire people, but he has to do it sometimes because he's the manager.*

Gross wages. The total amount of money earned before taxes and other deductions. *Ralph thought he would be making a lot of money when he heard what his gross wages would be, but unfortunately, he forgot to subtract his deductions.*

Human resources. The department in a company that deals with hiring and firing, as well as employee benefits, needs, and concerns. *If you want to learn about tuition reimbursement for continuing education, just ask human resources.*

Lay off. To dismiss a number of employees due to a reduction in business or need for their services. *I heard the company will be laying people off again later this month because business is so bad.*

Net wages. The amount of money paid to an employee after deductions. *Marion's net wages are high because she has so few deductions.*

Networking. A business information exchange between individuals, groups, or companies, meant to benefit all the parties involved. *Jan is starting her own home business, so she is networking to help her get a client base.*

Personnel. Everyone who works for the same company or employer. A division within the company that is concerned with the personnel, often called "human resources." *You'll need to go to Personnel to get an application.*

Professional. Conforming to good business ethics; a person trained specifically for a job or industry. *Ms. Williams dresses and acts very professionally, so she is often chosen to represent the company.*

Promotion. Advancement from one position to a higher one, usually with a pay increase. *It's about time Bill got a promotion; he's been such a loyal hardworking employee for a long time.*

Recruit. To actively seek new workers. *Jim was sent to several nearby colleges and universities to recruit college graduates.*

Reduction in force. A layoff, the elimination of employee positions. *If you read the financial section of the newspaper, you will see that a lot of companies are experiencing reductions in force.*

Time card. A card that keeps track of the time an employee works. *Remember to fill in your time card, or you may not get paid this month.*

Time clock. A clock that is used to punch an employee's time in and out on a time card. *Ask the manager to sign your time card because the time clock isn't working.*

16D ENGLISH UNDER THE HOOD

TOPIC 1: Passive and Past Forms of Infinitives and Gerunds

You've already seen active infinitives and gerunds, such as *to do* or *doing*. There are also passive infinitives and gerunds, *to be done* or *being done*. As you can see, the passive infinitive is formed with *to be* + past participle: *to be seen, to be taken, to be placed*. It is used with a main verb in the present tense to show an action that has not yet happened.

She wants to be given the opportunity to go to Europe.

I expect to be laid off this month.

If the main verb is in the past, the passive infinitive shows an action that (may have) happened after the action of the main verb.

He hoped to be seen at the beach, but no one was there.

They planned to be driven to the airport early this morning, and they left on time.

One common use of the passive infinitive with *be* as the main verb is to give instructions.

Time cards are to be inserted into the clock.

The pilot light is to be turned on before the gas.

The passive gerund is formed with *being* + past participle: *being seen, being taken, being placed*. The passive gerund can have the same functions as the active gerund—as subject or object.

I appreciate being driven to the airport.

Being stung by a bee is one of her greatest fears.

She mentioned being held up on the freeway.

There are also past forms of infinitives and gerunds. The past infinitive is formed with *to have* + past participle: *to have seen, to have taken, to have placed*. It expresses an action that happened before the time of the main verb.

The weather seems to have changed very recently.

It's so late; the guests are expected to have arrived already.

The past gerund is formed with *having* + past participle: *having seen, having taken, having placed*. It also expresses something that happened before the time of the main verb, and it can serve the same functions as the regular gerund.

As an adult he likes having had the chance to study abroad.

We discussed having received the wrong information yesterday.

Having already been laid off proved to be very helpful to Samantha.

PRACTICE EXERCISE 1: Finish each sentence with the correct form of the verb. First use the passive infinitive.

1. Nobody wants (take) _____ advantage of.
2. This product is (use) _____ sparingly.
3. Tom hopes (call back) _____ for the job that he interviewed for.

Now use the passive gerund.

4. Jack doesn't like (tease) _____ about his height.

5. Maria doesn't enjoy (ask) _____ to make photocopies.
6. Jan and Carol appreciate (help) _____ by their parents.

   Use the past infinitive.

7. Somebody seems (remember) _____ the cake for Marty's retirement.
8. The employees were expected (fill out) _____ their benefits forms by yesterday.
   Use the past gerund.
9. She denies (go) _____ to the boss with her story.
10. Georgia regrets (offer) _____ the job to her brother-in-law.

TOPIC 2: Passive Infinitives and Gerunds after *need*

Both passive infinitives and gerunds can be used after *need*. The implication is that it is either unknown or not important who is expected to perform the action.

This room needs to be cleaned, and I don't care who does it!

My office needs to be painted, but I'm not sure who'll do it.

This room needs cleaning, and I don't care who does it!

My office needs painting, but I'm not sure who'll do it.

The forms above are essentially interchangeable. However, the passive infinitive form is more emphatic than the gerund form. The gerund form often sounds less formal and more conversational. Many speakers limit its use to chores, tasks, or goals— especially household ones—while the passive infinitive is used more widely.

PRACTICE EXERCISE 2: Fill in the blanks with *need* + gerund. Pay attention to the tense of *need*.

1. The light bulb in this lamp (replace) _____.
2. The dog (walk) _____ every night.
3. The garden (weed) _____ before we can plant anything in it.
4. My bike (fix) _____ before I was able to use it again.
5. This tree (water) _____ if it doesn't rain soon.

   Now fill in the blanks with *need* + passive infinitive.

6. These files (move) _____ to the storage room if they're not current.
7. The position (fill) _____ before Monday.
8. We (drop off) _____ at the airport by 6 A.M., but we got there late.
9. The computer program (install) _____ before Monday.
10. This medicine (mix) _____ with water.

TOPIC 3: Using Possessives to Modify Gerunds

A possessive can be used to modify a gerund. If you remember that a gerund is a noun, then this structure will make more sense.

Did you know about our visiting you next week?

I decided what to do about John's meeting my friend.

This construction is also common with past gerunds.

Did you know about her having offered the job to someone?

I was concerned about Henry's not having called us in so long.

It is common to hear an informal form, with an object noun or pronoun instead of the possessive adjective. Note that this is a conversational form, and not a written form. Be careful about when you use it.

We told them about us going on vacation next month.

The interviewer asked about him leaving his last job.

PRACTICE EXERCISE 3: Fill in each blank with the correct gerund and possessive. Use the clues in parentheses.

1. I'm nervous about _____ surgery next week. (my mother, have)

2. The department is excited about _____ new offices. (everyone, get)

3. He was upset about _____ him the position. (his director, not offer)

4. Jack's wife is worried about _____ late. (he, be)

5. Sam often complains about _____ broken. (the photocopier, be)

6. Jordan was practicing the guitar until late at night, and _____ kept us awake. (he, play)

7. _____ a new car was an excellent idea. (they, buy)

8. _____ to human resources angered Julie's coworkers. (she, complain)

16E PHRASAL VERBS WITH *TAKE*

Take after.
To have similar qualities and physical features as an older relative. *Most people think my daughter takes after me; we're both a bit shy.*

Take back.
To reclaim as one's own. *After Cindy gave Jeff the promotion, she wished she could take it back!*

Take down.
To lower something physically. *We'll have to take the curtains down so that we can clean them.*

Take for.
To consider, to hold a particular opinion of someone. *The department really takes the new boss for a fool.*

Take in.
a) To learn; to absorb an idea. *Children take in too much violence on TV.*

b) To give someone a place to stay in a home. *When Marcy's cousin didn't have a place to live, the family took her in.*

Take on.
To add an additional responsibility; to hire. *Another project? You take on too much! You've got to start saying "no."*

Take over.

To assume control or possession of something. *The boss asked me to take over the leadership of the Henley project.*

Take off.

a) To remove something, such as clothing. *Jim took off his jacket and sat down at the conference table.*

b) To depart, as an airplane. *The plane took off five minutes late.*

c) To leave quickly. *When the vandals saw the security guard, they took off into the woods.*

d) To take a vacation, not to go to work for a period of time. *We took off the second week in January and flew to Curaçao.*

Take up.

To begin, as in studies or hobbies. *After Jenny traveled to Morocco she decided to take up Arabic.*

Take up with.

To discuss or confer with someone. *If you're not happy about your salary, you need to take it up with human resources, since they determine salary guidelines.*

16F REAL ENGLISH

I Really Work My Tail Off!

I've really been *swamped* at work lately. I've got a *stack* of papers on my desk, and I'm really *under the gun* to get through them all. My boss has been *breathing down my neck.* It's not like I'm *zoning out* or *surfing the net* all day, either. I really *work my tail off!* There's just too much work to do, and if my company keeps *downsizing,* they may be *in the black,* but all of us employees will *go out of our minds!* You can't *get blood from a stone,* after all. We're *stretched too thin* as it is, and it looks like things will only *get worse before they get any better.* On top of our having too much work, employee morale is *at an all-time low.* Everyone's waiting for the *axe to fall,* wondering if they're next.

I need to *get out of there.* I need a long vacation, time off to *recharge* and put some distance between me and this *cubicle farm.* But who am I kidding? After a vacation there would be an even bigger *pile of work* waiting for me!

16G BRING IT ALL TOGETHER

REVIEW EXERCISE 1: Vocabulary

Match the definition to the vocabulary word.

a) benefits, b) C. E. O., c) conference call, d) cubicle, e) deductions, f) fired, g) gross wages, h) human resources, i) laid off, j) net wages, k) networking, l) personnel, m) professional, n) promotion, o) recruit, p) reduction in force, q) time card, r) time clock

1. _____ A way employees can discuss business while not in the same office.

2. _____ Your total salary.

3. _____ A way to make business connections.

4. _____ A nicer way to say employees are being "laid off."

5. _____ A small semi-private working space in a large shared office.

6. _____ A machine that keeps track of time worked.

7. _____ Another word for "employees."

8. _____ The extras paid for by an employer.

9. _____ An office where an employee can go when he or she has questions or concerns about work.

10. _____ A person in a position that he or she was specifically trained for, usually involving a higher education.

11. _____ A company executive.

12. _____ A raise in position at work, usually involving more responsibility and a higher salary.

13. _____ Means the same thing as "dismissed from a job."

14. _____ Where an employee's time is tracked.

15. _____ A salary after deductions.

16. _____ Means that employees are let go because their positions are eliminated.

17. _____ Money taken out of a salary.

18. _____ To look for new employees.

REVIEW EXERCISE 2: Passive and Past Forms of Infinitives and Gerunds

First fill in each blank with the passive infinitive of the verb given.

1. Don't expect (hire) _____ so quickly.

2. The candidates for the job are waiting (interview) _____ in human resources.

Now use the passive gerund.

3. The applicant doesn't like not (call) _____ back after an interview.

4. The assistants are afraid of (give) _____ too much work.

Now use the past infinitive.

5. We were lucky (take) _____ a shortcut to work today.

6. You seem (find) _____ what you were looking for.

Finally, use the past gerund.

7. We talked about (go) our _____ to the same university.

8. Rob appreciates (get) _____ an honorary degree.

REVIEW EXERCISE 3: Gerunds or Passive Infinitives Following *need*

Use the passive infinitive with *need*.

1. Your medicine (take) _____ with water.

2. Everyone (give) _____ a chance to improve his or her job performance.

3. Your department (tell) _____ about your promotion.

4. These reports (submit) _____ to the marketing department.

Use gerunds with *need.*

5. The filing cabinet (clean) _____ out before we move to the eighth floor.

6. All of the offices (paint) _____ before anyone moves in.

7. The computer (debug) _____, so call I.T.

8. The plants in the reception area (water) _____ once a week.

REVIEW EXERCISE 4: Using Possessives to Modify Gerunds

Fill in each blank with the correct gerund and possessive. Use the clues in parentheses.

1. Yesterday I complained to my colleague about _____ too loud in her cubicle. (she, talk)

2. The director was anxious about _____ its budget. (the department, not meet)

3. Sandy's husband is proud of _____ a promotion. (she, get)

4. I look forward to _____ two weeks off for the holidays. (we, have)

5. Senior management regrets _____ to lay off so many people. (we, have)

6. _____ able to hire a new assistant is becoming a real problem. (we, not be)

7. You must feel excited about _____ published next week! (the book, be)

8. The board of directors was relieved to hear about _____ his resignation. (the chairman, submit)

REVIEW EXERCISE 5: Phrasal Verbs with *take*

take over, take in, took up, take for, take after, take off, take in, take on

1. What time do you expect the plane to _____ ?

2. There's too much information for me to _____ all at once.

3. Could you _____ some printer toner from that high shelf, please?

4. Who's going to _____ as head of sales after Sheila leaves?

5. Ralph _____ Spanish when he was in high school, and he's loved it ever since.

6. You're as stubborn as your father! You really _____ him!

7. Do you think you could _____ an additional project?

8. Do you _____ me _____ a fool?

16H LISTEN UP!

Listen to a short article on on-the-job romances, and then come back and answer the following questions.

1. Give two reasons why on-the-job romances may be on the rise.

2. What do companies encourage that makes on-the-job romances more likely?

3. What are two of the potential problems of on-the-job romances?

4. What is one good thing that can come out of an office romance?

16| WHY DO THEY DO THAT?

WATERCOOLER CONVERSATIONS

The American workplace has become a place for socializing as much as a place for work. During breaks, over lunch, and at the "watercooler," American workers enjoy socializing with their coworkers. Sometimes the discussions are political, or family related, or perhaps they're about the latest TV shows and movies. Gossiping about other coworkers or even the boss might also be common. But since office camaraderie can be cultivated under these circumstances, this could also be a forum for discussing work projects, and because it's a more relaxed environment, creative solutions to work often come up among coworkers in unexpected places. Whatever the case, more company executives say they believe that "watercooler conversations" focus more on business-related matters rather than gossip. Watercooler conversations are good for employees, since everyone needs a little socializing to get them through a day of hard work. And they're also good for business, since they encourage teamwork and creative exchanges of ideas.

Lesson 16: Answer Key

Practice Exercise 1	1. to be taken, 2. to be used, 3. to be called back, 4. being teased, 5. being asked, 6. being helped, 7. to have remembered, 8. to have filled out, 9. having gone, 10. having offered
Practice Exercise 2	1. needs replacing, 2. needs walking, 3. needs weeding, 4. needed fixing, 5. will need watering, 6. need to be moved, 7. needs to be filled, 8. needed to be dropped off, 9. needs to be installed, 10. needs to be mixed
Practice Exercise 3	1. my mother's having, 2. everyone's getting, 3. his director's not offering, 4. his being, 5. the photocopier's being, 6. his playing, 7. Their buying, 8. Her complaining
Review Exercise 1	1. c) conference call, 2. g) gross wages, 3. k) networking, 4. p) reduction in force, 5. d) cubicle, 6. r) time clock, 7. l) personnel, 8. a) benefits, 9. h) human resources, 10. m) professional, 11. b) C. E. O., 12. n) promotion, 13. f) fired, 14. q) time card, 15. j) net wages, 16. i) laid off, 17. e) deductions, 18. o) recruit
Review Exercise 2	1. to be hired, 2. to be interviewed, 3. being called, 4. being given, 5. to have taken, 6. to have found, 7. having gone, 8. having gotten
Review Exercise 3	1. needs to be taken, 2. needs to be given, 3. needs to be told, 4. need to be submitted, 5. needs cleaning, 6. need painting, 7. needs debugging, 8. need watering
Review Exercise 4	1. her talking, 2. the department's not meeting, 3. her getting, 4. our having, 5. our having, 6. Our not being, 7. your book being, 8. the chairman's submitting
Review Exercise 5	1. take off, 2. take in, 3. take down, 4. take over, 5. took up, 6. take after, 7. take on, 8. take ... for
Listen Up!	1. People spend a lot of time together at work; they spend less time socializing outside of work; they are often involved in emotional or exciting projects with their colleagues; the workplace is evenly split between men and women. 2. A team-like atmosphere. 3. Jealousy among coworkers, decreased productivity, bad feeling after a break-up, charges of harassment. 4. Coworkers may find greater job satisfaction.

This Diet May Work for You!

ARE YOU READY FOR THE LESSON?

Are you interested in health and nutrition? If so, then Lesson 17, *This Diet May Work for You!* has some information you'll find interesting. You'll hear friends discussing different diets in *English at Work*. You'll also learn what the new federal dietary guidelines are in *Listen Up!* And you'll learn a few important food customs in *Why Do They Do That?* And there's more. You'll also learn:

• The Real Conditional in the Present and Future
• The Unreal Conditional in the Present and Future
• The Past Unreal Conditional
• Phrasal Verbs about Food

You'll learn some good vocabulary words on the subject of food and eating along with some idioms that are also based on food. So let's get started with consonant clusters in *Say It Clearly!*

17A SAY IT CLEARLY!

Turn on your recording to practice pronouncing consonant clusters that contain the sounds *l* or *r*.

17B ENGLISH AT WORK

Dialogue: What are You Going to Get?

Three friends, Carol, Rosa and Glen, are having lunch together at a restaurant. Listen in as they look at the menu and decide what to order.

Carol   Hmm. So many things look good. What are you going to get, Glen?

Glen   I don't know yet. My doctor says I have high cholesterol, and he's got me on a low-fat diet. So, I have to think about it. Plus I'm trying to get back in shape, so I should stay away from the carbohydrates.

Rosa   You're not calorie-counting, are you?

Glen   No, not yet. But I'm trying to stay away from things that are high in carbs, especially in the evenings.

Carol   So, no bread or pasta for you tonight!

Rosa   Whoa. I'm afraid of what my doctor might say. I'm strictly a meat-and-potatoes kind of gal. I'll probably get the steak sandwich. What about you, Carol?

Carol   Actually I don't eat meat. I'm a vegetarian. And I probably can't have the soup because they usually make soup with chicken or beef broth.

Rosa   Oh, that's right. I forgot that you don't eat meat. But you can't even eat something with chicken broth? It must be hard for you!

Carol   Not really. You get used to it.

Rosa   But isn't it difficult for you to get protein and vitamins and minerals?

Carol   No, not at all. There's actually plenty of protein in vegetable sources, especially things like beans and tofu. And plants are full of vitamins and minerals.

Glen   Yeah, I read somewhere that there are just a few you have to be a bit careful about, like calcium, but you can get everything you need from plants.

Rosa   But don't you miss the flavor and variety of meat and fish?

Glen   Flavor and variety? Ha! I see you've never been to one of Carol's dinner parties! Trust me, if you could cook like she can, you wouldn't miss meat at all.

Carol   That's sweet of you to say, Glen.

Rosa   Okay, I'm game ... So, the next time we get together, why don't you cook for us? I'll bring a dessert.

Glen   And I'll bring the wine.

Carol   Well, sure. I love cooking for people. What should we have?

Rosa   Something vegetarian of course, but really interesting and flavorful.

Glen   And low-fat and low-carb.

Carol   Hmmm, maybe some kind of Thai curry, and we can go easy on the coconut milk and the rice.

Rosa   Oh, wow, that sounds great. I can't wait.

Waiter   So, have you decided?

Carol   We've decided about dinner sometime in the next few weeks, but not about lunch yet.

Glen   Could you give us a few more minutes?

Rosa   Sorry!

Waiter   Sure. I'll be back in a few minutes.

Rosa   Okay, so about dessert ...

Glen   Wait, we haven't figured out appetizers yet!

17C   BUILD YOUR VOCABULARY

A la carte. Food served on its own, an item on the menu that comes alone. *Would you like your enchiladas as an entrée with salad, rice, and beans, or a la carte?*

Appetizers. Starters, food served first and before the main course. *The Greek restaurant has wonderful appetizers.*

Appetizing. Appealing, well presented, having a good taste and smell. *It's difficult to choose because everything on the menu is so appetizing.*

Bitter. Having a harsh taste, one of the four basic tastes that is not sour, sweet, or salty. *Aspirin and unsweetened chocolate are both bitter.*

Bland. Lacking in flavor, with little taste. *This dish needs some salt or something because it's very bland.*

Calorie. A measure of energy in food. *If you want to lose weight, you have to be careful not to take in too many calories a day.*

Carbohydrates. Food sources found in grains and green plants that are primary sources of energy. *Foods that are high in carbohydrates give you energy, but they can also make you gain weight.*

Casserole. A main dish that is baked in the oven. *Each of us is bringing a casserole; I'm bringing lasagna.*

Cocktails. A mixed alcoholic drink, often served with ice. *The office staff often met at the lounge for cocktails on Friday nights.*

Cutlery. Implements used for cutting and eating food; silverware; flatware. *Fine restaurants serve their food with the best cutlery.*

Delicacy. An especially delicious, rare, or expensive food. *The blowfish is considered a delicacy in Japan.*

Diner. A small, inexpensive restaurant that serves American food for breakfast, lunch, and dinner. *Joe always takes Mildred to the diner for a burger and fries after a movie.*

Entrée. The main part of the meal. The main course. *We ate so many appetizers that we have no room for our entrées.*

Grill. To cook on a metal rack or grate over charcoal or gas flames. *How do you feel about grilling some vegetables tonight?*

Ingredients. The components of a recipe or dish. *If we're going to bake a pie, we need to make sure we have all the ingredients first.*

Junk food. Food that has little nutritional value but high fat, sugar, or salt content. *American kids eat too much junk food, and many of them are overweight.*

Leftovers. Food remaining after one meal and saved for another meal. *We've got a lot of leftovers, so maybe we should invite the neighbors to help us finish them off.*

Nutrition. The process by which the body takes in food and uses it for energy. *The path to good nutrition is through eating wholesome food.*

Savory. Palatable, well seasoned, appealing to the taste buds. *Mmmm, try this rice. It's really savory.*

Seasonings. The herbs and spices used to flavor food. *Shall we use fresh basil and oregano for seasonings?*

17D ENGLISH UNDER THE HOOD

TOPIC 1: The Real Conditional in the Present and Future

The real conditional is used to describe a real action that occurs as a result of another action. It can be compared to the following: If X happens, then Y happens. It looks just like the simple present tense, except one clause is introduced with *if.*

If I get up early enough, I eat a big breakfast.

If I finish my homework before dinner, I watch TV afterwards.

The order of the two clauses doesn't matter, but when the *if* clause is first, use a comma after it. When the *if* clause is second, do not use a comma.

If it rains, I take the bus to school.

I take the bus to school if it rains.

The future real conditional describes a future relationship. Notice that the verb in the *if* clause is in the present tense.

If I cut back on fats and carbohydrates, I will lose weight.

If I make cookies, the neighborhood children will come over.

The dog will bark if you make a lot of noise.

PRACTICE EXERCISE 1: Complete the sentences with the verbs in parentheses. First use the present real conditional.

1. If I work too hard, I (get) _____ very tired.
2. If the dog (exercise) _____ enough, she sleeps through the night.
3. A car (wear) _____ out faster if it isn't well cared for.
4. It always rains if you (wash) _____ your car!
5. If Amy sees something she likes on the menu, she (order) _____ it.

Now use the future real conditional.

6. If I have the time, I (go) _____ up to the mountains this weekend.
7. If Mary (go) _____ on a diet, she'll lose ten pounds.
8. We (catch) _____ the train if we arrive at the station on time.
9. You (miss) _____ your favorite TV show if you don't get home on time.
10. If you don't apply to the university on time, you (not get) _____ accepted.

TOPIC 2: The Unreal Conditional in the Present and Future

If the real conditional expresses real actions, then the unreal conditional expresses actions that are untrue, hypothetical, or contrary to fact. Notice that the *if* clause takes a past-tense verb, and the result clause takes a verb with *would*.

If I had the appetite, I would order the all-you-can-eat special.

If I had the time, I would make you a birthday cake.

Susan would quit her job if she had another one.

When using the verb *to be*, it's important to remember to use the form *were* in the *if* clause for both singular and plural.

If I were you, I would go to the movies with Jim.

If that food were more nutritious, I'd eat it too.

PRACTICE EXERCISE 2: Complete each sentence with the correct form of the verb in parentheses.

1. If your parents (be) _____ here, they (understand) _____ the problem better.
2. If Jan (know) _____ how to do it, she (not ask) _____ me.
3. I (buy) _____ a new sofa if I (have) _____ the money.
4. The children (not get) _____ so sick if they (eat) _____ better.

5. If you (make) _____ dinner, I (clean up) _____ the kitchen for you.

6. Everybody (feel) _____ bad if you (want) _____ to move out.

7. If I (be) _____ you, I (buy) _____ a better car.

8. If we (live) _____ in the country, the children (have) _____ a big yard to play in.

9. If you (have) _____ a better job, your salary (be) _____ higher.

10. I (watch) _____ TV if I (have) _____ one.

TOPIC 3: The Past Unreal Conditional

The past unreal conditional also expresses untrue, hypothetical, or contrary-to-fact actions. Use *had* plus a participle in the *if* clause and *would have* plus a past participle in the result clause.

If I had gone to work yesterday, I would have finished the project.

If you had followed your diet, you would have lost weight.

If they hadn't been late, we wouldn't have been angry.

PRACTICE EXERCISE 3: Complete the sentences with the verbs in parentheses.

1. If I (know) _____ you were in town, I (visit) _____ you.

2. The police (investigate) _____ if you (report) _____ the crime.

3. If we (buy) _____ the house last year, we (save) _____ a lot of money.

4. (answer) _____ you _____ the doorbell if it (ring) _____?

5. If the program (end) _____, I (turn off) _____ the TV _____.

6. If it (be) _____ sunny, we (go) _____ to the beach.

7. If you (invite) _____ me, I (go) _____ to the movies with you.

8. I (finish) _____ my homework if I (have) _____ the time.

9. We (ate) _____ by candlelight if the electricity (go) _____ out.

10. Jake (spend) _____ all his money if he (take) _____ the trip with his friends.

17E PHRASAL VERBS ABOUT FOOD

Bolt down.
To eat food very quickly. *Jack only had ten minutes before he had to go to work, so he bolted down his dinner and left.*

Burn off.
To use the energy supplied by food. *Since Gary ate a brownie for dessert at lunch, he jogged in the evening to burn it off.*

Chew up.
To chew food thoroughly before swallowing. *You'll get indigestion if you don't chew up your food first.*

Chop up.
To cut into very small pieces, such as tomatoes, potatoes, nuts, etc. *Could you help me by chopping up some nuts?*

Chow down.
To eat, usually with a group of people in an informal and relaxed setting. *We chow down at 6:30 on the ranch, so don't be late or the food might be gone.*

Come with.
To be included, as in a meal at a restaurant. *The entrée comes with salad and bread or rolls.*

Cut back on.
To decrease, to use less of something, as in a diet or on a budget. *Snacks are expensive and fattening, so we'll need to cut back on them.*

Cut up.
To cut into small pieces. *Please cut up some tomatoes and bell peppers for the salad.*

Do without.
To abstain from, to forgo, as in for religious reasons. *Muslims do without food from sunup to sundown during Ramadan.*

Eat/drink up.
To eat or drink something completely. *Drink up your coffee so we can get out of here.*

Pig out.
To overeat, often at parties or on special occasions. *I really pigged out at Polly's party last night, so I don't feel too hungry right now.*

Throw together.
To combine foods quickly and without following a recipe. *Mark always just throws things together, but his meals are amazing.*

Warm up.
To heat something before eating, such as leftovers. *I don't feel like cooking tonight, so I'll just make a salad and heat up the leftovers from last night.*

Wolf down.
To eat very quickly. *You shouldn't just wolf down such good food! Enjoy it!*

Work off.
To exercise in order to use the calories gained after eating something. *If you eat all of that cake, you'll have to work it off at the gym.*

17F REAL ENGLISH

This Is Your Cup of Tea

Hey, buddy, when were you going to *spill the beans?* Why didn't you tell me you were opening your own restaurant? So now you're going to be the *big cheese.* You'd better be careful because, *in a nutshell,* it won't be easy to *bring home the bacon* anymore. I just hope you won't be jumping *out of the frying pan and into the fire.* New businesses are risky and I hope you won't have to *eat humble pie* someday. But hey, this is really *your cup of tea.* You're a natural businessman, you know how to *use your noodle,* and I've seen that you can be as *cool as a cucumber* even in a tight situation. You aren't a *bad egg,* either. In fact, I think you'll be a success because you're *the cream of the crop.* Well, listen, I'm so glad we could *chew the fat* together for a while. See you around.

17G BRING IT ALL TOGETHER

REVIEW EXERCISE 1: Vocabulary

Across
2. Having little flavor.
5. How the body uses food for energy.
6. Another word for main course.
7. Food that remains after a meal.
11. The body's energy source.
14. An uncommon and expensive food.
16. Tasty and appealing.
17. What's used in a recipe.
18. A main course baked in a pan.

Down
1. A dish chosen and served on its own.
3. Food eaten before the main course.
4. Unhealthy snacks.
8. Add some of these for flavor.
9. Harsh tasting.
10. Food that's stimulating.
12. An inexpensive restaurant that serves a wide range of foods.
13. Knives, forks, and spoons.
15. Mixed drinks.

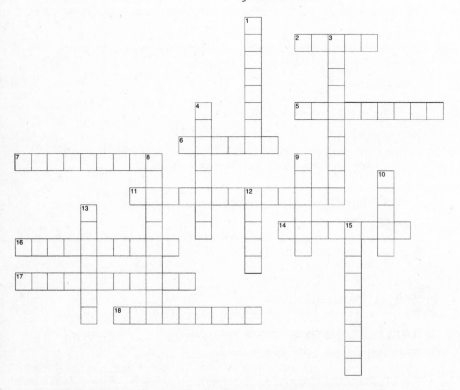

REVIEW EXERCISE 2: The Real Conditional in the Present and Future

Complete the sentences with the verbs in parentheses. First use the present conditional.

1. Students learn best if the teacher (know) _____ his or her subject well.

2. If Mark stops at the store after work, he always (get) _____ something for the kids.

3. You get things very quickly if you (order) _____ them on the Internet.

4. Jenny always takes aspirin if she (have) _____ a headache.

Now use the future conditional.

5. If you don't call me before Tuesday, I (call) _____ you.

6. You'll be hungry if you (not eat) _____ your dinner.

7. Ken will sleep better if he (drink) _____ chamomile tea.

8. If you don't pull the weeds out of the garden, it (become) _____ overgrown.

REVIEW EXERCISE 3   The Unreal Conditional in the Present and Future

Complete the sentences with the verbs in parentheses.

1. If it (rain) _____ more, it (be) _____ greener here.

2. You (be) _____ happy if he (call) _____.

3. The windows (look) _____ nicer if you (clean) _____ them.

4. I (hear) _____ better if you (turn) _____ up the radio.

5. We (visit) _____ you if we (see) _____ your car in front of your house.

6. This town (be) _____ better if we (have) _____ wider streets.

7. If I (be) _____ Jane, I (go) _____ on a diet.

8. If the neighbors (be) _____ quieter, the children (sleep) _____ at night.

REVIEW EXERCISE 4: The Past Unreal Conditional

Complete the sentences with the past unreal conditional forms of the verbs in parentheses.

1. It (be) _____ too late if I (wait) _____ for you to come back.

2. If Janet (tell) _____ the truth, everyone (not be) _____ upset with her.

3. It (rain) _____ by now if the weather report (be) _____ correct.

4. The kids (not feel) _____ sluggish and tired if they (eat) _____ more nutritious food.

5. The dinner (be) _____ ready if my sister (not call) _____.

6. The bookstore (close) _____ before this if it (not be) _____ so busy.

7. I (pay) _____ for the painting by now if I (have) _____ the money.

8. If you (hear) _____ his voice, you (love) _____ it.

REVIEW EXERCISE 5: Phrasal Verbs

Fill in the sentences with the following phrasal verbs:

bolt down, chew up, chop up, chow down, come with, cut back, cut up, do without, pig out, throw together, warm up, work off.

1. At Camp Paloma we _____ at 7:00 P.M., then it's lights out at 10:00 P.M.

2. This recipe calls for pieces of fruit to be _____ and arranged in the pan.

3. This apple skin is really tough, so be sure to _____ it _____ well before you swallow it.

4. During Lent, a lot of people _____ something they really like—for example sweets or coffee—as a gesture of sacrifice.

5. The mashed potatoes got a little cold, so we'll have to _____ them _____ before serving them.

6. Jimmy's always in such a hurry to get to football practice that he _____ _____ his dinner.

7. Does the lasagna _____ anything else, or is it a la carte?

8. I _____ over the holidays, so I gained about five pounds that I've got to lose.

9. For the spaghetti, I'll _____ the tomatoes and onions, and you can look for the seasonings.

10. If you want to lose weight, try to _____ on butter and other fatty products.

11. I'll need to get to the gym to _____ that dinner _____!

12. It's too late to cook. I'll just _____ something _____.

17H LISTEN UP!

🎧 Listen to the information about the Food and Drug Administration dietary guidelines, and then answer these questions.

📖

1. How many food groups are there in the food pyramid?

2. How many food groups were there in the old guidelines?

3. From which food groups should you eat the most servings?

4. From which food groups should you eat the fewest servings?

5. What are some of the diseases that might be prevented by following the food guide pyramid and exercising?

6. Which organization promotes the food guide pyramid?

17I WHY DO THEY DO THAT?

Food Manners

If you've ever been to an American's house for dinner, you may have noticed some differences in attitudes about offering food. In many countries, if you are having a meal with others it is considered good manners to reject food when a second serving is offered. Once rejected, food is offered and rejected several more times before the guest finally consents to having seconds. But when dining in an American home, if food is offered, accept it if you are hungry. If you say "no" and offer the explanation that you've eaten as much as you can, the food may be offered a second time and then not again. Americans are straightforward in their manners and usually mean what they say, so if they are hungry they will accept food when it is offered and will even ask for more if they are still hungry. Although this does not mean that one should eat more than everyone else, it is perfectly acceptable to be honest about your appetite.

Another food custom to be aware of is that when going to a restaurant with friends, payment of a meal may be divided among the members of the group so that each person pays for his or her own meal. This is sometimes called "going Dutch." If one person invites another to dinner, that person usually pays unless specified prior to the meal. If one person pays for the other's meal, then usually the other person offers to pay the next time. It's also common for a group of friends to divide a bill evenly, no matter what each individual ate or drank. This is usually simply called "splitting the bill."

If you are in a restaurant, it is customary to call the waitperson to your table by either holding up one hand, by saying "excuse me" when he or she passes the table, or by catching the eye of the waitperson. Americans consider it very impolite—even downright obnoxious—to snap one's fingers or whistle for the waitperson, so do not rely on this method to get an American's attention no matter how acceptable it is in your own culture! And don't forget that Americans usually tip their waitpersons 15 to 20 percent of the bill. If they do an especially good job, they could receive even more for their efforts.

Lesson 17: Answer Key

Practice Exercise 1
1. get, 2. exercises, 3. wears, 4. wash, 5. orders, 6. will go, 7. goes, 8. will catch, 9. will miss, 10. won't get

Practice Exercise 2
1. were . . . would understand, 2. knew . . . wouldn't ask, 3. would buy . . . had, 4. wouldn't get . . . ate, 5. made . . . would clean up, 6. would feel . . . wanted, 7. were . . . would buy, 8. lived . . . would have, 9. had . . . would be, 10. would watch . . . had

Practice Exercise 3
1. had known . . . would have visited, 2. would have investigated . . . had reported, 3. had bought . . . would have saved, 4. Would . . . have answered . . . had rung, 5. had ended . . . would have turned . . . off, 6. had been . . . would have gone, 7. had invited . . . would have gone, 8. would have finished . . . had had, 9. would have eaten . . . had gone, 10. would have spent . . . had taken

Review Exercise 1

```
                    A
                    L       B L A N D
                    A       P
                    C       P
                    A       E
            J       R   N U T R I T I O N
            U       T   I
            E N T R E E   Z
L E F T O V E R S   K   B   E
            E   F   I   R   S
        C A R B O H Y D R A T E S   P
        C   S   O   I   T   I
        U   S   O   N   D E L I C A C Y
A P P E T I Z I N G   E   R   O   Y
        L   I       R       C
    I N G R E D I E N T S   K
        R   G           T
        Y   C A S S E R O L E
                        A
                        I
                        L
                        S
```

Review Exercise 2
1. knows, 2. gets, 3. order, 4. has, 5. will call, 6. don't eat, 7. drinks, 8. will become

Review Exercise 3
1. rained . . . would be, 2. would be . . . called, 3. would look . . . cleaned, 4. would hear . . . turned, 5. would visit . . . saw, 6. would be . . . had, 7. were . . . would go, 8. were . . . would sleep

Review Exercise 4

1. would have been … had waited, 2. had told … wouldn't have been, 3. would have rained … had been, 4. wouldn't have felt … had eaten, 5. would have been … hadn't called, 6. would have closed … hadn't been, 7. would have paid … had had, 8. had heard … would have loved

Review Exercise 5

1. chow down, 2. cut up, 3. chew … up, 4. do without, 5. warm … up, 6. bolts down, 7. come with, 8. pigged out, 9. chop up, 10. cut back, 11. work … off, 12. throw … together

Listen Up!

1. Six. 2. Four. 3. Bread and cereals. 4. Fats, oils and sweets. 5. Some cancers, high blood pressure, heart disease, diabetes, and strokes. 6. The F. D. A. or the Food and Drug Administration.

Get Into Shape!

ARE YOU READY FOR THE LESSON?

You learned about diet and nutrition in Lesson 17, so you'll learn about health and fitness in Lesson 18: *Get Into Shape!* You'll read a dialogue with a health club fitness expert offering weight loss advice in *English at Work*. And you'll hear a doctor and patient discuss diet and exercise in *Listen Up!* You'll also learn some helpful vocabulary, idioms, and phrasal verbs on health. In *English Under the Hood*, you'll learn:

- Implied Conditionals
- Using *wish* in Conditionals
- Using *would* to Make Wishes

Then in *Why Do They Do That?* you'll learn about why so many Americans are joining fitness clubs. So let's get started with another pronunciation lesson on linking in *Say It Clearly!*

18A SAY IT CLEARLY!

Turn on your recording and listen to *Say It Clearly!* to practice an important kind of linking.

18B ENGLISH AT WORK

Dialogue: Let Us Design a Fitness Program for You!

Elvira is having trouble losing weight, so she is considering joining a fitness club. Right now she's on the phone with Debbie, a rep from the Day and Night Health Club, because she wants to get some information about what they offer. She also wants to get some advice about what kinds of exercise will help her take off the extra pounds. Let's listen.

Debbie	Day and Night Health Club, the club to shape you up! How can I help you?
Elvira	Hi, My name is Elvira Guzmon, and I'm calling because I'm interested in learning what programs you have to offer that will help me take off an extra twenty pounds.
Debbie	Well, you've just taken the best first step, because exercise along with proper diet is known to be the best way to lose weight. What you need to do is come in and we'll design a diet and exercise program that's right for you.
Elvira	Well, actually, I'd like some more information before I take it to the next level.
Debbie	Of course. Well, what we need to do, besides get you on the right diet, is to get you into an exercise program that includes cardio, strength training, and stretching. And we have some good classes for all of these.

Elvira   What is cardio?

Debbie   "Cardio" is short for "cardiovascular exercise," which means you work out hard enough that you increase the oxygen available to your body. That means that your body can work more efficiently. Cardio exercises are aerobic exercises—running, stair climbing, dancing, and the like. Besides helping you control your body fat, cardio along with strength training and the right diet can give you more energy and tone your muscles, which actually slims your body. And . . . oh, there are so many other benefits. You'll be more relaxed, you'll sleep better, and your mood will improve. An exercise program is known to reduce depression and anxiety, too.

Elvira   Wow! That sounds really good. But I'm really out of shape. I don't think I'll be able to do all those exercises.

Debbie   Well, the key is to start out slowly and build your way up. And if you think that you might be uncomfortable in classes, you could always have a personal trainer.

Elvira   What does that mean?

Debbie   A personal trainer is a coach trained to design an exercise program that's right for you and your fitness level. That way you wouldn't do more exercise than you're ready for, you won't hurt yourself, and you won't be discouraged.

Elvira   Hmmm. That sounds good, but it sounds expensive.

Debbie   You might be surprised. Why don't we set up an appointment for you? An interview won't cost you anything.

Elvira   Well, OK. If it doesn't cost anything . . .

Debbie   OK. Let's see, how's Friday?

18C   BUILD YOUR VOCABULARY

Abs. Abdominal muscles, the muscles below one's chest. *Dennis likes to take his shirt off at the beach and show off his abs.*

Addictive. Habit-forming, creating a physical or psychological dependency, as with smoking, alcohol, caffeine, and certain drugs. *It is so hard to quit smoking because nicotine is highly addictive.*

Adrenaline. A chemical substance in the body associated with bursts of speed or strength. *Working out gives Bob an adrenalin rush—he feels full of energy.*

Aerobics. Cardiovascular exercise that involves sustained movement to stimulate the heart. *Sarah goes to the gym for an aerobics class every day at lunch, and she's lost about ten pounds.*

Anxiety. Mental uneasiness, intense worry, fear, or concern. *Minnie suffered debilitating anxiety attacks whenever she thought about flying.*

Braces. Wires placed on the teeth that are tightened slowly in order to straighten the teeth over a period of one and a half to three years. *Rachel's braces not only straightened her teeth, they changed her smile, too.*

Bruise. An injury where the skin is not broken, but blood vessels are ruptured, causing a discoloration of the skin. *Although Ray looks terrible because of all the bruises he received, he really wasn't hurt too badly in the car accident.*

Crutch. A stick-like device that supports a person who cannot walk, usually held under the arms. *Greta had to use crutches to get around after breaking her ankle.*

Duffel Bag. A type of bag typically used to carry athletic clothing or equipment. *Michael always carries his duffel bag to work so he can go to the gym afterwards.*

Holistic. An approach that considers an entire person rather than individual parts, a type of alternative medicine that is concerned with the whole body and mind. *Doug took a holistic approach to getting over his divorce—he started to eat right and work out, he began to meditate, and he decided to take a Spanish class.*

Massage. Using the hands to rub the back or other part of the body for pleasure, relaxation, or physical therapy. *When Rita is stressed she treats herself to a massage.*

Obese. Very overweight. *There has been an increase in the number of obese children in the U.S., which many feel is a result of too much junk food and not enough physical activity.*

Push-up. An exercise performed stomach-down on one's hands and toes that involves pushing oneself up and away from the floor and back again. *Push-ups are a great way to build up chest muscles.*

Rash. A breakout of the skin, usually with small red bumps. *The first symptom of measles is a red rash.*

Sauna. A type of bath in dry heat to cause perspiration. *Valerie loves to sit in the sauna after working out at her gym.*

Sedentary. Not moving much; sitting more than moving. *Mabel's sedentary lifestyle has caused her to gain a lot of weight.*

Sit-ups. Abdominal exercises that involve the repeated movement of lying flat on the floor, then pulling oneself up into a sitting position. *Doing sit-ups is a very effective way to build up abdominal muscles.*

Steam room. A type of bath that uses heat and steam. *If you have sore muscles, it's a great idea to sit in the steam room and relax.*

Treadmill. A machine with a moving belt upon which a person can walk, jog, or run. *The treadmills are the most popular pieces of cardiovascular equipment at the gym.*

Weight lifting/training. Lifting weights in a repeated motion to strengthen and tone the muscles of the arms, chest, shoulders, back, or legs. *Some men like to bulk up their bodies by lifting weights.*

Yoga. A type of physical and spiritual exercise that involves positioning the body in various ways. *Rick has become much more relaxed and calm since he started doing yoga.*

18D ENGLISH UNDER THE HOOD

TOPIC 1: Implied Conditionals

It is possible to imply rather than state the *if* clause in a conditional. In these cases it is common to express the *if* clause using other words. Take a look at the following examples.

We would have gone to the movies last night, but we had a flat tire.

I couldn't have bought a new car without my parents' help.

Drake left the party early; otherwise, he wouldn't have been able to get up in time for work this morning.

PRACTICE EXERCISE 1: Rewrite the following conditional sentences as implied conditionals, following the clues given for each one.

Example: We would have waited for you if we had known you wanted to go.

We would have waited for you but <u>we didn't know you wanted to go.</u>

1. We would have arrived by now if it hadn't been raining.

   We would have arrived by now, but _____.

2. I wouldn't have known about your accident if Rosa hadn't told me.

   Rosa told me about your accident; otherwise, _____.

3. Dan wouldn't have gotten the promotion if you hadn't written such a good recommendation.

   _____ without your recommendation.

4. I never would have found the table I wanted if I hadn't decided to go to the new furniture store.

   I decided to stop at the new furniture store; otherwise_____.

5. We would have bought a new house by now if they weren't so expensive.

   We would have bought a new house by now, but _____.

6. Jane wouldn't have come to visit me last week if you hadn't helped her get here.

   _____ without your help.

   Now try rewriting these sentences with *if* clauses.

7. I wouldn't be here tonight without my wife's help.

8. I ran as fast as I could; otherwise, I wouldn't have made it on time.

9. I would have made you a cup of tea, but I didn't have any.

10. Jerry isn't interested in going out with me; otherwise, he would have called me by now.

TOPIC 2: Using *wish* in Conditionals

Wish expresses a strong desire, especially for conditions to be different from what they actually are. You can use *wish* to express a desire in the present, past, or future.

For a wish about the present, use *wish* + simple past, *could* + base verb or past continuous. Remember to use *were* instead of *was*, though.

I wish I were taller.

I wish I could go to a movie.

I wish I lived in New York.

I wish it weren't snowing.

For a wish about the past, use *wish* + past perfect or *wish* + *could* + *have* + past participle.

I wish I had seen him when he was here.

I wish Tanya could have stayed in this city.

For a wish about the future, use *were* + present participle, *were going to* + base verb, or *could* + base verb.

She wishes she were traveling to China next year.

I wish Delores were going to be there.

I wish I could take a trip next summer.

PRACTICE EXERCISE 2: Write the following sentences using *I wish . . .* and the clues in parentheses.

1. I can't travel to Paris this spring. (could)
2. Ralph will not be in town for the holidays. (be going to)
3. Sarah won't find a new job. (would)
4. You don't put effort into this job. (would)
5. I can't buy a new car this year. (could)
6. It's not going to be sunny this weekend. (be going to)
7. Mabel doesn't live closer. (I wish . . .)
8. My sister doesn't have a big house. (I wish . . .)

TOPIC 3: Using *would* to Make Wishes

Would after *wish* conveys a very strong desire—almost pleading—for something to happen in the future.

I wish you would stop talking during the movie!

Dimitri's boss wishes he would learn to speak English better.

They wish Tom would get here soon so they can go.

PRACTICE EXERCISE 3: Make wishes about the future using *would* using the clues.

1. Answer the phone. I wish you _____.
2. The neighbor's dog keeps barking. I wish the neighbor's dog (stop) _____.
3. Isn't anyone going to be home? I wish someone_____.
4. You need a new computer. _____ get a new computer.
5. We never go anywhere. _____ go somewhere.
6. Your radio is too loud. (turn down) _____ your radio.
7. I don't like the color of this room. I wish you_____ a different color.
8. The dog needs a bath. I wish you_____.

9. It's been too hot lately. _____ cool down.
10. I'm tired. (find) _____ a motel soon.

18E PHRASAL VERBS FOR HEALTH AND FITNESS

Black out.
To lose a part of one's consciousness or memory, to become unconscious. *Ted blacked out after he was hit in the head with the baseball.*

Break out.
To have skin eruptions such as acne, especially on the face. *Sally was embarrassed because she broke out right before the big dance.*

Bring around/to.
To help someone regain consciousness after blacking out. *Here, let's give her these smelling salts to help bring her around.*

Build up.
To increase. *The trainer taught me a series of exercises to build up my upper body.*

Come down with.
To get sick with the flu, a cold, the measles, etc. *I think I must be coming down with a cold because my nose is running and my throat hurts.*

Come to.
To regain consciousness. *Dan came to in the hospital two days after the accident.*

Flare up.
A recurrence of an old health problem. *Every time it rains, my arthritis flares up again.*

Pass out.
To lose consciousness temporarily, to faint. *Mark passes out whenever he sees blood.*

Shape up.
To strengthen and tone the muscles through diet and exercise. *Bill's thinking about joining the army, but if he does he'll have to shape up fast.*

Slim down.
To lose weight or body fat, to become slender. *American women usually think they need to slim down.*

Throw up.
To vomit. *Sonia had morning sickness when she was pregnant and threw up every day.*

Warm up.
To prepare the body for physical activity. *You should always warm up before you do any kind of exercise.*

Waste away.
To gradually lose body mass due to sickness. *Daniel's father wasted away as he got sicker and sicker.*

Wind down.
To slow down in order to gradually finish something. *After doing twenty minutes of aerobics, it's a good idea to wind down and cool off before stopping completely.*

Work out.

To exercise, usually to do an exercise routine. *Meg works out at the gym just about every evening after work.*

Work up to.

To start slowly and build oneself up to being able to do something. *Larry started out doing only twenty-five push-ups, but now he has worked up to one hundred-fifty.*

18F REAL ENGLISH

You're the Picture of Health!

Why, I haven't seen you *in ages!* Oh, my, you look absolutely marvelous. You are positively *glowing . . . the picture of health!* What happened? The last time I saw you, you looked like you were on *your last legs.* I thought it was only a matter of time before you would *meet your maker.* I mean, really, you looked like you were *at death's door.* But look at you now. I mean *my head is* positively *spinning!* You look *as fresh as a daisy, and in the pink!* And you're *on your feet,* too. What did you do? Did you *take it easy?* Has your doctor given you *a clean bill of health?* Whatever happened, *keep it up* because you *look like a million dollars.*

18G BRING IT ALL TOGETHER

REVIEW EXERCISE 1: Vocabulary

Fill in the sentences with one of the following words.

treadmill, adrenaline, sit-ups, anxiety, aerobic, weight lifting, yoga, holistic, sedentary, steam room, crutches, addictive, obese, duffel bag

1. Stress and _____ are two psychological conditions that cause sleeplessness.

2. Erik keeps his gym clothes and toiletries in his _____.

3. Gordon wants to lose fat around his stomach, so he went on a diet and does _____ every day.

4. If you'd like to do something that's both relaxing and physically challenging, why don't you take up _____?

5. It's difficult to stop drinking coffee because caffeine is so _____.

6. Sal used to be very small, but since he started _____ he's become big and muscular.

7. Usually Laura jogs in the park, but if it's raining she jogs on a _____ at the gym.

8. If you prefer a _____ approach to healing, you need to take into consideration all aspects of your physical and mental condition.

9. Eating poorly and leading a _____ lifestyle can cause serious health risks.

10. Many teachers have noticed a sharp increase in the number of _____ children and believe that fitness and nutrition need to be stressed more in school and at home.

11. There's nothing like sitting in a _____ and relaxing your muscles after a hard workout.

12. To lose weight, dietary changes are important, but some kind of _____ exercise is key.

13. I had to walk around on _____ for months after the accident.

14. The body releases _____ to help people flee from dangerous situations.

REVIEW EXERCISE 2: Implied Conditionals

Rewrite the following sentences using *if* clauses.

1. Jan would have gone jogging today, but he hurt his toe.

2. The doctor would have seen you by now, but he had an emergency.

3. My TV is broken; otherwise, I would have seen you on TV last night.

4. Ted wouldn't have finished his law degree without your help.

Now rewrite the following sentences by taking out the *if* clause.

5. Lettie wouldn't have gone to Mexico if she hadn't made enough money.

   Lettie _____ enough money; otherwise, she _____.

6. You would have gotten soaked if you hadn't worn your raincoat.

   _____ but _____.

7. Would you be here today if your parents hadn't met?

   Your parents _____ ; otherwise, you _____.

8. I wouldn't have stayed awake this long if I hadn't taken a nap.

   _____ but I _____ a nap.

REVIEW EXERCISE 3: Using *Wish* in Conditionals

Complete each of the following sentences.

1. It's not my birthday today, but I wish it _____.

2. It doesn't rain very much here, but we wish it _____ more.

3. Dan doesn't go to the gym with his girlfriend, but she wishes he _____ with her once or twice a week.

4. Sam didn't bring his coat, but he wishes he _____ it with him.

5. We can't go out tonight, but I wish we _____ dancing.

6. Larry isn't going to come up to the coast with me, but I wish he _____ with me.

7. Minnie didn't get a doll for Christmas, but she wishes she _____ one.

8. Joyce couldn't get the day off, but she wishes she _____ the day off.

REVIEW EXERCISE 4: Using *would* to Make Wishes

Complete each of the following sentences with the correct form of the verb in parentheses.

1. I wish you _____ soccer with me tomorrow. (come)

2. Paul's mother wishes he _____ to play the violin. (learn)

3. I wish you _____, or we won't make it to the theater on time! (hurry)

4. They wish their vacation to Chile _____ longer. (last)

5. Dana and Bart wish we _____ the new fitness club with them. (join)

6. Jack wishes his girlfriend _____ out to dinner. (go)

7. Danny wishes his physical therapy _____ results more quickly. (show)

8. We all wish you _____ us the truth. (tell)

REVIEW EXERCISE 5: Phrasal Verbs

Complete each of the following sentences with one of these words: *blacked out, breaking out, bring around, coming down with, came to, flare up, passed out, shape up, slim down, threw up, waste away, wind down, work out, work up to.*

1. When I _____, I was lying in a hospital bed, but I don't remember going there.

2. Hugh's memory of the accident is gone; he must have _____.

3. Dell was sick all morning, and then she finally _____.

4. Some fatal diseases are very slow, and patients _____ to skin and bones.

5. Teenagers are often embarrassed about their faces _____.

6. Let's _____ the party and go to bed. It's late.

7. Why don't you try doing some weight lifting if you want to _____?

8. After Sarah passed out, her friends tried slapping her to _____ her _____.

9. Rain often causes many health problems, like arthritis and bursitis, to _____.

10. It takes a while to _____ lifting heavy weights, so start with something light.

11. Paul looks like he might be _____ something, so he should go home and rest.

12. Ben donated too much blood, and when he tried to stand up he almost _____.

13. Many people _____ at this gym in the evenings before going home.

14. The best way to _____ is to change your diet and start to exercise.

18H LISTEN UP!

Listen to a discussion about diet and exercise between a patient and a doctor. Then answer these questions.

1. How has Mark been feeling lately?

2. Did any illnesses or diseases show up on his blood tests?

3. What is Dr. Leads concerned about, anyway?

4. What factors does Dr. Leads explain may contribute to fatigue?

5. What does Dr. Leads ask about Mark's diet?

6. What types of food contain fiber?

7. Did Mark stick to going to the gym?

8. How does Dr. Leads suggest he begin a more active lifestyle?

181 **WHY DO THEY DO THAT?**

The Fitness Craze

One thing that many people from other countries seem to notice about the United States is that there are a lot of overweight people. There's no denying this—many Americans have unhealthy diets, eat too much food, and have relatively sedentary lifestyles. But, strangely enough, visitors from other countries may also notice that the U.S. is home to some of the healthiest and most fitness-conscious people as well. Americans not only love recreational sports and spend time on the weekends playing baseball or swimming or hiking, but many Americans also go to extra pains to build better bodies through diet and exercise. Often this includes a regular fitness routine of cardiovascular exercise and weight training. And this usually means one thing— membership at the local fitness club.

Membership in fitness clubs—usually called "gyms"—is considered essential by many Americans. And there are good reasons for this. Monthly membership fees are low enough to be accessible to most people, and with such a membership comes a variety of opportunities to look better, feel better, stay healthier, and enjoy life more. Gyms offer the basics of weight training and cardiovascular exercise, but they also offer much more. Gym members can often swim, take dance classes, do yoga, or even learn about nutrition. Gyms are often open from very early in the morning until very late at night, and some even offer babysitting or child care facilities. To encourage membership in gyms, many companies in the U.S. offer their employees discounts or even money back for joining. They consider the benefits of gym membership very valuable, and they feel that better physical condition leads to fewer sick days, less money spent on health insurance, and greater productivity. So, it's no wonder that so many people are joining the fitness craze.

Lesson 18: Answer Key

Practice Exercise 1	1. it was raining, 2. I wouldn't have known (about it), 3. Dan wouldn't have gotten the promotion, 4. I never would have found the table I wanted. 5. they're so expensive. 6. Jane wouldn't have come to visit me last week, 7. I wouldn't be here tonight if my wife hadn't helped me. 8. I wouldn't have made it on time if I hadn't run as fast as I could. 9. I would have made you a cup of tea if I had had some. 10. Jerry would have called me by now if he were interested in going out with me.
Practice Exercise 2	1. I wish I could travel to Paris this spring. 2. I wish Ralph were going to be in town for the holidays. 3. I wish Sarah would find a new job. 4. I wish you would put effort into this job. 5. I wish I could buy a new car this year. 6. I wish it were going to be sunny this weekend. 7. I wish Mabel lived closer. 8. I wish my sister had a bigger house.
Practice Exercise 3	1. would answer the phone, 2. would stop barking, 3. were going to be home, 4. I wish you would, 5. I wish we would, 6. I wish you would turn, 7. would paint it, 8. would bathe the dog/give the dog a bath, 9. I wish it would, 10. I wish we would find.
Review Exercise 1	1. anxiety, 2. duffel bag, 3. sit-ups, 4. yoga, 5. addictive, 6. weight lifting, 7. treadmill, 8. holistic, 9. sedentary, 10. obese, 11. steam room, 12. aerobic, 13. crutches, 14. adrenaline
Review Exercise 2	1. Jan would have gone jogging today if he hadn't hurt his toe. 2. The doctor would have seen you by now if he hadn't had an emergency. 3. If my TV hadn't been broken, I would have seen you on TV last night. 4. Ted wouldn't have finished his law degree if you hadn't helped him. 5. made . . . wouldn't have gone to Mexico, 6. You would have gotten soaked . . . you wore your raincoat, 7. met . . . wouldn't be here today, 8. I wouldn't have stayed awake this long . . . I took a nap.

Review Exercise 3	1. were, 2. rained, 3. went, 4. had brought, 5. could go, 6. were going to come, 7. had gotten, 8. could have gotten
Review Exercise 4	1. would play, 2. would learn, 3. would hurry, 4. would last, 5. would join, 6. would go, 7. would show, 8. would tell
Review Exercise 5	1. came to, 2. blacked out, 3. threw up 4. waste away 5. breaking out 6. wind down, 7. shape up, 8. bring . . . around, 9. flare up, 10. work up to, 11. coming down with, 12. passed out, 13. work out, 14. slim down
Listen Up!	1. Tired, exhausted. 2. No. 3. High cholesterol. 4. Stress, sleeping patterns, diet, lack of exercise. 5. If he gets a lot of fiber. 6. Grains, oats, certain cereals, fruits, vegetables. 7. No. 8. Start slowly by walking, climbing stairs, going swimming.

Lesson 19

911, Emergency!

ARE YOU READY FOR THE LESSON?

If you want to know how to handle emergencies in the United States, then you may find Lesson 19: *911, Emergency!* helpful. You'll read a dialogue about visiting the emergency room in *English at Work.* You'll also hear a 911 operator help a woman whose child is choking in *Listen Up!* You'll also be learning some important vocabulary and phrasal verbs related to emergencies. Plus, you'll learn:

• Indirect Objects as Passive Subjects

• The Stative Passive

• Common Uses of *get*

And that's not all. You'll learn some idioms about accidents in *English for the Real World*, and you'll read about H. M. O.'s vs. the family doctor in *Why Do They Do That?* So let's get started by learning about words with silent sounds in *Say It Clearly!*

19A SAY IT CLEARLY!

🎧 Turn on your recording to practice another way to help your pronunciation sound natural.

19B ENGLISH AT WORK

Dialogue: Isn't This an Emergency?

📖 Korin Smiley has brought her 80-year-old mother, Maggie Woods, to the hospital emergency room after Mrs. Woods fell down her front stairs and hurt her shoulder. They have already met with the admitting nurse, who got a wheelchair for Mrs. Woods and told them to wait in the waiting room. They have been waiting to see the doctor for close to forty minutes, and Korin is starting to get irritated.

🎧   Korin   I don't understand. We've been waiting for nearly forty minutes. Isn't this an emergency? I wonder how long accident victims have to wait to see a doctor!

Mrs. Woods   Well . . . I'm sure there are more serious cases here. I'm just in a little pain.

    Korin   Mom, stop being so stoic. You really took a tumble.

Mrs. Woods   I suppose so. It does hurt quite a bit, and I can't move my arm at all. I'm starting to feel a bit odd.

    Korin   Are you going to pass out? That does it! I'm going to go see how much longer we have to wait.

After a few minutes . . .

    Korin   Well, when I told them you were about to pass out, the nurse said she'd take us right in. Here, let me push you back there. You look really pale.

Nurse	Here you are; you can go in room 3. See if you can get her in this gown. The doctor will see you next, Mrs. Woods. Just hold on a little longer.
Korin	OK, Mom.
Mrs. Woods	Ooh, it's hard to move.

A few minutes later . . .

Dr. Barat	Hello, I'm Doctor Barat. What happened here?
Mrs. Woods	Well, I was climbing the stairs to my porch, and I must have lost my balance or something.
Korin	She fell from the fourth or fifth step as far as I can tell. She landed on her shoulder and she's been in a lot of pain. I think she almost passed out in the waiting room.
Dr. Barat	I apologize again for the wait. We've had our hands a bit full this afternoon, after a pretty bad accident involving a few cars. But we don't want you to be in any pain, Mrs. Woods. Let's take a look at that shoulder.
Mrs. Woods	Oh, I feel silly taking your attention away from serious accidents.
Dr. Barat	This is a serious accident. A fall at your age can be serious.
Korin	Do you think it's broken?
Dr. Barat	It might be. Was there anything to break your fall, Mrs. Woods?
Mrs. Woods	Well, there used to be a lovely bush, but we had to get rid of it a few years ago when the foundation needed some work.
Korin	So, no, it was just a grassy patch that she fell on.
Dr. Barat	Yes, a tumble from a height of a few feet, nothing to break your fall . . . It looks like your shoulder might be broken, Mrs. Woods. We'll need to get an X-ray to be sure. If it is broken, we can't put a cast on it; you'll have to keep your arm in a special sling. And I'll give you a prescription for a painkiller. Here. You can take her down to the lab for an X-ray. The pharmacy is right next to the lab, so you can get this prescription filled while you're waiting. Take one immediately, Mrs. Woods. It should last about four hours, and you'll feel much better.
Korin	How often can she take them?
Dr. Barat	One every four hours or so, but no more than six in one day. OK? You'll need to see your regular doctor in a couple of days, and call me here at this number if the pain doesn't get better or if you have any other problems.
Mrs. Wood	Thanks.
Korin	Thank you, Doctor. Just point me in the right direction.
Dr. Barat	Oh, I'll get someone to help you with the wheelchair. The aide will show you where to go.

19C BUILD YOUR VOCABULARY

Atherosclerosis. Buildup of fatty deposits and blood platelets on the wall of the arteries, which forms plaques that slowly block the flow of blood. *A proper diet and exercise regimen can reduce the risk of atherosclerosis.*

Bandage. A strip of fabric used to bind wounds. *Recently scientists have made remarkable improvements in the effectiveness of bandages.*

Bleed. The action of blood exiting the body through a cut or wound. *Many people involved in the traffic accident on I-5 were bleeding and needed medical assistance.*

Cast. A plaster shell used to bind broken bones, often made of plaster that forms a hard shell around the area of the broken bone. *When Arend broke his arm skateboarding he had a plaster cast to keep the bones from moving while they healed.*

Choke. The action resulting from a blockage of the windpipe, such as by food. *If someone chokes, it's important to know the Heimlich maneuver, which forces air from the lungs to dislodge anything caught in the throat.*

C. P. R. Cardiopulmonary resuscitation, a technique used to help restore normal breathing by breathing air into the lungs and by placing pressure on the chest. *C. P. R. can be an effective method of helping restart breathing in victims who need emergency assistance.*

Defibrillator. An electronic device used to restore a normal heartbeat through electric shock. *More and more lives are being saved because places like shopping centers and movie theaters are installing defibrillators.*

Drown. To be suffocated by water filling the lungs. *Lifeguards have a big job every summer rescuing people from drowning in the ocean.*

Fracture. A breaking of bones. *The accident left the driver with several fractures in his legs.*

Heart attack. The result of an insufficient oxygen supply to the heart. *Although heart attacks are a leading cause of death in the United States, many victims wait up to three hours before seeking help for symptoms of a heart attack.*

Intoxication. An abnormal state that is essentially a kind of poisoning caused by an excess of drugs or alcohol. *Intoxication while driving often results in a car accident.*

Paramedics. Workers trained to give emergency medical treatment before or during transportation to a hospital. *When the paramedics arrived, they immediately began performing CPR on the heart attack victim.*

Pulse. A regular throbbing felt in the veins and caused by the contraction of the heart as it pumps blood through the body, especially noticeable in the wrist or neck. *After the man fainted, the paramedics first checked his pulse to be sure it was not too weak.*

Sling. A hanging bandage used to hold the arm in place in case of a broken bone or sprain. *When Ann broke her shoulder, the doctor put her arm in a sling rather than a cast.*

Stroke. An interruption of the blood supply to the brain, resulting in damaged brain tissue. *Mrs. Carpenter had a stroke and lost her ability to speak for a while.*

Tourniquet. A device, usually a bandage, twisted with a stick that cuts off blood supply through constriction and is used to stop heavy bleeding. *The paramedics applied a tourniquet to the patient's arm to temporarily stop the heavy bleeding.*

Wound. An open cut or sore on the skin. *Keep the wound clean and use an antibiotic cream in order to prevent infection.*

19D ENGLISH UNDER THE HOOD

TOPIC 1: Indirect Objects as Passive Subjects

As you've already seen, in a normal passive construction, a direct object becomes a subject.

Active	*The paramedics gave the man CPR.*
Passive	*CPR was given to the man by the paramedics.*

But there's another passive construction in English that allows the indirect object—the receiver of the action—to become a subject.

Indirect Passive	*The man was given CPR by the paramedics.*

Notice that the verb is the same as in a regular passive construction: a form of *to be* and the past participle. And as with the "regular" passive, it is not necessary to introduce the agent with *by*.

A bank teller was handed a note with the words "Give me the money!"

Jerry was shown the way out.

Not all verbs can accept indirect objects as the subject in a passive construction. Here are some of the more common ones: *give, write, hand, read, show, teach, tell, sell, send, lend, pass, ask, charge, offer, introduce.*

PRACTICE EXERCISE 1: Rewrite each sentence as an indirect passive construction.

1. Teena gave the Heimlich to one of the restaurant's guests.
2. Juan taught Denny Mexican cooking.
3. The teacher handed the students their papers.
4. Caroline sends memos to everyone.
5. The teacher read *Moby Dick* to the class.
6. The nurse brought the doctor the patient's chart.
7. Gordon passed the ball to Bill.
8. Didn't your mother tell you to eat your broccoli?
9. Annie sells gold jewelry to her friends.
10. Has the refund department sent me the check yet?

TOPIC 2: The Stative Passive

In the stative passive, an existing state or condition is described with a past participle used as an adjective. The stative passive gives a description of something that is the consequence of an action that happened previously.

When we went out to the car we saw that the window was broken. (Someone had already broken the window before we saw it.)

This dress is made of cotton. (At some point, someone made the dress.)

Don't worry, the dishes are already washed. (I washed them for you an hour ago.)

The agent (expressed with *by* in passive constructions) is never named in the stative passive.

PRACTICE EXERCISE 2: Complete the following sentences using the stative passive of the verbs given in parentheses. Watch out for clues about which tense to use.

1. He (confuse) _____ about the party; it's not tonight, it's next week.
2. It (crowd) _____ in here. Let's go!
3. All the money (spend) _____ on our vacation last month.
4. The milk (spoil) _____, so I threw it away.
5. Larry and Myra (divorce) _____ since last year.
6. Many of the accident victims (burn) _____ rather seriously.
7. Mel, your shirt (button) _____ wrong.
8. I thought you were home since the lights (turn) _____ on.
9. I don't think the computer (plug) _____ in.
10. Francis fell and broke her hip because the floor (wax) _____ earlier that day.

TOPIC 3: Common Uses of *get*

The verb *get* is used in many different ways in English. Its most common meaning is "to receive" or "to obtain," and it is often used with nouns.

The shopping center got a portable defibrillator for emergency use.

Can you get milk and bread at the store on your way home tonight?

If *get* is used with certain adjectives, it means "to become."

Frank got very pale right before he passed out.

The sky got terribly dark and it started to pour.

Get can be used with an infinitive to mean "have the opportunity" or "have the chance" to do something.

Jack wasn't hurt after his accident, but he was excited that he got to ride in an ambulance.

With the kids away at camp, John and Sarah will get to spend time alone.

Get can be used instead of *be* with a past participle in passive constructions, especially in spoken English.

My new pants got torn! (My new pants were torn!)

Jim got arrested for drunk driving. (Jim was arrested for drunk driving.)

Get can also be used with past participles to suggest "taking an action through to completion," or "achieving a certain result."

We'll get all our work done before it's time to go home.

You'd better get this room cleaned up before dinner, kids!

Another very common use of *get* is in what's called the "causative." You can use *get* with an infinitive to show that someone caused an action to happen through convincing or persuasion, rather than doing that action him or herself.

The kids got their parents to take them to the amusement park after a lot of begging.

I couldn't do it alone, so I got my friends to come help me paint.

PRACTICE EXERCISE 3: Use an appropriate form of get.

1. Dad said we _____ to go to a movie this coming Saturday.
2. Jane usually _____ tired after a long hard day at work.
3. Rosie _____ taken to the hospital after she fell and broke her arm.
4. Elena finally _____ her husband to buy them a new car.
5. I hope you haven't _____ too sleepy to drive home tonight!
6. Gretchen and Steve _____ married last June.
7. Jenny _____ to stay at her grandmother's house for a whole week.
8. The class _____ the teacher to postpone the test for a few days.
9. Ed drank too much last night and _____ too drunk to drive home.
10. I _____ worried when you don't _____ home on time.

19E PHRASAL VERBS RELATED TO EMERGENCIES

Check in/into.
To be registered and admitted into a hotel, conference, hospital, etc. *Everyone must check in when waiting for services in the emergency room.*

Check out.
To leave a place where one has been admitted through registration. *Upon leaving the hospital you are required to check out.*

Check up on.
To look at the progress of someone or something. *The doctor goes around and checks up on his patients in the hospital at least once a day.*

Cover up.
To hide; to put a blanket over someone. *When someone is in shock it is a good idea to cover them up to keep them warm.*

Fall down.
To trip over something or lose one's balance and land on the ground. *Nat fell down and broke his arm a few days ago.*

Keep up.
To continue doing something at the same speed or level without interruption. *If you don't keep up your physical therapy, you may never regain the full use of your arm.*

Keep on.
To continue to do something. *If you keep on drinking alcohol so often, you're going to have problems.*

Knock out.
To cause someone to lose consciousness. *Rocky was knocked out by the world-champion boxer in the first round.*

Pass out.
To lose consciousness. *Dmitiri passed out when the ball hit him on the head.*

Rest up.
To regain energy by relaxing. *Be sure to rest up before the marathon.*

Run over.
To hit someone with a car, truck, or other moving vehicle. *The old woman was run over by a taxi as she tried to cross the street.*

Slow down.
To decrease speed or activity. *The doctor says I have to slow down and relax a little more.*

Take care of.
To administer care for someone who is sick. *When Mr. Lange got sick, Mrs. Lange took care of him for several years before he died.*

Wear off.
To gradually lose potency; to gradually subside. *After getting her teeth worked on, Bev likes to drink a cup of coffee to help the novocaine wear off faster.*

19F REAL ENGLISH

Keep Your Cool!

Have you ever been in a car accident? Everything seems to happen in *slow motion*. Your *life passes before your eyes* when you think you're *at death's door* and *not long for this world*. When it's *all over*, it's really hard to *keep your cool* because that accident was just *too close for comfort*. You're probably *in shock* so you're kind of *out of it* even if you don't *pass out* from fright. So *take my advice*, if you want *to live to see tomorrow, buckle up* and slow down next time you're on the highway, or it might not be a *close call*.

19G BRING IT ALL TOGETHER

REVIEW EXERCISE 1: Vocabulary

Complete each of the following sentences with one of these words: *atherosclerosis, bandages, bleeding, cast, choking, C. P. R., defibrillator, drowned, fractured, heart attack, intoxication, paramedics, pulse, sling, stroke, tourniquet, wound.*

1. When Alison was pulled out of the pool, the lifeguard began _____ immediately.
2. Jack fell during a basketball game and ended up with a _____ finger.
3. Mel's arm was so badly burned that it became an ugly open _____.
4. To stop or slow the blood flow, apply a _____ to the wound.
5. Mr. Ramirez had a massive _____. He's in the hospital, but he may not survive.

6. It looks like you nicked yourself shaving. Your face is cut and _____

7. Remember to use a _____ to keep your arm from moving too much.

8. Even though the paramedics used a _____ on the accident victim, they were unable to get his heart working again, so he did not survive.

9. When you exercise hard, check your _____ every few minutes to be sure you are not overworking.

10. Someone call 911. This man is _____ on something he ate.

11. More traffic accidents are caused by _____ than by anything else.

12. You probably won't do much dancing with your leg in a _____.

13. You can lower your risk of _____ by changing your diet and exercising.

14. A _____ victim can be left with the inability to speak, read and write, or walk.

15. Did you hear about the child that _____ but came back to life several hours later?

16. When the _____ arrived, they quickly administered some basic first aid and brought Mrs. Zhou out of her swoon.

17. Every household should have several varieties of _____ available in case of an accident.

REVIEW EXERCISE 2: Indirect Objects as Passive Subjects

Make the indirect object the passive subject in the following sentences. Do not use the agent.

1. Jim lent me his car for a few days.

2. Hedy passed a note to Reg during class.

3. The paramedics asked the woman many questions to keep her conscious.

4. The parking lot charges customers a fee for parking.

5. My boss offered me a better position.

6. Dana introduced her mother to Erik.

7. Tanya gave Letty a dog for her birthday.

8. Joe read the children a story every night.

REVIEW EXERCISE 3: The Stative Passive

Use the stative passive of the verbs given in each sentence.

1. A lot of nice houses (burn) _____ to the ground in the last big fire.

2. Did you know that your dress (tear) _____?

3. The meeting (schedule) _____ for 3:00 PM today, but we had to change the time.

4. The clothes (fold) _____, so you don't have to do it.

5. The needle (stick) _____ on the compass; I think it's broken.

6. Hank's leg (break) _____ before his vacation even began.

7. This carpet (soil) _____, so we need to get it cleaned.

8. I hope you know how to fix drains because the kitchen sink (plug up) _____.

REVIEW EXERCISE 4: Common Uses of *get*

Rewrite the following sentences using *get*. Change the underlined portions.

1. You'd better <u>make yourself</u> busy, because the boss is coming.
2. I called you as soon as I <u>finished</u> with my dinner.
3. No one <u>has the chance</u> to go swimming this year because of dangerous tides.
4. Everyone <u>will have an opportunity</u> to try out the new computer.
5. The nurse <u>took</u> a needle from the cabinet and gave the patient an injection.
6. Drake <u>returned</u> home after four days in the hospital.
7. I can't believe he <u>persuaded</u> me to loan him some money!
8. Joan <u>becomes</u> tired easily since she's on chemotherapy.

REVIEW EXERCISE 5: Phrasal Verbs

Complete each of the following sentences with one of these words: *check into, check out, check up on, cover up, fell down, keep up, keep on, knocked out, rest up, run over, slow down, take care of, wear off.*

1. I'm waiting for the doctor to release me so that I can _____ of here.
2. I _____ at work and broke my leg.
3. The anesthetic is starting to _____, and I'm starting to feel some pain.
4. If you don't _____ your exercise program you'll gain some weight.
5. It always takes a long time to _____ the hospital when you go to the emergency room first.
6. Everyone needs to _____ and relax in order to release tension.
7. Be sure to _____ over the holidays so that you can feel better soon.
8. If you need me to, I can _____ you while you're recuperating from surgery.
9. We'll need to hire a nurse to _____ Mother when she gets home from the hospital.
10. You need to be very careful with your medications in order to _____ your health.
11. A softball hit your son on the head and _____ him _____.
12. Nurse, could you please _____ my feet? They're getting cold.
13. Did you hear that the neighbor got _____ and is in the emergency room right now?

19H LISTEN UP!

Turn on your recording to listen to a 911 call. Then answer the following questions.

1. What is wrong with the woman's son?
2. What caused this?
3. Is the boy unconscious?
4. Who does the 911 operator send to the woman?
5. What does the operator tell the woman how to do?

191 WHY DO THEY DO THAT?

HMOs vs. the Family Doctor

Health care in the U.S. has changed dramatically over the last 20 or 30 years. Perhaps the most notable change has been the steadily rising costs associated with it, and these costs have prompted a number of other changes. Years ago, for example, people went to their family doctors for just about everything. Sometimes the family doctor would even make house calls, which meant that if a patient was too sick to go to the doctor, the doctor went to the patient's home. But nowadays, except for in some very rural areas, doctors no longer make house calls. And in fact, the idea of a "family doctor" isn't the norm for most people, as most Americans have to rely on their jobs to provide them with health insurance to cover the costs of even basic healthcare. Therefore, the family doctor has in many cases been replaced by a healthcare provider who participates in the particular medical plan offered by a person's employer.

Most insured Americans are covered by what's called an HMO, or a health maintenance organization. Companies contract with HMOs to organize and control medical treatment for their employees, and most HMOs have approved lists of doctors who participate in their medical plans. So, a person who works for Company X will have his or her medical care managed by HMO Y, and that person will be able to choose Doctor Z from a list maintained by the HMO. Does that sound a bit, well, cold and impersonal? Many people feel that it is, especially when compared to the family doctor of years ago, who treated every member of a family, and perhaps even several generations in a family, with familiarity and personal warmth.

It's probably safest to say that there are good things and bad things when it comes to HMOs. On the bad side, there's a lot of paperwork, there's a narrower range of choice among doctors, doctors' visits are often cold and impersonal, and medical procedures are subject to approval by the HMO for full coverage — and that approval process seems at times to value cost cutting above high-quality healthcare. But on the good side, HMOs are one way to help control the soaring costs of medical care in the U.S., they offer companies a cost-conscious way of providing health coverage to their employees, and in the end, their cost-consciousness may help cut down on unnecessary medical procedures, which in the absence of an HMO would have cost the individual patient a great deal of money. In the end there's no easy way to compare today's time of HMOs to the time of the family doctor; too many factors have changed in healthcare and in American society in general. But there's no denying that many Americans are less than satisfied with healthcare in the United States, and perhaps a better solution to the problem of meeting such basic needs of American citizens has yet to emerge.

Lesson 19: Answer Key

Practice Exercise 1
1. One of the restaurant's guests was given the Heimlich (by Teena). 2. Denny was taught Mexican cooking (by Juan). 3. The students were handed their papers (by the teacher). 4. Everyone is sent memos (by Caroline). 5. The class was read *Moby Dick* (by the teacher). 6. The doctor was brought the patient's chart (by the nurse). 7. Bill was passed the ball (by Gordon). 8. Weren't you told to eat your broccoli (by your mother)? 9. Her friends are sold gold jewelry (by Annie). 10. Have I been sent the check (by the the refund department) yet?

Practice Exercise 2
1. is confused, 2. is crowded, 3. was spent, 4. was spoiled, 5. have been divorced, 6. were/are burned, 7. is buttoned, 8. were turned, 9. is plugged, 10. had been waxed

Practice Exercise 3	1. get/will get, 2. gets, 3. got, 4. got, 5. gotten, 6. got, 7. gets, 8. got, 9. got, 10. get … get
Review Exercise 1	1. C. P. R., 2. fractured, 3. wound, 4. tourniquet, 5. heart attack, 6. bleeding, 7. sling, 8. defibrillator, 9. pulse, 10. choking, 11. intoxication, 12. cast, 13.,atherosclerosis, 14. stroke, 15. drowned, 16. paramedics, 17. bandages
Review Exercise 2	1. I was lent Jim's car for a few days. 2. Reg was passed a note during class. 3. The woman was asked many questions to keep her conscious. 4. Customers are charged a fee for parking. 5. I was offered a better position. 6. Erik was introduced to Dana's mother. 7. Letty was given a dog for her birthday. 8. The children are read a story every night.
Review Exercise 3	1. were burned, 2.was/is torn, 3.was/had been scheduled, 4.are/have been folded, 5. is stuck, 6. was/had been broken, 7. is soiled, 8. is plugged up
Review Exercise 4	1. You'd better get busy, because the boss is coming. 2. I called you as soon as I got done with my dinner. 3. No one gets to go swimming this year because of dangerous tides. 4. Everyone will get to try out the new computer. 5. The nurse got a needle from the cabinet and gave the patient an injection. 6. Drake got home after four days in the hospital. 7. I can't believe he got me to loan him some money! 8. Joan gets tired easily since she's on chemotherapy.
Review Exercise 5	1. check out, 2 .fell down, 3. wear off, 4. keep on, 5. check into, 6. slow down, 7. rest up, 8. check up on, 9. take care of, 10. keep up, 11. knocked … out, 12. cover up, 13. run over
Listen Up!	1. He's choking. 2. A piece of candy. 3. No. 4. The paramedics. 5. The Heimlich maneuver.

Lesson 20

Just Shooting the Breeze

ARE YOU READY FOR THE LESSON?

If you're interested in learning about how Americans interact with friends and neighbors, then Lesson 20: *Just Shooting the Breeze* will help you know more. You'll hear a dialogue between two neighbors discussing a block party, and you'll also hear a story about how communities come together to help one another. The vocabulary in this lesson is about friends, acquaintances, and community. Here are a few more topics in this lesson:

• Participial adjectives
• Verbs of perception
• Reflexive pronouns
• Phrasal verbs with *get*
• Idioms about friendship and dating

In another reading, *Why Do They Do That?*, you'll read about the significance of facial expressions and body language. Now let's get started by learning about English intonation in *Say It Clearly!*

20A SAY IT CLEARLY!

One of the most important elements in the natural pronunciation of any language is its intonation. Turn on your recording to practice some intonation patterns typical of American English.

20B ENGLISH AT WORK

Dialogue: A Block Party

Let's listen as Gabby calls Annie, her neighbor, on the phone to talk about an upcoming block party that's been organized in their neighborhood.

Annie   Hello?
Gabby   Hi, Annie. This is Gabby. How are you?
Annie   Gabby! Hi! I'm doing well. What's going on? I haven't talked to you for ages.
Gabby   I know. I've just been so busy with my kids.
Annie   I know what you mean. How's Lillie doing?
Gabby   Oh, she's doing great. She's applying for college right now. She's really been pushing herself. How about Trent?
Annie   The same. He just took his SATs, so he's looking around right now. He's not sure whether he wants to stay close by for college or go far away.
Gabby   Yeah, that's always a big question. Listen, Annie. We're going to have a block party on the 23rd; can you come?
Annie   Oh, I'd love to. What should I bring? Where is it?

Gabby   It's going to be in the park. Yeah, it's a potluck, so you can bring a main dish or salad, if you like.

Annie   Oh, I have a great salad recipe that I made up myself. I'll bring salad.

Gabby   Good. I'm going to bring homemade bread. But I'm not making it myself. My mother's making it for me.

Annie   So are we going to do anything else besides eat and socialize?

Gabby   Yeah. We've got some games planned. You know, things like a three-legged race, horseshoes, Frisbee throwing, maybe we'll get a baseball game going, stuff like that.

Annie   A three-legged race? I haven't done that since high school. But it all sounds so fun. What a great way to get to know some of the neighbors we don't already know!

Gabby   And we're going to have a no-host coffee bar.

Annie   A no-host coffee bar? Oh, I love it!

Gabby   I know. Isn't it a great idea? Oh, and there's a band, a salsa band, so there'll be some dancing.

Annie   A salsa band? I don't know how to dance. I'll just watch everybody else dance.

Gabby   Don't worry. We got a teacher to come and teach us. We're also going to have a karaoke machine, so we can listen to people sing. Do you like to sing?

Annie   Oh, no. I can't carry a note at all. I'm a pretty boring singer. What about you? Can you sing?

Gabby   I don't think so, but other people say I can. Maybe the karaoke machine will help me see if I really can . . . Oh, I just remembered. There's going to be someone photographing everybody so we can buy pictures if we want to. It should be a good time all around. I think we're going to enjoy ourselves a lot.

Annie   I love this neighborhood! It's such a fun place to live.

20C BUILD YOUR VOCABULARY

Acquaintance A person who is known to you but who is not close enough to be a friend. *Nora and Annie work together but are not close enough to be friends; they are only acquaintances.*

Block party. A party organized by and for people who live on the same block or in the same community. *It's Tina and Larry's turn to put together the block party this year.*

City Council. A body of elected officials who help govern a city. *John Hartley is running for city council as someone who wants to improve neighborhoods.*

Community. A group of people who share some aspect of their identities; a neighborhood, a religion, an ethnicity, etc. *There is a large Ethiopian community in this city, so there are a lot of great Ethiopian restaurants.*

Confidant. An intimate and trustworthy friend to share secrets with. *Jenny always found solace in talking to her best friend and confidant.*

Congenial. Pleasant, agreeable, compatible. *The relationship between the Drummond sisters was congenial.*

Courtesy. Considerate behavior, good manners, politeness. *It's important to show courtesy and call before visiting a friend or neighbor.*

Dinner party. A party among friends, coworkers, or other associates that revolves around dinner, usually cooked by a host at his or her home. *Eleanor loves giving formal dinner parties because she likes to show off all her nice crystal, china, and silverware.*

Fair-weather friend. Someone who is friendly when things are going well but who does not show friendship during difficult times. *Andy was a great friend until I started having financial problems-now I never see this fair-weather friend.*

Familiarity. Friendship, a feeling of knowing someone well, lack of formality in a relationship. *The feeling of familiarity is one reason Sara and Jenny have remained close friends for so many years.*

Fraternize. To mingle as brothers, to associate or interact closely with others. *Lately, Dale's been fraternizing with the kids at the local YMCA.*

Kindred. A group of people who are related, or who have a similar nature. *People who love art are kindred spirits, because they understand one another so well.*

Neighborhood watch. An organization set up in neighborhoods where neighbors watch over one another's property by being alert to potential thieves. *Because of the neighborhood watch program, a burglary was averted when the next-door neighbor called the police.*

Neighborly. Friendly, helpful, congenial, amicable. *The people in small towns are very neighborly, bringing cookies or casseroles to welcome new people into town.*

Newcomer. Someone who is new to an area. *Since they are newcomers, Paul and Brenda don't know many people in town.*

Potluck. A party where everyone brings a dish of food to share with everyone else. *Block parties are usually potlucks because it would be too expensive for one person to feed everyone.*

Sociable. Enjoying being with and interacting with people. *Tom's really sociable tonight; he's been talking to everybody.*

Street fair. A neighborhood party that usually involves live music, food, and crafts for sale. *The Adams Avenue street fairs have become a tradition every spring and fall.*

20D ENGLISH UNDER THE HOOD

TOPIC 1: Participial Adjectives

Both the present participle and the past participle can be used as adjectives, but they have different meanings. The present participle, which is an -*ing* form of the verb, is active and describes an action that is happening during the time of the sentence.

There is a wonderful smell of baking bread in the air. (The bread is baking at this moment.)

A very damaging storm passed through the area. (It caused a lot of damage.)

I love the smell of brewing coffee. (I love to smell coffee while it is brewing.)

The past participle, which is the *-ed* form of regular verbs but may also be an irregular form, is a passive adjective that describes something that happened to the noun it modifies.

Samantha brought freshly baked bread to the dinner party. (She, or someone else, had baked the bread before the party.)

We saw many damaged houses after the storm. (The houses had been damaged by the storm.)

There's some freshly brewed coffee for you. (The coffee has been brewed already.)

PRACTICE EXERCISE 1: Complete each sentence with the correct participial adjective of the verb given in parentheses.

1. This is a really _____ movie. (bore)
2. Jerry looked really _____ at the party last night. (bore)
3. The elevator was very _____ this morning. (crowd)
4. There were _____ cups all over the floor after the party. (break)
5. The neighbors are playing loud and _____ music. (annoy)
6. We'll need to hire someone to fix the _____ wall. (crack)
7. My friends told some _____ jokes. (embarrass)
8. My little sister was always a _____ child. (frighten)
9. All the runners were absolutely _____ after the marathon. (exhaust)
10. Climbing the mountain was a _____ adventure. (thrill)

TOPIC 2: Verbs of Perception

Verbs that describe how a person perceives or senses actions or events are called "verbs of perception." The most common ones are: *see, look at, watch, observe, notice, hear, listen to, feel, taste, smell.*

They can be followed either by the base form of a verb or the *-ing* form. As a general rule of thumb, it's more natural to use the *-ing* form to emphasize something that is or was happening during the time of perception, or to emphasize that the action is a process and lasts over a period of time. The base verb form, on the other hand, is often used to make a general statement or to show that the action happens once or quickly. However, in practice, these forms are often interchangeable.

I saw John riding his bicycle to work the other day.

I always see John ride his bicycle to work in the morning.

Mary listened to my friends singing in a karaoke bar last night.

She had never listened to anyone sing so poorly.

Sarah feels something crawling across her foot.

Sarah hates to feel something crawl across her foot.

Also, in general, only the *-ing* form is used with *smell*.

Do you smell something burning?

PRACTICE EXERCISE 2: Complete each sentence with the verb in parentheses. Follow the general rule of thumb to choose which form to use.

1. Did you see anyone (photograph) _____ people at the event?
2. Marilyn noticed Jake (talk) _____ to another woman.
3. The teacher always watches her students (take) _____ the exam.
4. Look at everyone (dance) _____!
5. I have never observed anyone (work) _____ on the house.
6. Does anyone hear the birds (sing) _____?
7. We always listen to reporters (interview) _____ the president.
8. I feel the cool wind (blow) _____ across my face.
9. Mmmm. I smell cookies (bake) _____ in the oven.
10. Tory tasted the wine (get) _____ more and more bitter.

TOPIC 3: Reflexive Pronouns

Reflexive pronouns are pronouns that refer back to the subject rather than another direct object. They are: *myself, yourself, himself, herself, itself, ourselves, yourselves, themselves.* They're used to show that the doer of the action does that action to him or herself.

Tom prepared himself to ask his boss for a raise.

The surgeon steadied himself to begin the long surgery.

They can also be used to emphasize that the subject is doing something unusual or unexpected, or that the subject did something alone and without help.

I made this dress myself instead of buying it at the store.

Her housekeeper was sick, so Linda cleaned the house herself.

To emphasize that the subject performed an action alone, you can add *by* in front of the reflexive pronoun.

Nobody was home, so I ate dinner by myself.

Jenny likes to go to the movies by herself.

PRACTICE EXERCISE 3: Finish each sentence by using the correct reflexive pronoun. Use *by* when the context calls for it.

1. Jean watched _____ in the windows as she walked down the street.
2. I enjoy _____ more when it's not so hot and humid.
3. She lived _____ for about five years before she got married.
4. Mindy and Ted bought _____ a new car.
5. You don't have any reason to feel sorry for _____.
6. I made and ate breakfast _____; no one else was awake.
7. Ralph taught _____ Spanish with books and CDs.
8. I can't believe you and Daryl built this cabin _____! No one helped you?

9. We should pat _____ on the back for doing such a great job.

10. The deer looks like it hurt _____.

20E PHRASAL VERBS WITH *GET*:

Get after.
To reprimand. *Molly got after her son because he left the car windows open overnight.*

Get along with.
To have a good relationship with another person. *Marta's children seem to get along with each other better than most brothers and sisters.*

Get around.
To go to many places, to travel from place to place. *Even though Shauna doesn't have a car, she still gets around easily by public transportation.*

Get at.
To suggest a meaning, to allude to. *I don't understand what you're getting at. Can you explain it a little better?*

Get away with.
To avoid punishment. *My brother used to get away with everything because he knew how to make everyone else look guilty.*

Get back.
To return. *When did you get back from your vacation?*

Get back at.
To repay mistreatment. *Tina got back at her sister for breaking her new doll.*

Get back to.
To come back into contact with a person about a particular issue. *When can you get back to me about the question I asked you?*

Get by.
To manage financially. *Young married couples usually find that it's difficult to get by, even when both work.*

Get in.
To enter, to return to one's home. *Jack is tired because he got in so late last night.*

Get into.
To become involved or interested in something. *Jessica really got into reading after she read* Gone with the Wind.

Get off.

a) To leave a train, bus, or airplane. *Mrs. Gareth gets off at First Avenue and 34th Street.*

b) To stop working. *We get off at 5:30, so I should be home by 6:00.*

c) To rationalize or justify a particular behavior, used most often with "Where . . . ?" *Where do you get off telling him that's he's dishonest, when you lie so much?*

d) To derive pleasure or excitement from, sometimes in a sexual sense, but not always. *Everyone in the department thinks that the new boss really gets off on making people feel little and stupid.*

Get on with.
To resume. *Meredith decided she had to get on with her life, even though she was still grieving over the loss of her husband.*

Get out.
To go somewhere for pleasure, not to stay at home. *It's time for Mary to start getting out more. She's been staying home too much.*

Get over.
To overcome feelings for another, to resolve; to recover from an illness. *I know, Mary really needs to get over Barry and move on with her life.*

Get through.
To overcome difficult times. *It's difficult to imagine how people got through the Great Depression.*

Get through to.
To communicate effectively with someone. It took some work, but Mary finally got through to Jerry that she doesn't feel as deeply for him as he does for her.

Get together.
To join up socially, to link as in a relationship. *It's hard to believe that Liza and Anthony finally got together and now they're getting married.*

Get up.
To rise from bed in the morning. *What time did you get up this morning?*

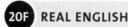 **REAL ENGLISH**

Shooting the Breeze

The other day, I was *hanging out* with my neighbor, *shooting the breeze.* Well, you know how it is, *birds of a feather flock together,* and so we *got to talking* about a mutual friend of ours, Mimi, whom I haven't seen *for ages* because we just haven't *kept in touch* much lately. Well, Mimi's son, who's *the apple of her eye* and a real *egghead,* is studying to be a doctor. He was really needing some *R & R,* so he went to Miami just to *hang out* at the beach for a while. Well, it turns out that Mimi's son *ended up* going out on a *blind date* and *falling for* this gal. Mimi was really happy about that because he and the girl he'd been *seeing* had just *broken up.* It turns out he and his new girlfriend are just like *two peas in a pod* — they're so much alike. And now they're getting *hitched.* Mimi must be *bursting with pride,* so now I'll just have to *drop her a line* to congratulate her on her son's good luck!

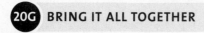 **BRING IT ALL TOGETHER**

REVIEW EXERCISE 1: Vocabulary

Complete each of the following sentences with one of these words: *acquaintances, block party, city council, community, confidant, congenial, courtesy, dinner party, fair-weather friends, familiar, fraternize, kindred, neighborhood watch, neighborly, newcomer, potluck, sociable, street fair.*

1. _____ are easy to find during the good times, but disappear when the problems begin.

2. Everyone likes to be around _____ people because they are so easy to be with.

3. I think it's a lovely idea to have a formal _____ just for the "girls."

4. There's something _____ about that woman. I know I've met her before.

5. It's great to find a _____ spirit who knows you better than anyone else.

6. Did you see the invitation to the _____? It's going to be next Saturday from 1:30 to 7:00 PM in Jameson Park.

7. Why don't you be _____ and take some fruit from the garden to the new family next door?

8. Are you going to the _____ over on Sixth? I hear they're going to have a lot of blues and Cajun music there.

9. As a_____, the local grocery store gives a 10 percent discount to new families in the neighborhood.

10. I have a few very close friends and lots of _____ that I don't see all that often.

11. I've lived here a while, but when I was a _____ all the neighbors made me feel very welcome.

12. Every _____ has a grocery store, a Laundromat, a bar, and at least one church.

13. The robbery across the street was stopped because a neighbor was watchful. Thank goodness for _____.

14. The _____ agreed that a library was more important for the city than a football stadium.

15. Maria's taking spaghetti, Toni's taking a salad, and I'm taking a cake to the _____.

16. Here, you go _____ with the guests and I'll finish up in the kitchen.

17. Caroline is my _____. I tell her all my innermost secrets.

18. I'm feeling _____, so let's invite the neighbors over for dinner.

REVIEW EXERCISE 2: Participial Adjectives

Use the verb in parentheses for both forms of participial adjective.

1. (confuse) Don't worry if you feel _____. This is a _____ class.

2. (satisfy) Are you _____? Was the meal _____ enough?

3. (excite) Isn't this an _____ game? I'm so _____ to be here.

4. (frighten) This movie is so _____ I think anybody would be _____ by it.

5. (exhaust) I'm _____. I didn't realize how _____ it was to chop wood.

6. (bore) I'm almost always _____ in that class because he's such a _____ teacher.

7. (interest) Isn't this an _____ painting? I've always been _____ in this artist.

8. (disappoint) I think Jack was _____ that he didn't get into Harvard. It's always _____ when you don't get into the school you want.

REVIEW EXERCISE 3: Verbs of Perception

Fill in the sentences with the verbs given in parentheses. Follow the general rules of thumb to decide which form to use.

1. The children were laughing while they watched the dog _____ his tail. (chase)
2. I noticed you _____ here by yourself, so I decided to come talk to you. (sit)
3. What would you do if you heard someone _____ for help? (cry)
4. I think I see someone _____ us in my rearview mirror. (follow)
5. Grandpa likes to listen to the birds _____ every morning. (sing)
6. Do you smell bread _____ in the oven? (bake)
7. The teacher observed the students _____ on their tests. (cheat)
8. Don't just look at me _____ here. Help me! (stand)

REVIEW EXERCISE 4: Reflexive Pronouns

Finish each sentence with an appropriate reflexive pronoun and verb from the list. Use *by* if necessary.

promised, took, fixed, told, live, sits, reward, stay

1. Tom _____ he would never fall in love again after he got hurt so badly the last time.
2. I got up early and _____ some breakfast before going out for a run.
3. Do you want to _____ for the rest of your life, or do you want to live with someone?
4. The Garcia's saved their money and _____ to Disneyland for their last vacation together.
5. There are no other houses around. The house _____ on top of a hill just outside the city.
6. You've all done such a good job that I think you should _____ with dinner and a movie.
7. Mary _____ she would lose ten pounds by February.
8. To really relax, we like to _____ in a cottage by the ocean.

REVIEW EXERCISE 5: Phrasal Verbs with *get*

got after, get around, get along with, gets off, getting at, got away with, get back at, got back, get by, get in, got into, get on with, get out, get over, get through, get through to, get together, get up

1. I can't believe the robbers _____ so much money and won't be caught!
2. What time did you _____ last night? I didn't hear you come in.
3. I have to _____ earlier than usual tomorrow because I have to be at work an hour early.
4. The teacher _____ the students who were fighting on the playground.
5. The movie was so good that we really _____ it.
6. What time shall we _____ for dinner at Merle's tomorrow night?

7. Many young people barely _____ on their low salaries.

8. It's difficult to _____ in California if you don't have a car.

9. Having a loving family makes it easier to _____ the most difficult problems.

10. I _____ early this morning after a two-week vacation.

11. Wendy was too sick to _____ much over the last few weeks.

12. George was so in love with Melinda that it took years to _____ her after they broke up.

13. It took a long time to understand what the professor was _____. He just didn't explain it very well.

14. It's so difficult to _____ to teenagers sometimes; they just don't understand.

15. Drake decided that he would try to _____ Tina for going out with another guy.

16. It's time for you to _____ your life; you have to forget about her!

17. I heard that Bill and Jane don't really _____ each other and that they may be getting a divorce.

18. Frank normally _____ at 5:00, but he had to stay at the office late tonight.

20H LISTEN UP!

🎧 Listen to a story about how one community of friends and neighbors helped each other during a devastating fire. Then answer these questions.

📖

1. How did San Diegans know there was a fire?

2. Why did residents have to stay at home for a week?

3. What made so many people want to help the fire victims?

4. What were some of the ways people helped one another?

20I WHY DO THEY DO THAT?

Body Language, Personal Space, and More

Like spoken language, gestures and body language in a new culture can be confusing. Every culture has its own certain unwritten rules that people from other cultures need to be aware of, and the U.S. is no exception. There are many very common and important gestures and body signals that are helpful to know while dealing with Americans.

For example, Americans' sense of personal space — a comfortable distance between oneself and others — is between eighteen and thirty inches depending on the closeness of the relationship. If others stand within that personal space, it makes Americans feel uncomfortable, and they may take a step back to recover an acceptable distance. Standing "too close" to an American while in coversation is just one pitfall to avoid. Here are few others:

Eye contact — Americans usually look each other directly in the eyes, looking away briefly from time to time. A failure to maintain "acceptable" eye contact may be interpreted as a lack of self confidence, or — worse — as a sign that you are guilty of something and are trying to hide it.

Touch — Americans are not as openly affectionate as those from some other cultures may be, but a brief touch on the arm could be interpreted in various ways, ranging from flirtatious to sympathetic or reassuring depending upon the situation.

Beckoning — It is common to beckon by holding the upturned palm out and up while wiggling one or two fingers or even all together towards oneself. This is acceptable in most situations and is not considered rude. However, in a restaurant, it's more polite to simply hold the index finger up while trying to catch the eye of a server. Do not snap your fingers to get someone's attention.

Saying goodbye — Usually, the hand is held up with the palm down with the fingers together as they wave up and down, or the hand is held straight up, palm out bending at the wrist from side to side.

Kissing hello or good-bye — It is very unusual for some Americans to kiss one another when they say "hello" or "good-bye," and they may consider it downright bizarre. However, this does occur sometimes, especially in urban settings where people are more comfortable with a mix of cultural norms. The best thing to do is follow the example set by the person you're with.

Handshake — The handshake is firm and bobs up and down two or three times. This is a standard greeting among people from most regions, regardless of gender or situation.

Laugh — There is a range of types of laughter among Americans, from "big" and hearty to "small" and softer. Loud, open laughter is not usually considered odd or offensive; instead it may be interpreted as coming from a person who enjoys life.

Pointing — Point with the index finger, the one next to the thumb. Do not point with the middle finger as this is considered an obscene gesture in the U.S. And some people consider it rude to point directly at other people, so it's best to point to people with the full hand, palm facing nearly upward.

OK — This is a gesture made with the index finger and thumb forming a circle with the other fingers extended. It means *OK*, or *that's right*, or *perfect*.

Thumbs up or down — The thumb turned up means "everything is good;" down means the opposite.

There are some other cultural behaviors to be aware of. For example, Americans may interrupt a conversation at any time, especially when it is highly animated and among friends or coworkers. You also may have noticed that men usually stand up when a woman enters the room. This is considered very polite but is occurring less and less in the changing roles of women and men in American society. And although some Americans do not always follow these rules, spitting and burping are not publicly acceptable. Try to suppress burps and always say "Excuse me" afterwards. Find a private place to spit if needed.

And last but not least, the smile. A common criticism of Americans is that they smile too much. But for many Americans, smiling is a gesture of courtesy to others, because it is a way to present a happy face to others, and perhaps to brighten other people's moods as well. Americans in many regions believe that it's less than polite to allow oneself to be seen as angry or in a bad mood. A nice smile — even if it's not entirely genuine — is thus considered proper behavior among other people.

Lesson 20: Answer Key

Practice Exercise 1	1. boring, 2. bored, 3. crowded, 4. broken, 5.annoying, 6. cracked, 7. embarrassing, 8. frightened, 9. exhausted, 10. thrilling
Practice Exercise 2	1. photographing, 2. talking, 3. take, 4. dancing, 5. working, 6. singing, 7. interview, 8. blowing, 9. baking, 10. getting
Practice Exercise 3	1. herself, 2. myself, 3. by herself, 4. themselves, 5. yourself, 6. by myself, 7. himself, 8. by yourselves, 9. ourselves, 10. itself
Review Exercise 1	1. Fair-weather friends, 2. congenial, 3. dinner party, 4. familiar, 5. kindred, 6. block party, 7. neighborly, 8. street fair, 9. courtesy, 10. acquaintances, 11. newcomer, 12. community, 13. neighborhood watch, 14. city council, 15. potluck, 16. fraternize, 17. confidant, 18. sociable
Review Exercise 2	1. confused . . . confusing, 2. satisfied . . . satisfying, 3. exciting . . . excited, 4. frightening . . . frightened, 5. exhausted . . . exhausting, 6. bored . . . boring, 7. interesting . . . interested, 8. disappointed . . . disappointing
Review Exercise 3	1. chasing, 2. sitting, 3. cry, 4. following, 5. sing, 6. baking, 7. cheating, 8. standing
Review Exercise 4	1. told himself, 2. fixed myself, 3. live by yourself, 4. took themselves, 5. sits by itself, 6. reward yourselves, 7. promised herself, 8. stay by ourselves
Review Exercise 5	1. got away with, 2. get in, 3. get up, 4. got after, 5. got into, 6. get together, 7. get by, 8. get around, 9. get through, 10. got back, 11. get out, 12. get over, 13. getting at, 14. get through to, 15. get back at, 16. get on with, 17. get along with, 18. gets off
Listen Up!	1. The sky was orange, there were ashes everywhere, air smelled like smoke. 2. It was dangerous to be outside breathing the air. 3. Because they would want others to do the same for them. 4. Collecting and distributing food and clothing, lobbying for public money, putting up sand bags to stop erosion.

Irregular Verbs

Each of the following verbs appears in the infinitive, the simple past, and the past participial forms.

arise / arose / arisen
awake / awoke / awoke (n)
be (am, are, is) / was, were / been
beat / beat / beaten
become / became / become
begin / began / begun
bend / bent / bent
bet / bet / bet
bid / bid / bid
bind / bound / bound
bite / bit / bitten
bleed / bled / bled
blow / blew / blown
break / broke / broken
bring / brought / brought
build / built / built
burst / burst / burst
buy / bought / bought
cast / cast / cast
catch / caught / caught
choose / chose / chosen
cling / clung / clung
come / came / come
cost / cost / cost
creep / crept / crept
cut / cut / cut
deal / dealt / dealt
dig / dug / dug
do / did / done
draw / drew / drawn
eat / ate / eaten
fall / fell / fallen
feed / fed / fed
feel / felt / felt
fight / fought / fought
find / found / found
fit / fit / fit
flee / fled / fled
fling / flung / flung
fly / flew / flown
forbid / *forbade / forbidden
forget / forgot / forgotten
forgive / forgave / forgiven
freeze / froze / frozen
get / got / **gotten
give / gave / given
go / went / gone
grind / ground / ground
grow / grew / grown
hang / hung / hung
have / had / had
hear / heard / heard

hide / hid / hidden
hit / hit / hit
hold / held / held
hurt / hurt / hurt
keep / kept / kept
kneel / knelt, kneeled / knelt, kneeled
know / knew / known
lay / laid / laid
lead / led / led
lean / leaned, leant / leaned, leant
leave / left / left
lend / lent / lent
let / let / let
lie / lay / lain
light / lit, lighted / lit, lighted
lose / lost / lost
make / made / made
mean / meant / meant
meet / met / met
misspell / misspelled / misspelled
mistake / mistook / mistaken
misunderstand / misunderstood / misunderstood
overthrow / overthrew / overthrown
pay / paid / paid
prove / proved / proven, proved
put / put / put
quit / quit, quitted / quit, quitted
read / read / read
rid / rid / rid
ride / rode / ridden
ring / rang / rung
rise / rose / risen
run / ran / run
say / said / said
see / saw / seen
seek / sought / sought
sell / sold / sold
send / sent / sent
set / set / set
shake / shook / shaken
shine / shone / shone
shoot / shot / shot
show / showed / shown
shrink / shrank / shrunk
shut / shut / shut
sing / sang / sung
sit / sat / sat
sleep / slept / slept
slide / slid / slid
speak / spoke / spoken
speed / sped, speeded / sped, speeded

*Some speakers often use *forbid* for simple past.
**Some speakers often say *have got to* meaning *must,* and in British English the form *gotten* does not exist.

spend / spent / spent
spin / spun / spun
spread / spread / spread
spring / sprang / sprung
stand / stood / stood
steal / stole / stolen
stick / stuck / stuck
sting / stung / stung
stink / stank / stunk
strike / struck / stricken
swear / swore / sworn
sweep / swept / swept
swim / swam / swum
swing / swung / swung
take / took / taken
teach / taught / taught
tear / tore / torn

tell / told / told
think / thought / thought
tread / trod / trod, trodden
throw / threw / thrown
understand / understood / understood
undertake / undertook / undertaken
upset / upset / upset
wake / woke / woken
wear / wore / worn
weave / wove / woven
weep / wept / wept
win / won / won
wind / wound / wound
withdraw / withdrew / withdrawn
wring / wrung / wrung
write / wrote / written

Adjectives Followed by Prepositions

absent from
accustomed to
acquainted with
addicted to
afraid of
angry at/with
annoyed with
associated with
aware of
blessed with
bored with
capable of
cluttered with
committed to
composed of
concerned about
connected to
content with
convinced of
coordinated with
crazy about
crowded with
dedicated to
devoted to
disappointed in/with

discriminated against
divorced from
done with
dressed in
engaged to
enthusiastic about
envious of
equipped with
excited about
exposed to
faithful to
familiar with
filled with
finished with
fond of
friendly toward/with
furious about
furnished with
glad about
grateful to/for
guilty of
hidden from
innocent of
interested in
involved in

jealous of
known for
limited in / by
made of
married to
opposed to
patient with
polite to
prepared for
provided with
proud of
ready to / for
related to
relevant to
remembered for
responsible for
safe from
satisfied with
scared of
terrified of
tired of
upset with
used to
worried about

Verbs Followed by Prepositions

accuse of
agree with
apologize for
apply to/for
approve of
argue with/about
arrive in/at
ask for
beg for
believe in
blame for
care about/for
compare to/with
complain about
consist of
contribute to
count on/upon
cover with
decide on
depend on/upon
die from
distinguish from

dream of/about
drink to
escape from
excel in
excuse for
fall in love with
feel like
fight for
forget about
forgive for
hide from
hope for
insist on/upon
know about
listen to
look after
look forward to
object to
participate in
pay attention to
pray for
prevent from

prohibit from
protect from
provide with
recover from
remind of
rescue from
respond to
search for
shoot at
stare at
stop from
subscribe to
substitute for
succeed in
talk about
take advantage of
take care of
thank for
think of
vote for / against
wait for
warn against / about

Real English Idioms

All over with. Finished, finalized.

All over. Everywhere.

All stressed out. Nervous; feeling stress.

All thumbs. Clumsy or awkward.

All-time low. A situation that has never been worse.

Apple of someone's eye. An adored person, most often one's child.

As fresh as a daisy. Well rested; new looking.

At death's door. Close to death.

Axe to fall (To wait for the...). To expect to lose one's position.

Bad egg. One bad thing among others that are good.

Bargain basement. A store featuring inexpensive products, often on sale.

Bargain rack An area of a store devoted to reduced prices; cheaper products.

Bear market. A stock market that is not performing well; pessimism about the market.

Birds of a feather flock together. People who have similar ideas, feelings, and behaviors are more likely to become friends.

Blast. A lot of fun.

Blog. A forum on the Internet for sharing one's views. A "Web log."

Boot up. To start a computer.

Boxed in. Trapped on all sides.

Bread. Money.

Break away. To take a break from hard work. To remove oneself from stress.

Break in. To use something until it begins to operate smoothly.

Break laws. To violate laws.

Breathe down someone's neck. To pressure someone to work.

Bring home the bacon. To bring home one's salary to pay for a family's living.

Buckle up. To wear a seat belt.

Build. A person's physique.

Bull market. A stock market that is performing well; optimism about the stock market.

Bursting with pride. Feeling very full of pride.

Chat room. A special "space" on the Internet for conversing or sharing opinions.

Check out. To look at something carefully.

Chew the fat. To make conversation or small talk.

Clean bill of health. A pronouncement of good health, made by a doctor.

Close call. A near-accident, an accident that was barely avoided.

Cool as a cucumber. Calm and relaxed.

Crash. To stop working, said of a computer.

Crash. To fall asleep suddenly and anywhere; to lose energy.

Crazy. Wild, different from the majority. Also, insane.

Cruise along. To drive in a relaxed manner.

Cry all the way to the bank. To be without money and in need of a loan.

Cubicle farm. Office space made of cubicles; semi-private work spaces separated by partitions.

Cut out for. Naturally suited to do something.

Do all your homework. To study something carefully in advance.

Dough. Money.

Down on one's luck. In a difficult financial situation.

Downsize. To cut back on employees.

Dressed to kill. Dressed very well and looking good.

Drop a line. To write a short letter or note to someone.

Eat humble pie. To have to admit one is wrong.

Egghead. One who is extremely intelligent; an exceptional student.

End up. To finally result in.

False alarm. Expected danger that does not happen.

Feel two inches shorter. To lose confidence.

Filthy rich. Extremely rich.

Fix up. To repair; to make better or more livable.

Fixer-upper. A property in need of repairs.

Flame. To send an angry or hostile e-mail message.

For ages. For a very long time.

Freak out. To become upset and agitated.

Geek. An often disliked intellectual; a person who knows a lot about computers.

Get blood from a stone. To work someone more than they are capable.

Get hitched. To get married.

Get into. To become involved or interested in.

Get it. To understand.

Get to talking. To begin talking about something.

Get out of here/there. To leave.

Get worse before something gets better. Things will not improve immediately, and they may get worse.

Give it away. To sell for a very low price.

Glow. To look healthy; to look good.

Go all out. To do something with intensity or enthusiasm.

Go blank. To momentarily be unable to recall something.

Go broke. To run out of money.

Go bust. To lose all one's money.

Go down. When the computer network one is using is not working or can't be accessed.

Go out of one's mind. To go crazy because of some problem.

Go postal. To act rashly.

Going out. Dating.

Go over someone's head. To go higher in the chain of command.

Good catch. Better than average.

Goof off. To relax; to play.

Hacker. Someone who illegally breaks into a computer system.

Hang out. To spend time together, socializing informally.

Have a nervous breakdown. To lose control of oneself.

Have a night on the town. To go out for an evening of entertainment.

Have what it takes. Have the necessary qualities for something.

Heart sinks to one's feet. A sudden feeling of fear or worry.

Helper unit. A rental house or apartment in back of a main house that helps pay the bills when rented.

High-end. Higher-priced.

Highway robbery. Profits derived from items that are extremely expensive or overpriced.

Hit the books. To study.

Home sweet home. Your own home.

Hot date. A date with someone exciting.

In a nutshell. In a few words.

In ages. In a long time.

In love with. Having strong feelings for someone or something.

In shock. Surprised; a state the body goes into to protect itself after an accident or tragic or frightening event.

In the black. Making money.

In the pink. In good health; having rosy colored skin.

Keep in touch. To communicate from time to time.

Keep it up. To continue doing something.

Keep one's cool. To remain calm.

Kick back. To relax.

Kick up one's heels. To let go of inhibitions and have fun.

Knockout. A gorgeous woman.

Laugh all the way to the bank. To make more money than most people, especially suddenly.

Lead foot. A "heavy foot" that presses too hard on the accelerator. A fast driver.

Lemon. A poorly manufactured product that breaks down a lot more than it should.

Life passes before your eyes. A rapid review of one's history prior to death, said to happen when one is about to die, as in an accident.

Live it up. To have a good time.

Live to see tomorrow. To continue living.

Long arm of the law. The power and influence of law enforcement.

Look forward to. To anticipate something pleasurable.

Look in the eye. To look at someone directly and/or without fear.

Look like a million dollars. To look fantastic and richly dressed.

Make (someone's) day. To allow or cause something exciting and memorable to happen to someone.

Make money. To earn money.

Man! An expression about a feeling, similar to *wow!*

Meet your maker. To die.

Mess up. To ruin; to harm.

Miss the boat. To be too late; to lose a chance.

My head is spinning. I have too much information to think about.

Neighborhood specialists. Ones who know a specific neighborhood well.

No strings attached. Without secondary expectations or complications.

Nose to the grindstone. Working very hard.

Not long for this world. Having little time before one's death.

Off the top of one's head. Expressed without much forethought or research.

Online. On the Internet.

On your feet. Out of bed; not sick.

On your last legs. Worn out; close to death.

Open house. A time when a house or apartment is "open" for prospective buyers to visit.

Open up. To click on a message so that it can be read.

Out of it. Not thinking clearly; not paying attention.

Out of nowhere. Unexpected; with unknown origins.

Pack. To carry a weapon.

Package deal. Several things that come together for one price.

Paint the town red. To have fun and do a lot of things for evening entertainment.

Pass out. To lose consciousness temporarily.

Pay through the nose. To pay a lot for something.

Pile of work. A lot of work to do.

Priced out of the market. Not having enough money.

Pride of ownership. Home ownership that causes people to care for a home.

Pull over. To stop one's car along the side of the road.

Push the envelope. To push something beyond what is expected; to go to the limit.

Put your nose to the grindstone. To work tediously and with much effort.

Rain or shine. Steady; Regardless of obstacles.

Recharge. To revitalize oneself.

Rip off. To pay more than is necessary for something of low value.

Rise to the top. To become the most popular or most qualified.

Roll around. To arrive, as with a particular time.

Rule out. To exclude or eliminate.

Scene of the crime. The place a crime was committed or where something wrong was done.

Secondhand store. A store that sells used products, especially clothing or books.

Seeing someone. Dating someone.

Serve a purpose. To be useful.

Shades. Sunglasses.

Shoot the breeze. To pass the time by talking about nothing in particular.

Shopaholic. Someone who can't stop spending money.

Shopping spree. Outing in which one buys a lot of things all at one time.

Skyrocket. To go up in value quickly.

Slow motion. Movement that appears slower than normal, as in a slow-motion film.

Smooth operator. Someone who knows how to get what he or she wants through manipulation.

Snail mail. "Regular" mail, not e-mail.

Sort out. To go through and organize one's problems until some resolution begins to occur.

Spam. Unsolicited e-mail.

Spill the beans. To tell all that you know, usually about a secret or surprise.

Squeak out. To speak in an unnaturally high-pitched voice.

Stamp of approval. Approval from someone more knowledgeable or more experienced.

Stand a chance. Have a good possibility.

Stand to reason. To be reasonable.

Stars in your eyes. Idealization of someone or something.

Stars. Famous movie personalities; actors that are very popular.

Stay on someone's mind. To remain thought about.

Steal. Inexpensive, very cheap price.

Stick it out. To continue doing something that is difficult or uninteresting.

Stick to. To follow through on something without wasting time.

Stop by. To visit, especially for a short while.

Straighten up. To improve, especially behavior.

Surf the net. To look at different Web sites for pleasure.

Swamped. Having too much work.

Sweat buckets. To be very nervous.

Sweet talk. Flattery used to get what is wanted.

Take (someone's) advice. To listen to someone.

Take it easy. To relax.

Take my advice. To accept someone's suggestion.

Take one's time. Not to rush to finish something.

Take the bull by the horns. To take care of things in an assertive or determined fashion.

Take your breath away. Experiencing something so fast and exciting that breathing momentarily stops.

TGIF. Thank God it's Friday.

The big cheese. The most important person.

The cream of the crop. The best of a group.

The works. Everything. All of the optional extra features or ingredients.

This is your cup of tea. Something is especially suitable or enjoyable for you.

Throw one's hat in the ring. To join other candidates trying for the same position.

Throw the book at someone. To give someone the greatest punishment possible.

Ticket. A traffic citation.

Time to kill. Extra time.

To learn by heart. To memorize.

Too close for comfort. In a place where an accident almost happens.

Under the gun. Uunder time pressure.

Under the table. Not reported to the IRS in order to avoid paying taxes, as with money.

Upgrade. To improve with higher-quality products.

Use your noodle. To think.

Vintage store. A secondhand store that sells antique clothing.

Want in the worst way. To desire something very much.

What a deal! What a good price!

Win by a landslide. To win by a large majority.

Won't cut it. Not good enough.

Work one's tail off. To work very hard.

You're the picture of health. You look like you're healthy.

Zone out. To stare into space; to waste time doing nothing.

Index

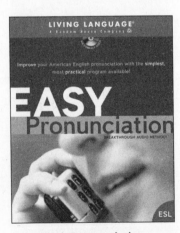